Shakespeare and Early Modern Drama

RELATED TITLES

English Renaissance Tragedy, Peter Holbrook
Essential Shakespeare: The Arden Guide to Text and Interpretation, Pamela Bickley and Jenny Stevens
Hamlet: Language and Writing, Dympna Callaghan
Performing King Lear: Gielgud to Russell Beale, Jonathan Croall
Romeo and Juliet: A Critical Reader, edited by Julia Reinhard Lupton

Shakespeare and Early Modern Drama: Text and Performance

*Pamela Bickley
and Jenny Stevens*

Bloomsbury Arden Shakespeare
An imprint of Bloomsbury Publishing Plc

B L O O M S B U R Y
LONDON · OXFORD · NEW YORK · NEW DELHI · SYDNEY

Bloomsbury Arden Shakespeare

An imprint of Bloomsbury Publishing Plc

Imprint previously known as Arden Shakespeare

50 Bedford Square	1385 Broadway
London	New York
WC1B 3DP	NY 10018
UK	USA

www.bloomsbury.com

BLOOMSBURY, THE ARDEN SHAKESPEARE and the Diana logo are trademarks of Bloomsbury Publishing Plc

First published 2016

© Pamela Bickley and Jenny Stevens, 2016

Pamela Bickley and Jenny Stevens have asserted their right under the Copyright, Designs and Patents Act, 1988, to be identified as authors of this work.

All rights reserved. No part of this publication may be reproduced or transmitted in any form or by any means, electronic or mechanical, including photocopying, recording, or any information storage or retrieval system, without prior permission in writing from the publishers.

No responsibility for loss caused to any individual or organization acting on or refraining from action as a result of the material in this publication can be accepted by Bloomsbury or the authors.

British Library Cataloguing-in-Publication Data
A catalogue record for this book is available from the British Library.

ISBN:	HB:	978-1-4725-7714-6
	PB:	978-1-4725-7713-9
	ePub:	978-1-4725-7715-3
	ePDF:	978-1-4725-7716-0

Library of Congress Cataloging-in-Publication Data

Typeset by RefineCatch Limited, Bungay, Suffolk
Printed and bound in Great Britain

CONTENTS

Using this book vii
Introduction viii

1 Defining the self 1

Romeo and Juliet 7
Getting over the language: *William Shakespeare's Romeo + Juliet* (1996) 19
The Duchess of Malfi 24
Moving performances: *Malfi* at the Blackfriars and the Globe 35

2 Money and the modern city 41

The Merchant of Venice 47
Playing the Jew: Al Pacino in Michael Radford's *The Merchant of Venice* (2004) 61
Volpone, or the Fox 65
Volpone as beast fable 79

3 Performance and performativity 85

The Taming of the Shrew 90
Shakespeare goes to Hollywood: Burton and Taylor (1966) 105
The Tragedy of Mariam, The Fair Queen of Jewry 109
Closet drama 123

4 Servants, masters and service 129

Othello 133
Performing *Othello* in the twenty-first century 145
The Changeling 150
Compulsion (2009) 164

5 Fatherhood, state and the dynamics of revenge 171

The Spanish Tragedy 178
Things on stage 191
Titus Andronicus 195
Julie Taymor's *Titus* and the aesthetics of revenge 205

6 Transgressive desire 211

Measure for Measure 218
Casting Isabella 231
'Tis Pity She's a Whore 234
The Cook, the Thief, his Wife and her Lover: Peter Greenaway's theatre of blood 247

7 Damnation 253

Doctor Faustus 260
Performing *Doctor Faustus*: Stage on Screen (2010) 274
Hamlet 278
A Soviet *Hamlet*: Grigori Kozintsev (Lenfilm, 1964) 289

Glossary 295
References 301
Index 333

USING THIS BOOK

This book is organized around historical topics or critical areas which inform the study of early modern texts, each chapter exploring a play by Shakespeare alongside one by his contemporaries. While it is not intended as a comparative study, affinities between texts of the period will inevitably present themselves, thereby developing an alertness to dramaturgical fashions, textual nuances, as well as to key signifiers of the age.

A wealth of early modern texts is now easily accessible online, thanks in part to the initiatives of early modern scholars to take advantage of the opportunities offered by new technologies. Digital texts, such as the British Library's facsimiles of Shakespeare **quartos**, are especially useful for research and for understanding more about the way plays were presented in published form. This book references early editions of works such as treatises, conduct books and scientific studies, and these can be readily found by an internet search. Original spelling has been retained for texts for which there is no accessible modern edition.

Each chapter features one film adaptation of an early modern drama; all of these are available on DVD to enable them to be viewed alongside the book's commentary. There is also frequent reference to stage performances, some of which can be researched further on the appropriate theatre website (the RSC and National Theatre websites offer plentiful material on past performances).

A range of critical approaches is represented, including close analysis of both film and drama texts in each chapter. Further reading suggestions provide useful secondary sources that have not been cited within the chapter, with some interesting examples of creative reworkings of the featured works.

INTRODUCTION

Text

Students of *Hamlet* are probably accustomed to debating whether the protagonist refers to 'solid', 'sullied' or 'sallied' flesh in his first soliloquy. Such textual variants offer subtly nuanced differences and individual readers, actors or directors exercise their own choices from these possibilities. There is, of course, no 'authentic' text of any one of Shakespeare's plays in that no manuscript editions survive. The modern relationship between author, text and publisher bears no similarity to the situation of the early modern playtext. Plays were first for performance and the scripts were the property of the acting company, open to whatever changes were considered expedient or artistically desirable. The life of the author's handwritten manuscript was an uncertain one; it was vulnerable to ephemeral changes in popularity as well as being physically fragile. Texts were copied, in the first place, probably by a professional scribe, from the original 'foul papers' for use as a working promptbook (by which point a number of transcription errors had doubtless been introduced). This fair copy would need to be approved by the Master of the Revels before it could be licensed for performance. At this stage, the text could be subject to considerable alteration: music, songs, prologues and epilogues could be added, and actors might themselves suggest changes to the written text or add necessary stage directions. By the time the play had been successfully performed – and perhaps revived – there would have been several manuscript versions of the same play in existence at any one time. In these circumstances, the text was far from a fixed product; it evolved and changed to meet the exigencies of the moment – whether theatrical, political or just practical. Popular plays might then be published, although very few of the huge number performed did reach the printing house. But precisely who delivered the manuscript to the printers and what exactly *was* delivered is a vexed question. It seems that 'Bad Quartos' of some of Shakespeare's texts were the result of 'memorial reconstruction', the attempt to recall the play in its entirety from cue scripts (or from memory) in order to scramble together a sellable commodity. Heminge and Condell, the editors of Shakespeare's First **Folio**, refer to 'maimed and deformed' copies with which unscrupulous 'imposters' had 'abused' the public. Authorial rights to the original was not a concept recognized at the time and certainly Shakespeare appears to have shown no consistent interest in seeing his plays through the printing house. Indeed, without the efforts of Heminge and Condell there are some eighteen plays that would have disappeared entirely; their first printed appearance is in the 1623 First Folio. As these include some of Shakespeare's most highly esteemed works – *Macbeth*, *The Tempest*, *Antony and Cleopatra* – the notion of the author caring deeply about publication seems not to exist. The usual explanation is that Shakespeare was the quintessential man of the theatre, always concerned with the next play. So, was there any notion of the play continuing for posterity? *Hamlet* raises questions that move beyond the theatrical moment: the play as it exists in its Second Quarto form (Arden 3) is far too long for afternoon production on the early modern stage; did Shakespeare, therefore, revise it with 'reading' rather than acting in mind? The answer might possibly lie with the printing of texts such as Elizabeth Cary's *The Tragedie of Mariam* in the early seventeenth century. Cary's text was never intended for commercial performance; it could be recited as closet drama or privately read. The editors of Shakespeare's First Folio imply as much for their text: they advise purchasers to 'Reade him ... and againe and againe.' Arguably the extraordinary vibrancy of the theatrical texts of this period began to establish an entirely new culture of preserving and reading vernacular playtexts.

Shakespeare's contemporaries

Textual indeterminacy also impacts on questions of authorship: the absence of an author's name on the title page of a quarto text reveals a great deal about the status of the writer, and, to an extent, the genre. Readers of T.S. Eliot's essays on early modern drama might be surprised to discover that *The Revenger's Tragedy* was attributed to Tourneur rather than Middleton. Modern scholarship has done much to clarify textual uncertainties and issues of authorship, often with a view to exploring ideas of collaborative working. Light years away from the chaotic nature of the early modern written text is the world of modern digital research. This offers a means of intertextual analysis through metadata specific to the genre, offering a network of verbal similarities and parallels. The forensic investigation of text also has a bearing on questions of canonicity: the relative popularity of Shakespeare's contemporaries has seen significant changes. For Hazlitt, the great Romantic critic, there was a clear hierarchy of early modern dramatists: in his 1821 lectures he singles out Jonson and Beaumont and Fletcher while describing as 'nearly obsolete' Marlow [*sic*], Middleton and Rowley, Marston, Webster, Deckar [*sic*] and Ford, all of whom are now available in modern scholarly editions and all of whom have been represented in recent Globe theatre productions. A century after Hazlitt, Eliot, who did much to revive the reputations of Elizabethan and seventeenth century dramatists, broadened the discussion of early modern writers and included Massinger, Heywood, Chapman and Tourneur – but still concludes that Elizabethan art is 'impure'. The canonization of Shakespeare as the elusive genius towering above his contemporaries still exists to some extent but there is a much more sophisticated understanding of Shakespeare's role among his contemporaries. There is no doubt that the growth of London as a thriving commercial world and the concomitant flourishing of the new theatres played a significant part. Andrew Gurr, theatre historian, has estimated that in the years between 1580 and

1640 up to 25,000 people per week attended various public or private performances. In this context, the exuberant variety of writing for the theatre is perhaps as striking as the fact of Shakespeare's vitality and linguistic complexity. His exact contemporary, Marlowe, arrived on the scene in 1587 with *Tamburlaine* Part I and it is quite feasible that his entire oeuvre was performed before Shakespeare's first recorded play. Equally, the lively and satiric city comedies of Jonson, Dekker, and Beaumont and Fletcher pursued a genre which clearly did not excite Shakespeare whose comedies tend to be located elsewhere. There was, in other words, a thriving and changing theatre world in which Shakespeare's plays existed in a fruitfully symbiotic relationship with those of his contemporaries.

Early modern drama in its time

Much of what we know about theatrical practices in the early modern period is based on what can be learnt from the playtexts themselves and from documentary sources such as theatre company accounts, legal documents and antitheatrical tracts. There is, though, a great deal of fact and detail that remains irrecoverable and research approaches often require a degree of speculation and imaginative reconstruction. Today's theatre scholars work energetically with and around the manifold uncertainties of early performance to illuminate areas such as the materiality of performance (cosmetics, props, costume, stage places and spaces), the practices of theatre companies (training, rehearsal, acting styles), and the interrelatedness of performer and audience. As the field has diversified, so it has involved more and more interdisciplinary investigation. Geometric calculation has helped academics to estimate the proportions of the original Globe; historians of clothing have advised on the cut, contour and textiles of the costumes to be worn in original practices productions; studies into early modern actors' line-learning has been informed by neurobiological theory focused on brain capacity.

So what can be assumed about the experiences of player and playgoer in early modern England? An actor would join a company well before his voice had broken and receive training delivered primarily by its more experienced members. Graduating to ever more demanding roles, he would be expected to work independently to prepare his 'part': a document containing only his lines and the cues for when he should deliver them. Most companies would put on several plays in a week, obliging actors to keep multiple roles in their heads, aided no doubt by the mnemonic qualities of **blank verse**, rhyme and rhetorical patterning. Part conned, a player would usually give his first performance after only one run-through. Once on stage, he would have to be fleet of foot to cover the large expanse of the outdoor stage and adaptable to the more constricted space of the indoor playhouses. Sharing the same light as the audience, he could observe their responses to his performance as a means of honing his craft – though he would also need to be prepared to keep his concentration in the event of crowd trouble and other disruptions. He would have moved about the stage, playing to spectators at both the front and the sides, unhampered by the kind of blocking that today's performers are often obliged to follow – if only to keep in synch with the lighting plan.

The spectators watching these movements may well have been drawn to attend the performance by the relative novelty of the playhouse. Commercial theatres only came into existence in the late 1560s (and only then in London) and the thriving competitiveness of the new enterprise meant that there would have been numerous productions all vying for attention. Unlike today, public theatre was a popular form of entertainment, with outdoor audiences being made up from all social strata. With no pre-booking to worry about – or critical reviews to consider – early modern theatre allowed for the spur-of-the-minute attendance only rarely managed by modern playgoers.

Performing early modern drama today

In Tom Stoppard's play, *The Real Thing*, one character mockingly sums up another's literary elitism in the line: 'Shakespeare out in front by a mile, and the rest of the field strung out behind trying to close the gap'. The speaker's racing **metaphor** succinctly captures the privileged place that Shakespeare has come to inhabit over the course of four centuries or so. Shakespeare's literary monopoly is evidenced in Britain's theatre establishment, its tourist and media industries, as well as in school and university curricula across the globe. With this in mind, considerable energy is currently being invested in repositioning Shakespeare and his work. Scholars are moving away from the conventional stance of seeing the author as a lone genius towards a rather broader vision of early modern drama, focusing more on the affinities between Shakespeare and his peers and less on their differences. This shift in approach should not be mistaken for 'icon-bashing'. As well as paying close attention to the works of long-neglected dramatists, academics are also examining Shakespeare's works with fresh eyes, unpicking some of the distortions that have been inflicted on them in the name of adulation.

How far the current scholarly imperative to move away from reading early modern drama texts through the lens of Shakespeare will influence the cultural consciousness depends to some extent on how far it filters through to the world of performance. While theatres such as the Wanamaker Playhouse and the RSC Swan are committed to staging plays hitherto confined to library bookshelves, these venues are not easily accessible to the majority of would-be playgoers. However, one recent innovation that holds the potential to bring early modern plays to a wider audience is live stage-to-screen broadcasts. Pioneered by the National Theatre in 2009, the live broadcasting of hot-ticket performances to cinema audiences across Britain and around the world via satellite technology looks set to open up to millions an art form often regarded as the reserve of the few. While the National Theatre Live initiative has been warmly welcomed by some, it has also met with some resistance. Despite sophisticated camera work that ensures cinema audiences enjoy a 'best-seats-in-the-house' view, and the synchronizing of stage and screen to preserve the 'liveness' of the piece, some have expressed doubts about how far the experience of live performance can be captured on film and how far actors and audiences can remain uninhibited by the presence of film apparatus. For others, recording a live staging works against one of theatre's defining characteristics: its ephemerality. As the distinguished Shakespearean actor, Ben Kingsley, commented in a radio programme which brought together both director and cast of Peter Brook's landmark production of *A Midsummer Night's Dream* (1968), 'theatre is a very beautiful and gentle way of introducing us to mortality ... recording something that is ephemeral is actually dodging the issue' (transcribed from *The Reunion*, broadcast on BBC Radio 4, 3 May 2015).

Moving away from a Shakespeare-focused perspective also depends on how far adaptive media such as the visual arts, fiction writing, poetry and film are prepared to engage with a range of early modern plays. Screen adaptations in particular have the potential to bring the work of Shakespeare's contemporaries to the attention of a broader and larger audience than would be possible with stage performance. As things stand, though, film versions of Shakespeare's major tragedies and best-known comedies far outweigh those based on the work of his fellow playwrights, partly on account of Shakespeare being regarded as commercially more viable. Yet as screen adaptations such as Mike Figgis's *Hotel* (based around *The Duchess of Malfi*), Derek Jarman's *Edward II* and Alex Cox's *Revenger's Tragedy* demonstrate, there is much in the category of 'non-Shakespeare' to stimulate the creative imagination.

1

Defining the self:

Romeo and Juliet and *The Duchess of Malfi*

In Western societies today, various words and phrases relating to selfhood circulate freely to describe the experience of individuals and their relationships with others. People are judged as 'selfless' or 'selfish', 'self-possessed' or 'self-obsessed', 'self-deluded' or 'self-aware' and are prone to feelings of 'self-consciousness' or 'self-hatred'. All such terms operate in a relatively unproblematic way, with the concept of the 'self' taken as read: the essence or core of a person which generates everything that is said, done or thought and which distinguishes them from everyone else. In one of the most extensive explorations of the self written in recent decades, the philosopher Charles Taylor defines what generally passes for modern subjectivity:

> We think of our thoughts, ideas, or feelings as being 'within' us, while the objects in the world which these mental states bear on are 'without'. Or else we think of our capacities or potentialities as 'inner', awaiting the development which will manifest them or realize them in the public world . . .

> We are creatures with inner depths; with partly unexplored
> and dark exteriors.
>
> TAYLOR, *Self*, 111

However, as Taylor goes on to examine, understanding the self and its histories is rather more complex than this commonsensical definition might suggest.

Enquiry into the nature of selfhood has given rise to a number of highly complex questions, all of which tend to elude definitive answers. Is the 'inner self' a natural part of every individual or an effect of the network of authorities at work on the individual? Does our sense of self develop from an original source or does it only come into being when it offers resistance to the forces which seek to contain it? Has the experience of interiority remained constant, with only the way it is represented and respected being liable to change? Any consideration of inwardness as treated in early modern drama will inevitably lead to such questions, requiring alertness to the very considerable changes in the way the self has been conceptualized over the centuries. While histories of the subject stretch as far back as Plato, the emergence of what might be called the 'modern self' tends to be pinned at around the time of the Enlightenment. Mid- to late seventeenth-century philosophical, political and religious thought is seen to encourage a conscious disengagement of the material body from the immaterial mind: a dualistic model often attributed to the French philosopher, René Descartes, and one which encourages the idea of psychological inwardness. In the late nineteenth century, psychoanalytic theory overturned belief in the mind as something under an individual's control. Freud's tripartite model of the id, the ego and the superego insists on the inseparability of body and mind; the repression of certain physical desires, for example, has an unavoidable impact on the psyche. Moreover, the mind itself is never master of its own processes. Thoughts and actions are always prone to pressures of which the individual is entirely unaware, forming what Freud termed the 'unconscious'. As psychoanalytic theory developed, so the idea of a fixed and immutable selfhood began to appear as antiquated as a flat earth: the split between body and mind had become a split within the mind of the subject itself.

The second half of the twentieth century saw another major shift in conceptualizing subjectivity. Post-structuralist theorists, strongly influenced by the ideas of the French philosopher and historian Michel Foucault, sought to expose as a delusion the notion of the individual as unique – human beings are, inescapably, a product of the state institutions which repress and control them. For Foucault, even apparently instinctual experiences are determined by external rather than internal forces:

> We believe ... that the body obeys the exclusive laws of physiology and that it escapes the influence of history, but this ... is false. The body is molded by a great many distinct regimes; it is broken down by the rhythms of work, rest, and holidays; it is poisoned by food or values, through eating habits or moral laws ... Nothing in man – not even his body – is sufficiently stable to serve as a basis for self-recognition or for understanding other men.
>
> FOUCAULT, 'Nietzsche', 87–8

Foucauldian theory attracted particular interest from academics working in early modern literary studies. Stephen Greenblatt recalls the impact that a seminar led by Foucault had on his thinking about human identity:

> This vision of the nature of the inner life was deeply pessimistic – the hidden place into which one might hope to retreat in order to escape a totalizing institution was itself created by that institution – but the pessimism seemed constructed around a small, irreducible core of hope: it was possible to see how it was done and therefore it was in principle possible to see how it might be undone.
>
> GREENBLATT, *Self-fashioning*, xv

Greenblatt's *Renaissance Self-fashioning: From More to Shakespeare* ([1980] 2005), a cornerstone of new historicism, followed Foucault in its exploration of culture as a social practice, inseparable from the power structures of the day. Greenblatt pinpoints the sixteenth century as the time when, in England, 'there appears to be an increased self-consciousness about the fashioning of human identity as a manipulable, artful process' (Greenblatt, 2). Such 'self-fashioning' is not, however, borne out of an individualistic desire for self-expression, but is determined by the cultural, social and political prescriptions of the period.

Revisionist debates surrounding early modern subjectivity have continued to develop over the past three decades or so. Informed by Foucauldian anti-essentialism, cultural materialist and new-historicist critics have produced readings of Renaissance texts which have radically challenged the liberal humanist assumptions of earlier interpretations. Shakespeare's *Hamlet* has proven to be one of the most popular foci of attention, not least for its hero's reputation as the progenitor of modern consciousness, more in step with the modern age than his own. Greenblatt sees the play as marking 'an epochal shift . . . in Western drama . . . as if the play were giving birth to a whole new kind of literary subjectivity' (Greenblatt *et al.*, 1661). Others have insisted that the interiority located in the figure of Hamlet is no more than the anachronistic imposition of modern thinking on an early modern playtext. In *The Tremulous Private Body: Essays on Subjection* (1984), Francis Barker claims Hamlet's reference to an interior self – 'that within which passes show' (1.2.85) – is no more than 'gestural', belonging to 'a historical order whose outline had so far only been sketched out' (Barker, 36, 37); and in *The Subject of Tragedy* ([1985] 1993) Catherine Belsey, broadly in agreement with Barker, cautions against imposing an 'imaginary interiority' on Renaissance creations (Belsey, 48).

As might be expected, given their tendency towards the polemical, the cultural materialist and new-historicist writings of the 1980s have not gone uncontested. In *Inwardness and the Theater in the English Renaissance* (1995), Katharine Eisaman Maus returns to the arguments of the 1980s to explore her own 'complex relationship to recent new-historicist and cultural-materialist attempts "to write the history of the subject"' (Maus, *Inwardness*, 3). Maus argues that Hamlet's distinction between inwardness and outwardness, far from being an anachronism, would have been an entirely commonplace idea in Shakespeare's day, to be found in a wide range of early modern writing. Convinced that the materialist standpoint of critics such as Belsey and Barker had given too little attention to the religious context of the period, she partly accounts for what she views as the age's preoccupation with the internal/external in terms of competing Christian doctrines: 'Sixteenth- and seventeenth-century Catholics and Protestants, Anglicans and sectarians endlessly debate whether priests ought to wear vestments, whether communicants should kneel when they receive communion, whether infant baptism is acceptable ... Protestants typically describe themselves as cultivating internal truths while accusing Catholics of attending only to outward "shows"' (Maus, *Inwardness*, 15).

The medievalist, David Aers, also takes issue with the Foucauldian critics of the 1980s, objecting to their reductive 'master narrative of Dark Ages to Renaissance' (Aers, 197). More scrupulous and open-minded attention to medieval history, culture and texts, and a rather more critical reading of Foucault, Aers argues, would have shown that a history of the subject which denied pre-Renaissance interiority was entirely untenable: '[S]oliloquies and concern with inward states of being are abundant in courtly literature . . . such concerns were a fundamental aspect of mysticism and the literature of self-examination and self-fashioning in late-medieval culture' (Aers, 190).

Perhaps the most polemical response to the cultural materialist and new-historicist histories of the subject has been Harold Bloom's *The Invention of the Human* (1999). In a volume of over 700 pages, Bloom insists on treating Shakespeare's characters as free, self-defining beings – not the decentred subjects of Foucauldian discourse. Disassociating himself entirely from what he calls the 'School of Resentment', Bloom makes the rather grand assertion that: 'Shakespeare essentially invented human personality as we continue to know and value it' (Bloom, 290), enshrining Hamlet as the inventor's supreme achievement.

Unsurprisingly, given the predominantly anti-essentialist underpinnings of the literary academy of the late 1990s and beyond, a sizeable number of scholarly readers regarded Bloom's volume as embarrassingly old-fashioned and reactionary. Its contentions, though, sit quite comfortably with today's theatrical practices. Dramatic representation of character still tends to focus around a Stanislavskian model of psychological realism and a firm belief in the immutability of human emotion and selfhood. Interviewed about the experience of playing in the RSC's production of *Richard II* (2013–14), one of the company's youngest actors, Elliot Barnes-Worrell, expresses just such a paradigm: 'The characters are three-dimensional and real ... I don't think Shakespeare wrote from his head, he wrote from the gut, and that's why his plays are so timeless. Our guts don't change, and emotions – fear, lust, anger, jealousy – are universal' (*Bringing Richard to Life*, RSC programme, 2013).

While such an approach to character and selfhood is likely to be judged naive by the majority of early modern drama scholars, there are some efforts afoot in the academy to narrow the gap between theatre practitioners and literary critics. The editors of *Shakespeare's Sense of Character: On the Page and From the Stage*, for example, describe the volume as representing the current scholarly impetus to reconsider the 'importance of character as a critical category, particularly in the light of postmodern ideas that have dominated academic thinking in the past quarter century' (Ko and Shurgot, 1). The disparity between academic writing and stage performance is perhaps inevitable, given that the very nature of theatre precludes the indeterminacy of so much scholarly interpretation: a director cannot be in two minds if he hopes to keep his audience.

> This chapter explores a range of recent approaches to the subject of selfhood through a study of two female tragic protagonists who seem to become 'themselves' through resisting the social and political order into which they are born: Shakespeare's Juliet and Webster's Duchess of Malfi.

Romeo and Juliet

With the possible exception of *Hamlet*, *Romeo and Juliet* is Shakespeare's best-known play, described by Stanley Wells as 'one of the great myths of the Western world' (Wells, 1). Having found its way into innumerable art forms, as well as the discourse of advertising and tourism, the work has become 'familiar to the point of cliché' (Roberts, 1). The play's many admirers are sometimes surprised, if not disappointed, to learn that its central narrative did not come directly from Shakespeare's imagination, but was just one of several reworkings of a well-known story. The analogue which bears the closest resemblance to the drama is Arthur Brooke's verse poem *The Tragical History of Romeus and Juliet* (1562), dismissed nowadays as dull, moralistic and, at over 3,000 lines, far too long. While Shakespeare's drama is unanimously held to be the aesthetic superior of its predecessor, it has not always received the kind of sustained critical attention afforded to the tragedies of the playwright's more mature years. There are a number of reasons for this relative neglect, most of which can be attributed to the historical development of Shakespeare studies. The youthful and unworldly figure of Romeo, for example, did not fit neatly into the paradigm of the tragic hero laid down in A.C. Bradley's *Shakespearean Tragedy* (1904) that held sway in the early decades of the twentieth century; and where today's critics interpret the script's rhetorical excesses in terms of linguistic self-reflexivity, earlier commentators were inclined to regard them as a form of Shakespearean juvenilia.

Young lovers defying the wishes of their family to pursue amatory desires was a common theme in a range of early modern dramas from Thomas Dekker's rumbustious city comedy *The Shoemaker's Holiday* (1599) to the multi-authored domestic tragedy *The Witch of Edmonton* (1621). The scenario of lovers struggling against the oppressive forces of their social milieu was the stuff of absorbing drama, made even more so in *Romeo and Juliet* by Shakespeare freezing the lovers' relationship in a highly romanticized love-death which, according to one critic, saves them from experiencing the 'banal, humdrum, lacklustre lassitude of a tired and cynical collusion: that is the normal marriage' (Kristeva, '*Romeo*', 75). While not everyone would concur with Kristeva's particular view of married life, few would deny that the power of *Romeo and Juliet* lies in its presentation of the impetuousness and idealism of youth. The very speed of the play – it takes place over four days compared to about nine months in Brooke's version – seems to present the development of the self in fast forward, what the Romantic critic, William Hazlitt, memorably described as 'a beautiful *coup-d'œil* of the progress of human life' (Hazlitt, *Characters*, 141). Such compression heightens the sense of a free, desiring self, coming into being through opposition to the social forces which threaten to contain it.

While modern views of selfhood would tend to see the controlling of desire as a denial of the self, scholars such as Michael Schoenfeldt argue that this would have been far from the case in the early modern period:

> The Renaissance seems to have imagined selves as differentiated not by their desires ... but by their capacity to control these desires. Psychoanalysis and early modern psychology are linked in that both require fastidious attention to the inner promptings of various appetites and urges. But where psychoanalysis tends to locate identity in terms of which objects are desired ... how intensely they are desired, and how these desires have been fashioned by the experiences of early infancy, the Renaissance locates

identity in the more or less successful regulation of a series of desires shared by all.

SCHOENFELDT, 17–18

Theoretical writings such as Schoenfeldt's provide an interesting framework for considering where the sympathies of Elizabethan playgoers would have lain when contemplating the plight of Shakespeare's lovers. Would they – as modern audiences invariably do – have sided with the headstrong adolescents or would they have looked past the allure of the narrative to settle on the side of convention? Brooke's version leaves no room for being in two minds; its initial address to the reader makes clear that the story is to be read as a warning of the fatal consequences of yielding to 'unhonest desire' and, lest they forget, provides regular reminders via the omniscient speaker. Regarding Renaissance attitudes to immoderate emotions, the historian Lawrence Stone suggests that:

To an Elizabethan audience the tragedy of Romeo and Juliet ... lay not so much in their ill-starred romance as in the way they brought destruction upon themselves by violating the norms of the society in which they lived ... An Elizabethan courtier would be familiar enough with the bewitching passion of love to feel sympathy with the young couple, but he would see clearly enough where duty lay.

STONE, *Family*, 70

Yet such an evaluation is perhaps more fitting for Brooke's version of the tale than for Shakespeare's. The verse poem offers a reasonably sympathetic picture of the lovers in the main body of the text, but this is framed by a resolutely didactic preface: Stone's exemplary courtier is allowed to feel the 'bewitching passion of love' only through the prism of moral duty.

Of course, when considering Brooke's poem alongside Shakespeare's drama, it is important to bear in mind the differences between their respective genres. While some poems feature the voices of individual speakers, most are authorial monologues which address the reader directly and, to some extent, control their responses. Drama, though, by its very nature, is multivocal, with at least two main levels of communication: that between the playwright and the audience and that between the *dramatis personae*. In most early modern playtexts, audiences are not provided with one overarching moral viewpoint; rather they are offered numerous perspectives generated by characters of varying subject positions, speech habits and backgrounds. It is true, of course, that playgoers are always at liberty to settle moral certainties on individual characters, though to do so is surely to resist the dialogic energies of the drama. As Kiernan Ryan has argued, '[t]he moralistic interpreter can invoke Friar Lawrence's warning that "these violent delights have violent ends"'; yet in so doing, they make the error of equating 'one character's viewpoint with the perspective formed by the play' (Ryan, *Shakespeare*, 73). The complexity of this perspective is far removed from the univocality of Brooke's poem – a compelling example of Shakespeare's ability to craft 'literary gold from dross' (Weis, 2).

'I should have been more strange' – Juliet and the gendered self

For decades now, the relationship between gender and identity has been a key concern in Shakespeare studies. Complex questions about the representation of men and women on the early modern stage have been explored from a wide variety of perspectives, with feminist, psychoanalytic and historicist approaches, often in combination, proving especially popular. All of these critical methods have served to illuminate *Romeo and Juliet* which, with its sustained dual focus on a male and female character of similar age, raises questions about how far gender shapes how people experience the world and, consequently, an individual's sense of self. Where Romeo encloses himself 'private in his chamber' (1.1.136) in order to live the script laid down for the courtly lover, he is nonetheless at liberty, even encouraged, to roam freely with his bachelor friends. Juliet, on the other hand, is confined to her maidenly quarters and to the company of married or widowed women. Yet if Juliet's selfhood is restricted by societal norms, so too is Romeo's: Verona's insistence on male bonding and its cynical and aggressive attitudes towards sex could be seen as having an equally stultifying effect on individuality. Conforming to gender expectations in revenging Mercutio's death, Romeo also expresses, in a despairing lover's **apostrophe**, the traditionally held belief that masculinity is undermined by the state of being in love:

> O sweet Juliet,
> Thy beauty hath made me effeminate
> And in my temper softened valour's steel!
>
> 3.1.115–1

The text undoubtedly offers ample evidence to support the general view that Juliet is more successful in transcending the limits of her circumstances than her lover, as well as being a more complex dramatic presence – a notable exception to Phyllis Rackin's generalization that '[w]omen's roles in Shakespeare's plays are far more limited than men's, both in size and number ... In fact, Shakespeare's representations of women often seem less sympathetic than those of other playwrights working at the same time' (Rackin, *Women*, 48).

Juliet is one of only three women to share a place in a Shakespearean title and one of only five women to have more than 500 lines of the play. And while it is true that Romeo has the longer part (by about eighty lines), she easily matches him in the number and range of her soliloquies. From the outset, Juliet seems to embody the potential for female power. The Nurse's account of her precocious babyhood seems to prefigure the courage of her early adulthood: making her own decisions about a marriage partner (and the arrangements for the wedding); taking the Friar's potion and, when accident prevails, choosing to take her own life. By the play's close, Juliet has surely become its main focus and it is *her* name, not Romeo's, that is placed first in the final line, the female possessive pronoun seeming to reverse the conventionally male prerogative of ownership:

> For never was a story of more woe
> Than this of Juliet and her Romeo.
>
> 5.3.309–10

Shakespeare's presentation of Juliet could, then, be seen as dramatizing a radical female selfhood as it emerges through conflict and adversity, a reading that raises concerns at the heart of some of today's major critical-theoretical debates. One such is Judith Butler's contention, expounded in *Gender Trouble: Feminism and the Subversion of Identity* (1990), that gender is 'performative' and does not exist 'behind the expressions of gender' (Butler, *Gender*, 25). Far from being at the self's core, gender (which Butler sees as entirely distinct from the biological sex of a person) is imposed from without. Shakespeare's decision to make Juliet three years younger than Brooke's heroine could indicate a desire to explore the impact of intense passion on a female on the very cusp of the social conditioning which will prepare her for the performance of womanhood.

One of the reasons why Juliet's role is thought to portray a rapidly maturing interiority is its relatively high number of soliloquies, positioned in four of the five acts of the tragedy. While the idea that soliloquies were intended to reveal inwardness has been challenged as anachronistic by some critics, there is no doubt that for today's audiences at least, they create the illusion of someone thinking aloud, of expressing an inner self. The soliloquy most frequently cited as articulating Juliet's innermost desires is that delivered as she waits for the consummation of her marriage.

📖 *Read the soliloquy (3.2.1–31) closely and consider the following questions:*

- *How and for what reasons might critical responses to Juliet's expression of sexual longing have changed over the centuries?*
- *This soliloquy has undergone frequent bowdlerization. Which lines and phrases are most likely to have been cut by prudish editors?*
- *How does the language and structure of the soliloquy convey the urgency of Juliet's desire?*

Critical responses to what is sometimes referred to as Juliet's **'epithalamium'** (wedding song) have inevitably been shaped by thinking about female physiology and psychology at any given time. Comparing how the speech has been glossed in editions published over successive generations reveals how increasing emphasis has been placed on the erotic tenor of the lines, as consideration of sexuality has become more open. Yet that is not to say that the liberalizing of attitudes to sexual desire has followed a strictly chronological line. The way Elizabethans viewed female desire was in some respects closer to modern-day thinking than it was to that of, say, the mid-nineteenth century. While the common Renaissance belief that the female orgasm was a prerequisite for conception is regarded now as folklore, it did acknowledge women's equality in the domain of sexual desire. Juliet's speech stresses the reciprocity of the sexual act: it will involve the loss of 'a pair of stainless maidenhoods', with the lovers co-owners of the 'mansion' to be 'possessed . . . and . . . enjoyed'.

The idea of female desire – especially that of a thirteen-year-old – being as urgent as that of the male was troubling for eighteenth- and nineteenth-century audiences. The actor and director David Garrick increased Juliet's age to seventeen in his 1748 adaptation of *Romeo and Juliet* and removed some of the more overtly erotic language from the epithalamium (see below). As with any age of course, sensibilities around the sexual content of the speech were by no means uniform. The Romantic critic, William Hazlitt, praised it for 'combining warmth of imagination and tenderness of heart with the most voluptuous sensibility' (Hazlitt, *Characters*, 146), whereas just over a decade later, Anna Jameson sought to play down any 'voluptuous' elements by emphasizing its poetic qualities: 'The fond adjuration, "Come night! Come Romeo! *come thou day in night!*" expresses that fulness of enthusiastic admiration for her lover, which possesses her whole soul; but expresses it as only Juliet could or would have expressed it, – in bold and beautiful metaphor' (Jameson, I, 123).

* * *

Compared with the bawdy of Mercutio and the Nurse, Juliet's speech is relatively demure, yet as Weis observes, some of the lines are striking in 'their sheer sexual candour' (Weis, 14). Such candour went through varying degrees of dilution as time went on. Garrick removed the most unambiguously sexual language (lines 8 to 16 and 'and though I am sold,/Not yet enjoyed') and, about half a century later, in Thomas Bowdler's *Family Shakespeare*, the speech appeared cut by half, losing from the middle of line 5 down to and including line 16 (with the exception of 'Come, civil night ... all in black') and the final six lines. Hazlitt regarded the bowdlerization of the soliloquy as the work of those who '[w]ithout refinement themselves, ... confound modesty with hypocrisy' (Hazlitt, *Characters*, 145). Yet regardless of the voices raised against such censorship, expurgated editions of the text continued to circulate well into the twentieth century: that Juliet was a sexually aware and desiring being would have come as quite a shock to several generations of school students. It is interesting to note, though, how lines 21 to 25 of the speech usually escaped the blue pencil. Today, these lines are frequently read as expressive of the female orgasm, with critics and actors alike picking up on Juliet's quibble on 'die' – a verb which commonly connoted sexual climax for the Elizabethans. This is a moot example of how a historicist approach to the language of the text can alert critics to its potential richness. It is also an example of how sexual innuendo tends to be firmly rooted in a specific time frame; while it is unlikely that the majority of audience members today would pick up on the double meaning of 'die', they may well find a like significance in the frequently repeated and emphatically placed imperative, 'Come'.

* * *

Juliet's soliloquy moves swiftly from apostrophe to apostrophe, with 'fiery-footed steeds', night, and Romeo all serving as addressees. This dramatic device underlines Juliet's solitariness, her lack of a female companion in whom to confide, as well as exteriorizing feelings that would usually only be communicated between intimates. The speech has an urgent, incantatory pulse running through it, created through the insistent repetition of words such as 'night' and 'come', and through frequent deviations from the **iambic** rhythm. Metrical stress often falls on imperative verbs placed at the start of lines ('Spread', 'Leap', 'Hood', 'Come', 'Give', 'Take'), these initial **trochees** conveying a sense of impatience even more pressing than that expressed in Juliet's earlier soliloquy, spoken as she awaits the arrival of the Nurse (2.5.1–17).

Feelings of sexual desire are suggested not only through the pulsating verse rhythms, but also through imagery which draws attention to the senses. The image of lovers performing 'their amorous rites/By their own beauties' throws emphasis on erogenous sensation. While nowadays the idea of making love in the dark is associated with modesty or coyness, as it is presented here, the absence of clear vision suggests a consequent intensification of other senses – the smell, touch, taste and sound of sex. Reading the line in the context of the Elizabethan belief that eyes emitted light, adds an extra dimension: the lovers, eyes wide open, see only as far as the object of their desire. Juliet's heightened sensory consciousness is also conveyed through the protean nocturnal imagery and its phantasmagorical shifts from spreading curtains to 'sober-suited matron' to a kind of dark angel, bearing Romeo on its wing. Yet for all its erotic fervour, the speech insists on the sexual inexperience of the speaker; her 'bating' blood is both a sign of passion and virginal shyness, one of the soliloquy's several paradoxes. However desirous she may be, she is yet to 'learn' the lessons of the amatory.

In its foregrounding of physical desire, the soliloquy recognizes the erotic as a key part of a woman's identity, not merely a physiological necessity for procreation, and in this sense could be seen as presciently modern. Although, as a recent critical study observes, 'it is difficult to decide whether the text is self-consciously offering a different "type" of woman that did not exist, whether it is constructing a woman who was just becoming possible at the time, or whether it is presenting a recognizable type that modern gender relations have obscured' (Hunter and Lichtenfels, 135).

As is made clear in the quotation, contextualized readings of early modern playtexts are bound to be provisional, not least because the contemporary non-fiction texts that offer insights into what life was like for the early modern woman tend to be male-authored and didactic (sermons, conduct books, antifeminist tracts), and thus by no means wholly representative.

Language and identity

The connection between language and identity is a major field of modern linguistics, as well as preoccupying much of the post-structuralist theory that has informed literary studies. It was also a key area of interest for Renaissance thinkers, who viewed speech as a defining characteristic of human beings. *Romeo and Juliet* is one of Shakespeare's most linguistically self-conscious plays. Its numerous puns range across the play from the lewd innuendo of servants, to the scintillating wordplay of Mercutio, to Romeo's final quibble on 'die' as he breathes his last. In the homosocial world of Shakespeare's Verona, being smart with puns is a crucial means by which a young man can project a self worthy of respect; as Jonathan Hope underlines in *Shakespeare and Language*, 'such wordplay was a sign of intelligence and social engagement in the Renaissance' (Hope, 43). Given this social context, Romeo's layering of **oxymora** in the play's opening scene appears more a conventional demonstration of the 'feelings' expected of a courtly gentleman than an expression of genuine suffering.

Juliet's relationship with language is markedly less conformist than her lover's. What is arguably the most famous (and most frequently parodied) scene in the play sees her exhort Romeo to separate his 'real' self from his given name:

> What's in a name? That which we call a rose
> By any other word would smell as sweet;
> So Romeo would, were he not Romeo called,
> Retain that dear perfection which he owes
> Without that title. Romeo, doff thy name,
> And for thy name, which is no part of thee,
> Take all myself.

2.2.43–9

Here Juliet imagines an 'essential' Romeo existing beyond the symbolic order of naming. Derrida's deconstructionist reading of the speech dismisses Juliet's onomastic wrangling as futile, caught up in the very language system it seeks to evade: 'She does not say to him: why are you called Romeo, why do you bear this name (like an article of clothing, an ornament, a detachable sign)? She says to him: why *are you* Romeo? She knows ... his name is his essence. Inseparable from his being' (Derrida, 426).

Other critics, such as Ryan, regard the lovers' attempts to divorce themselves from the language of their society as demonstrating 'the tragedy's estrangement from its era, the imprint of its commerce with futurity' (Ryan, *Shakespeare*, 83). Certainly, the tragedy invites its audience to contemplate at least the possibility of dismantling the linguistic discourses that constrain Romeo's self-expression. It is frequently observed that, thanks to Juliet's influence, Romeo is able to shed the **Petrarchisms** of his Rosaline period. Indeed, as the more linguistically daring and nonconformist of the pair, Juliet is quick to point out the absurdities of his courtly clichés; not only does she assert the inappropriateness of swearing by 'th'inconstant moon' (2.2.109), she also advises him to 'not swear at all' (2.2.112), an attempt, perhaps, to move their love beyond the constraints of language and the contaminating influence of tradition. As events take their course, so Juliet becomes increasingly adept at accommodating her language to the quickly changing circumstances, so that word becomes mask, a vital means of preserving a secret self.

📖 *Read the dialogue between Lady Capulet and Juliet (3.5.68–104).*

In what ways does this scene contribute to the play's consideration of the relationship between language and identity?

Lady Capulet's promise that Romeo will be hunted down and murdered comes immediately after the **aubade** and Juliet's premonition of Romeo's death, a sequence which underscores the ironic doubleness of the situation: Romeo is both villain and adored husband; Juliet both bride-to-be and married woman. The dilemma of Juliet's split identity is especially keenly felt when Romeo is given the **epithet** of 'villain' by her mother – a term of abuse that ironically echoes the daughter's earlier naming of him as an 'honourable villain' (3.2.79), an oxymoron generated by her short-lived anger at the news of Tybalt's murder. Most editors follow Thomas Hanmer (an early editor of Shakespeare) in marking the first line of Juliet's response to her mother's use of the term as an aside, a theatrical convention which indicates a disparity between the external and internal. The use of the adverbial 'asunder' in the aside is not only a poignant reminder of the liturgy of the marriage service and of Juliet's premature estrangement from her new husband, it also marks the moment in the encounter when Juliet's words begin to operate solely on the level of double meaning.

Juliet's sustained equivocality allows her to appear the vengeful Capulet while at the same time remaining the faithful

Montague wife. The precarious balance between these identities is sometimes reflected in the verbal balance of the syntax: 'Dead' is placed between the end of the sentence spoken as the grieving cousin and the start of the sentence intended by the grieving wife – a Janus-like hinge to enable both Juliets to speak at once. In other instances, the equivocality comes from the **polysemy** of individual words: 'satisfied' signifies the reward of both revenge and sexual pleasure; the verb 'temper' signifies both the fury of the avenger intent on making a substance fatally toxic, or the lover's desire to render the substance harmless through dilution. There is, though, nothing in the play's situation here that demands such linguistic contortions: Juliet could just as easily act the role of the grieving, angry Capulet without them. However, her manipulation of words seems in keeping with the tragedy's preoccupation with the nature of language itself. While speaking with 'double tongue' generally carries associations of deception, the scene demonstrates how language play can be employed to hold faith as well as to betray. Furthermore, it draws attention to the **performative** force of the word: for Juliet, to speak ill of her husband directly, without recourse to ambiguity, would constitute an act of treachery.

Getting over the language: *William Shakespeare's Romeo + Juliet* (1996)

One of the 'extras' included in the Special Edition DVD of *William Shakespeare's Romeo + Juliet* features the director, Baz Luhrmann, recounting how, at the pitching stage of the film's development, he was warned by his producer: 'Don't mention the language ... don't mention it's Shakespeare ... until the end'. It is a warning grounded in hard economic reality: transforming an Elizabethan script into commercially profitable entertainment will always be a high-risk venture. Yet Luhrmann's conviction that 'funky Shakespeare could work', proved entirely justified. Not only was the finished product the highest grossing Shakespeare film of the twentieth century, earning $46,351,345 over the duration of its theatrical release (Hindle, 244), it has also succeeded in attracting a good deal of scholarly attention – and admiration.

For those inclined to take a more reverential approach to Shakespeare, Luhrmann and Pierce's radical editing of *Romeo and Juliet* to about a third of its original length seemed more an act of artistic barbarism than a triumph of postmodern wit and ingenuity. Such a view, of course, does not take into account that the very notion of an 'original' text is highly problematic. It is generally accepted that, like the vast majority of early modern dramas, *Romeo and Juliet* does not have a definitive text, stamped with the imprimatur of the playwright. First published in **quarto** in 1597 (Q1), it was succeeded two years later by a second version 'Newly corrected, augmented, and amended' (Q2), which would form the basis of two more quarto editions (Q3 and Q4), as well as that included in the First **Folio** of 1623. Generally accepted to be the most reliable, Q2 is the text that today's readers and audiences are most likely to encounter. It is also the text that Luhrmann chose to chop, shift around, splice and, occasionally, update.

Luhrmann's professed intent to bring *Romeo and Juliet* to audiences as heterogeneous as those attending the play's original performances is achieved through making its language as accessible as possible. From the outset, key lines from the text appear on the screen in a variety of formats, made more familiar by virtue of being both seen and heard. Lengthy speeches by characters such as the Prince, Friar Lawrence and the Apothecary are either cut completely or stripped down to their bare essentials, even Mercutio's set-piece 'Queen Mab' speech being cut by just over a half. That is not to say, though, that the film script is no more than a simple synopsis of the drama, with the more archaic language features removed. Luhrmann does not shy away from its linguistic artifice, preserving some of Romeo's Petrarchisms, the lover's shared sonnet and a good proportion of its rhyming lines (of all the tragedies, *Romeo and Juliet* has by far the highest percentage of rhyme). Nor is Luhrmann afraid to retain some of the more obscure quibbles that characterize the banter between Mercutio and his companions – *jeux de mots* frequently cut in stage performances. Preserving these features contributes to the film's self-conscious anachronism, something very much in keeping with the postmodern mood.

It is often the case that the Shakespearean lines that survive the screenwriters' cuts are moved, adapted or redistributed in order to appeal to modern sensibilities. Romeo's line 'Thy drugs are quick' (5.3.120), apostrophized to the Apothecary before he drinks his poison, becomes in the film '*Your* drugs are quick', spoken as he pops what appears to be an ecstasy tablet, prior to gate-crashing the Capulet ball. In other instances, a line is kept in place, but put into the mouth of another character. Some of Montague's lines expressing his concerns about Romeo's reclusiveness (1.1.135–8) are given to his wife, the shared parental concern perhaps being more in step with twentieth-century conceptions of the family. A more significant line shift comes in the third act when Capulet's 'And so did I' (3.4.4), referring to loving Tybalt, moves to Lady Capulet, reminding the viewer of her sexual encounter with her nephew at the fancy-dress ball, and furthering Luhrmann's interpretation of her as a young wife, unsatisfied by her ageing husband. Where these changes have a significant impact on how we interpret the relationships in the play, there are others made solely for the sake of clarity. So, for instance, when the marriage arrangements are being made, the word 'shrift' is replaced by 'confession', a substitution which, while still in keeping with early modern lexis, ensures intelligibility for twentieth-century cinema-goers.

A parallel reading of film and play scripts only goes part way to revealing the reasons for Luhrmann's success in reaching such a huge audience. As scholars of screen Shakespeare frequently observe, it is the director's ability to translate the play's imagery so exuberantly into the language of film that gives *Romeo + Juliet* its enduring appeal. Romeo's declaration that he will be 'new baptized' (2.2.50) and Juliet's that her 'bounty is as boundless as the sea' (2.2.133), though omitted from the film script, are translated to the imagery of the screen. Both lovers are associated with water from the outset. The audience first sets eyes on Juliet as she emerges out from under her bath water, a shot echoed by Romeo dousing his head in a tub of water to shake off the effects of recreational drugs, leaving his party-mask floating on the surface, a clear visual marker that he is about to leave his 'false' self behind. From the moment the lovers' eyes meet in silent communication across an enormous fish tank, water becomes their element, protecting them from the surveillance cameras as they immerse themselves in the swimming pool beneath Juliet's balcony – their baptism into a new life. The play's iterative imagery of light is literalized through the candles which burn in various locations, including in their thousands in the cathedral where the lovers take their own lives; and the starbursts of fireworks let off at the Capulet ball provide a visible prefiguration of Juliet's invoking night to cut Romeo 'out in little stars' (3.2.22). Perhaps most striking of all is how Luhrmann's casting – like Zeffirelli's before him – brilliantly captures the youthfulness of the lovers. While references to Juliet's age are cut from the play text (doubtless to avoid the uncomfortable discrepancy with today's age of consent), the sixteen-year old Danes and the twenty-year-old DiCaprio have a physical flawlessness that captures the extreme youth of Shakespeare's eponymous pair.

The film's soundtrack is equally crucial in interpreting the play's language for a cinema audience. Having promised the studio financing the film project 'more hits than you can possibly imagine' to offset the perceived difficulty of the Elizabethan dialogue, the completed soundtrack plays a major part in holding the attention of the audience at the same time as interpreting the Shakespearean text. The lyrics of popular hits such as Kym Mazelle's cover of 'Young Hearts Run Free', and the Wannadies' 'You and Me Song', interleave with the play's verse, lending emphasis to the timelessness of the love story (Luhrmann's postmodernism does not stretch as far as resisting the lure of universality). Other song lyrics engage more directly with the specifics of the text. Stina Nordenstam's 'Little Star', plays faintly as Juliet speaks her epithalamium (the first nineteen lines cut so that it starts with the image of cutting Romeo 'out in little stars') and One Inch Punch's 'Pretty Piece of Flesh', a grunge rearrangement of the clash between the Capulet and Montague servants in the opening scene of the play, provides the signature tune for the Montague 'boys'.

The two most pervasive tracks of the film, however, are Des'ree's 'Kissing You' and Radiohead's 'Talk Show Host', both of which play a vital role in pointing up the tragic irony of the love story. 'Kissing You', written specifically for the film, is very much the lovers' tune, dominating their first meeting, where it supplies both **diegetic** sound (performed directly to the guests at the Capulet ball) and **non-diegetic** sound (as background music for the 'fish tank scene'). Strains of the love song continue to track the hectic development of the lovers' relationship, a musical reminder of the *coup de foudre* moment. Likewise, Radiohead's plangent 'Talk Show Host' tracks Romeo's interior state from self-conscious melancholy, as he pens courtly love-thoughts to Rosaline in his notebook on Verona Beach, to more mature expressions of feeling for Juliet, penned in the same notebook, as he sits in the dusty wasteland of his exile. However, the lover's final scene together, set in a candle-filled cathedral that literalizes Romeo's figurative 'feasting presence full of light' (5.3.86), is played against a more traditional background music: Wagner's *Tristan and Isolde*. Perhaps a concession to those members of his audience who might be unfamiliar with the more popular elements of the soundtrack, this piece of classical music is the last to be heard in the film, providing an unabashedly emotive accompaniment to the lovers' last moments. Wagner's *liebestod* not only provides a highly charged climax to the soundtrack, it also translates into musical phrase the play's closing quibbles on sex and death: Romeo's final 'Thus with a kiss I die' (5.3.120) and Juliet's 'O happy dagger!/This is thy sheath; there rust, and let me die' (5.3.169–70).

Those who examine Shakespeare at pre-university level often complain that candidates' essays on *Romeo and Juliet* are more faithful to Luhrmann's work than Shakespeare's. Undeniably, its cinematography (an exhilarating combination of slam-zoom shots, zip pans, freeze-frames, rapid-image montages and slow motion) goes all out to leave a lasting impression. Rarely allowing the viewer time to draw breath, it is hardly surprising that *William Shakespeare's Romeo + Juliet* holds more appeal for a youth audience than a sedate saunter through the full text of Q2. The twenty-first century is still to produce a worthy successor.

Further reading

Dympna Callaghan (ed.), *Romeo and Juliet: Texts and Contexts* (Boston, 2003)

Anthony R. Guneratne, *Shakespeare, Film Studies and the Visual Cultures of Modernity* (Basingstoke, 2008)

James N. Loehlin, '"These violent delights have violent ends": Baz Luhrmann's Millennial Shakespeare', in Mark Thornton Burnett and Ramona Wray (eds), *Shakespeare, Film, Fin de Siècle* (Basingstoke, 2000)

Ben Power, *A Tender Thing: Adapted from William Shakespeare's* Romeo and Juliet (London, 2009)

Gillian Woods (ed.), *Shakespeare: Romeo and Juliet* (Basingstoke, 2013)

The Duchess of Malfi

The Duchess of Malfi is one of the few eponymous heroines of early modern drama. Where the female protagonists of tragedies such as *Romeo and Juliet* and *Antony and Cleopatra* are locked firmly in the titular embrace of their lovers, the Duchess stands alone. Why Webster chose to isolate his heroine from her partner is open to speculation. One reason might be that he was simply observing the distinctions of class: unlike

Antony or Romeo, Antonio is not his lover's social equal and thus not appropriately elevated in society to earn a place in the tragedy's title. Another might be that he was directly signalling to an audience the dramatic treatment of a well-known story of a historical duchess which had already undergone various retellings, most familiarly for an early seventeenth-century audience in William Painter's compendium of translated stories *The Palace of Pleasure* (1567). Whatever Webster's reasons for his choice of title, there is no doubt that the Duchess has held centre stage from the earliest days of performance. The **paratextual** material in the first printed edition of the play includes verses penned by two of the author's sometime collaborators, William Rowley and Thomas Middleton. Both fellow authors fix their praises on the figure of the Duchess, responding to her as she embodies real, lived experience. Middleton asks 'who'er saw this Duchess live and die/That could get off under a bleeding eye?' and Rowley avers that the historical figure had been 'lively bodied' – brought to life by the power of Webster's dramaturgy.

The Duchess continues to hold the spotlight today, both in performance and in scholarly readings. Webster's play has generated a wealth of highly diverse feminist readings, with some – but by no means all – viewing the author as a proto-feminist, more radical in his portrayal of female subjectivity than many of his contemporaries. The figure he chooses to dramatize is undoubtedly a complex one, inhabiting as she does multiple subject positions in the course of the play: ruler, mother, sister, twin, widow and wife. Where Juliet's transgression in the name of love moves along a swift, unhampered course from dutiful daughter to secret bride, the Duchess's is presented through a series of complicated, often tortuous, negotiations with the different roles and responsibilities she has taken on as a mature woman. Equally contrasting are the means by which the interior lives of the two women are suggested. As demonstrated above, the part of Juliet was unusual for the drama of the day in containing almost as many lines of soliloquy (the dramatic mode most readily associated with interiority) as that of the male lover. Yet despite occupying the title role, the Duchess has only one soliloquy in I.2 (256–64) – and even this is questionable. Indeed, the textual uncertainty as to Cariola's positioning on stage at this point in the drama has led some critics to regard *Malfi* as 'a play where the protagonist *never* speaks in soliloquy' (Caldwell, 152 [my italics]).

The Duchess's decision to marry outside the limits of class, family and religion is often taken as a defiant act of self-determination, especially by modern audiences who find in the Duchess someone in tune with post-Romantic notions of selfhood – a woman who values personal fulfilment above all else. Yet for all her pursuit of individuation, the play persists in presenting her as a character inextricably bound to others: she is identified by the title of her first husband, emotionally tied to her second husband and, as the relationship takes its course, physically attached to the couple's offspring *in utero*. The remainder of this chapter examines how far these ties that bind serve to shape or inhibit selfhood.

'The misery of us that are born great!': The double life of the Duchess

Literary treatments of female rulers attempting to seduce their male servants are plentiful. Those in Webster's audiences who had attended a performance of *Twelfth Night* would surely have noted the parallels between the forged letter of seduction from Olivia to her steward, and the situation between the Duchess and Antonio; some might have recognized as analogous the biblical story of Potiphar's wife's attempted seduction of her servant Joseph (Gen. 39.7–23) – a story reframed with irreverent comic brio in Henry Fielding's novel *Joseph Andrews* (1742). However, *Malfi* differs in one important respect from the seduction narratives cited above in that the desire between servant and mistress is reciprocal and the relationship is consummated. Painter's version is implacably unsympathetic towards the union of the Duchess and Antonio and lays the blame squarely at the feet of the mistress: 'And above all modesty ought to be kept by Women, whom as their race, Noble birth, auchtority and name, maketh them more famous, even so their vertue, honesty, chastity and continencie more prayse worthy' (Painter, III: 3–4).

Reimagined through the generally more dialogic genre of tragic drama, the lovers' story takes on an altogether more nuanced hue. Moving determinedly away from the didacticism of analogues such as Painter's, Webster explores the experience of leading a double life in all its complexities.

Read the dialogue between the Duchess and Antonio (1.2.276–322).

- *What different forms of 'doubleness' operate in this scene?*
- *Consider this extract in the light of the Duchess's line 'I am Duchess of Malfi still' (4.2.137).*

The most obvious form of doubleness lies in the Duchess playing the part of both ruler and seducer: a mistress in both senses of the word. Her halting commands at the start of the extract seem forced in their peremptoriness and that it is difficult for her to sustain the register of the ruler is shown by how quickly she loses her composure: 'What did I say?' As the scene unfolds, so commands give way to questions; the royal 'we' shifts to the personal 'I'; and there is a move away from Antonio's brief, dutiful responses to more expansive speeches exploring personal feelings about marriage and fatherhood. The shared lines (303–4) mark a clear turning point in the dialogue, as the two voices playfully interact and the focus shifts from mistress to servant. The Duchess's transition from prince to lover is pictured on stage by the giving of the ring, an action which prompts Antonio to make his first unguarded statement: 'You have made me stark blind'.

Another feature of doubleness in the scene is that which comes from equivocation and innuendo. Where Juliet equivocates in 3.5 to keep her mother at arm's length, the Duchess quibbles to draw Antonio into a more intimate communication, culminating in a clandestine marriage. As the social superior of the two, it is left to her to make the first move, to play the male role in the ritual of courtship; she is the first to draw attention to the ambiguous potential of words, stalling the conversation by completing Antonio's line and settling on his use of the phrase 'beauteous Excellence'. Rapidly converting Antonio's words from a standard honorific to a literal reference to her person, she extends their dual signification to inform Antonio that it is for his sake that she keeps a youthful appearance: a statement that he can choose to read as the praise of a mistress for a servant's job well done or a declaration of desire. As the Duchess moves to what is purportedly their meeting's purpose – arranging her will – so the scene settles on one of the most polysemous words in the Jacobean lexis. As brilliantly displayed in Shakespeare's Sonnet 135, the word 'will' could mean: 'to wish', to 'desire sexually', to project into the future, a testament, as well as a slang term for both male and female genitals. Similarly here, the Duchess and Antonio play on 'will' as a legal document and the word's connotation of desire, a quibble which also evokes the Jacobean use of 'to die' as a colloquialism for orgasm. While the Duchess leads the way in double-talk, Antonio too, as he grows more certain of his mistress's intentions, begins to exploit the potential of language to signify two or more meanings at once. He might employ the conventional rhetoric of a confirmed bachelor, but the fondness suggested by his use of the diminutive 'little' and the verb 'chatter' points in quite a different direction.

* * *

The subjectivity of the Duchess is inevitably influenced by the constraining forces of her social and political world. Her resistance to such forces could be seen as demonstrative of a strong inner self already fully formed or as the process by which selfhood comes into being. Much of the dramatic force of the play derives from the complex and precarious relationship between the Duchess's public and private spheres of existence. Once she passes her 'sovereign' ring to Antonio, she confers on him the husband's conventional right to rule and her 'excellent self' occupies at once the position of ruler and subject: the body politic and the body feminine. The tensions generated by this duality of role seem to heighten the sexual excitement between the couple. In the lovers' erotic banter in 3.2, Antonio is cast as the 'Lord of Misrule' (7), whose mastery is 'only in the night' (8), the innuendo serving to reinforce the idea that 'Love mixed with fear is sweetest' (3.2.65).

Fear soon eclipses sweetness, however, as the Duchess's secret world is exposed and the brothers assert the full power of church and state. As punishment for 'looseness' (3.4.30), the Duchess is stripped of her sovereign power by Papal authority. Yet while the 'two bodies' of the ruler are reduced to one at a stroke, it is a reduction that she refuses to acknowledge, insisting to Bosola as tomb-maker 'I am Duchess of Malfi still'. One of the stand-out lines of the drama, it is often read as a defiant expression of the immutability of the unique core of every individual. Yet such a reading is complicated by the fact that the title by which she continues to identify herself is not taken from the husband she has married in a private, self-determined ceremony, but from the husband chosen for her by male relatives. At this moment in the play, then, she defines herself by a title that appears ill-suited both to her inner sentiments and her political circumstances. At the same time, the Duchess appears at her most regal and authoritative *after* she has been stripped of her title, facing death with supreme composure and stoicism. Ultimately, then, the play deconstructs the binary opposition in Cariola's question of '[w]hether the spirit of greatness or of woman/Reign most in her' (1.2.410–11), offering up a hero whose selfhood cannot be located solely in the personal or the public.

Sex, selfhood and the companionate marriage

The Duchess's love for Antonio is inextricably bound up with her sexual desire for him and her remarriage is an act of self-definition inseparable from the life of the body. In this sense, she could be viewed as conforming to the figure of the 'lusty widow' (1.2.255), a staple of Western literature over several centuries. Such a figure embodied the threat posed to male society by a financially independent woman whose libido persisted beyond the death of the husband. While early modern attitudes to female sexuality, by their very remoteness and complexity, are difficult to pin down, the evidence supplied in the medical writings of the time suggests that strong female desire was considered to be God-given, a means of ensuring copulation and procreation. Nature's demand for erotic sensation was considered highly dangerous if not kept in check, however. In *The Secret Miracles of Nature*, sixteenth-century Dutch physician Levinus Lemnius writes of women as man's natural inferiors, whose innate physical and mental frailties lead all but an honourable few to be 'shamelesse, foolish, fierce, and imperious ... slippery, various, mutable; and as for lust of the flesh, and pleasure ... insatiable' (Lemnius, IV: 272).

How far Webster upholds normative views of female sexuality has been vigorously argued in scholarly writing. Linda Woodbridge casts the Duchess as a 'hero of desire' (Woodbridge, 'Malfi', 162) and Webster as an author intent on challenging contemporary views of female sexuality. In the course of her argument, she demonstrates how modern critical views of the Duchess's 'dogged sexiness' (Woodbridge, 'Malfi', 161) tend to polarize: some regarding her erotic attachment to Antonio as natural and healthy, others insisting on grounding it more firmly in the misogynist outlook of the day. The latter view, Woodbridge argues, has emerged partly because of a tendency to focus more on the political than the personal – a tendency that has led to some stagnation in critical thinking: 'Sex was once something you shouldn't talk about in front of children. To make it something you shouldn't talk about in front of feminists isn't doing us any favors' (Woodbridge, 'Malfi', 164). As arguments such as Woodbridge's make clear, attitudes to sexuality and its relation to selfhood are imbricated in an ever-changing social and cultural climate. Inevitably, then, plays such as *Malfi* will accumulate diverse readings, both synchronically and diachronically.

Webster's presentation of the Duchess's sexual self emphatically resists Painter's depiction of her as like 'a female Wolfe or Lionesse (when they goe to sault)' (Painter, III, 27). The Duchess's erotic longing for Antonio is presented as an integral part of her identity so that, after his supposed death, the object of her desire removed, she appears as 'like some reverend monument' (4.2.32), finally willing to become the 'figure cut in alabaster' (1.2.364) that kneels at her husband's tomb. Webster's anchoring of the Duchess's sexuality in an enduring marriage is in itself quite unusual in early modern drama, which tends to confine sexual desire to illicit liaisons, with marital sex defined by its lack of passion. In *King Lear*, the illegitimate Edmund sneers at the 'dull stale tired bed' (1.2.13) in which legitimate offspring are conceived, and the Duchess of *The Revenger's Tragedy* complains of her elderly husband's 'slack' performance in bed (1.2.75). And where there *is* erotic pleasure in marriage, it is often short-lived, cut short by untimely death or infidelity. In some instances, marital desire is shown as a disturbing phenomenon: Hamlet is repelled by the thought of Claudius and Gertrude 'honeying and making love/Over the nasty sty –' (3.4.91–2) and the sexual energy that passes between Macbeth and his wife is ineluctably bound up with the act of regicide.

It is, then, noteworthy that *Malfi* presents marital sexuality as generous, joyful and satisfying, not unlike the way it is portrayed in Protestant writings about the companionate marriage. In *Of Domesticall Duties* (1622), William Gouge refers to conjugal relations as 'benevolence': 'This *due benevolence* . . . is one of the most proper and essentiall acts of mariage: and necessary ... for increasing the world with a legitimate brood ... it must be performed with good will and delight, willingly, readily, and cheerefully' (Gouge, 222). And while the Duchess and Antonio do not always heed Gouge's caution against 'provoking, rather then asswaging lust' (Gouge, 223), they succeed in producing, 'living monuments' (Gouge, 210) to their mutual devotion. Antonio's declaration to Delio that the Duchess is 'an excellent / Feeder of pedigrees' (3.1.5–6) affirms the success of their companionate marriage – one of several instances where the couple seems to be defined in terms of Protestant values, standing in contrast to the corrupt Catholicism that surrounds them.

Pregnancy and the maternal body

The feminist critic and philosopher, Julia Kristeva, has suggested that '[p]regnancy seems to be experienced as the radical ordeal of the splitting of the subject: redoubling up of the body, separation and co-existence of the self and of another' (Kristeva, 'Women's Time', 456). Yet in the case of the Duchess, it is the determination of male authority to discover the 'secret' that lies within the pregnant body that is the eventual cause of 'the splitting of the subject', as the private life which brings integrity to her existence is discovered and destroyed.

📖 *Read Bosola's description of the Duchess (2.1.69–77) and analyse how it contributes to the play's treatment of the female self.*

Despite the Duchess not being on stage when Bosola is speaking, she is nonetheless placed as the object of the male **gaze**, her pregnant body defined by its changeability: it 'wanes' and 'waxes' and operates as if independent from an autonomous 'self'. Written at a time of rapidly emerging enquiry into the science of reproduction, Bosola's speech offers an interesting parallel to the ever-increasing scrutiny of the maternal body by the male physician and the concomitant desire to unlock the mysteries of its perceived instability. Bosola's observation that the Duchess's 'eyelids look most teeming blue' suggests an unnervingly close-up surveillance of the physical form; it also conforms to the advice given in Jacques Guillemeau's childbirth manual, *Childbirth, or, The Happy Delivery of Women* (first translated into English in 1612) that 'as Hippocrates saith, if thou canst not find by any meanes whether a woman be with childe, or no, her very eies wil tel thee' (Guillemeau, 5).

Yet for all the disturbing nearness of Bosola's regard, there are some vital signs which he cannot access. For the early modern male the uncertainties surrounding conception were highly troubling, not least because final proof of a viable pregnancy was deemed to lie with the woman – a sex not noted for its honesty. In Ford's *'Tis Pity She's a Whore*, the servant Puttana, when asked by Giovanni how she knows Annabella is pregnant, responds with a succinct list of physical signs very similar to those noted by Bosola: 'changing of colours, queasiness of stomachs, pukings, and another thing that I could name' (*'Tis Pity*, 3.3.14–15). The 'thing' that rests unnamed is the cessation of menstruation: a crucial, though by no means definitive, diagnostic sign that can only be confirmed by the woman whose womb is in question. In addition, the foetal movements which provided almost certain proof of pregnancy remained the inner secret of the mother at least until the final weeks before birth when, as Bosola acknowledges, it is possible to see the 'the young springal cutting a caper' (2.1.156) in an unclothed belly. Thus the 'loose-bodied gown' which prevents Bosola from seeing the Duchess's secret manifest in flesh is also a physical sign of the female proclivity for mystery and deception.

Webster's presentation of the pregnant Duchess could be regarded as diminishing her individuality: she is watched with an almost **scopophilic** intensity, her voracious eating of the 'wondrous fair' (2.1.138) apricots seeming to present her as a mirror image of Eve, her appetite beyond control. However, while pregnancy endangers and eventually exposes the secret life that has enabled the Duchess to express her inner desires, it also brings a rich new dimension to her sense of self. The Duchess's maternal affection is often seen as one of her defining features, aligning her somewhat anachronistically with modern conceptions of motherhood. *Malfi* was composed at a time when the classical belief that a child was formed solely from male seed, with the woman carrying out the subordinate role of incubator, was being increasingly held up to question. Lemnius, for example, warns that if mothers 'must endure the tedious time of nine Moneths, as if the womb were hired by men, as Merchants ships are to be fraited by them' they would 'grow luke-warm, and lose all humane affections toward their children' (Lemnius, I: 9, 10). Webster's presentation of the Duchess makes clear that she is far from a 'luke-warm' mother. Her fondness for her children is often seen to culminate in the maternal solicitude she displays just moments before she faces her own death:

> I pray thee, look thou giv'st my little boy
> Some syrup for his cold, and let the girl
> Say her prayers ere she sleep.
>
> 4.2.196–8

Judith Haber reads these lines in terms of the unsettling of contemporary notions of the tragic, observing that 'it is surely remarkable for a "tragic heroine" to die neither attempting wholly to "personate masculine virtue," nor wholly focused on her male partner . . . but concerned instead with the mundane comforts of her children' (Haber, 83).

To say that the Duchess's main focus is on her children rather than her male partner is, though, to overlook one of the play's more unique features: its presentation of parents who *both* display tender feelings towards their children. The couple's affective final scene together suggests dual parenting. Before parting, the Duchess tells Antonio that he resembles a 'dying father' (3.5.86) and he exhorts her: 'Be a good mother to your little ones' (3.5.83). Considered in the light of this scene, the Duchess's solicitude for her children shortly before her death could be read as a wife fulfilling her husband's last wish.

However, what Haber terms the 'extraordinary ordinariness' (Haber, 83) of the Duchess's last requests for her children is complicated by one of several of the play's textual puzzles: why does the Duchess speak of her children as living beings, when she has been presented with physical evidence to the contrary? Some editors suggest that she has by this point discovered the truth about Ferdinand's cruel trick with the wax effigies, though this begs the question of why the audience is kept in the dark about such an important discovery, as well as sitting oddly with her reaction to Bosola's revelation that the dead bodies were faked: 'Mercy!' (4.2.342). Alternatively, if the Duchess has 'forgotten' that her children are deceased, then her motherly concern for them in her final moments could be – though it rarely is – taken as heart-rending evidence that her mind has finally collapsed under the weight of her suffering. That a director of *Malfi* must choose between presenting the Duchess's instructions as coming from an ever-mindful mother, or one deluded and traumatized by loss, is a telling example of what Emma Smith terms the 'tragic opacity' of Webster's female lead (Smith, 'Shakespeare', 140). But for all the uncertainties which surround her motivation, actions and dramatic statements, at the close of the drama, audiences often feel that they have come to 'know' the inner life of its hero. This illusion of familiarity with the Duchess's interior world derives largely from the dialogic exchanges she has with others, both intimates and adversaries, as well as from the inclination of each generation of playgoers to 'dress themselves in her' (1.2.123).

Moving performances: *Malfi* at the Blackfriars and the Globe

The early performance history of *Malfi* owes a considerable debt to the paratextual materials provided in the First Quarto of 1623. Its title page states that it was performed by the King's

Men 'privatly, at the Black-Friers; and publiquely at the Globe' and its list of actors helps peg the date of the first performance at no later than December 1614, when one of the named cast-members, William Ostler, is thought to have died. Though it is not known for sure which theatre first hosted Webster's tragedy, it is considered likely that its earliest performance was at the Blackfriars. The rebuilding of the original Globe, accidentally burnt to the ground in a performance of Shakespeare's *Henry VIII* during the mid-summer season of 1613, did not reach completion until the spring of 1614 and the King's Men are likely to have used the Blackfriars as an alternative space. Speculation also has it that Webster may have felt more inclined for his play to premier in front of the generally well-to-do spectators of the indoor theatre than the demographically broader audiences found outdoors, especially given that his earlier tragedy, *The White Devil*, had met with less than rapt attention from the 'ignorant asses' in attendance at the open-air Red Bull theatre (see Webster, 5).

How far venue would have influenced *Malfi* in performance has been an enduring question for performance scholars and, for want of firm evidence, answers to the question are usually couched in the grammar of conjecture. In the introduction to the Arden edition (2013), Leah Marcus notes how 'recent research suggests that playing conditions at the two venues may have been more similar than earlier theatre historians had thought' (Marcus, *Duchess*, 92). Evidence of such similarity can be found in the example of the second Globe, which is known to have adopted some indoor theatre practices, such as frequent act breaks filled with musical entertainment; the playing areas were also comparable in terms of structure, if not size, with both offering 'discovery spaces' and a balcony for dual-level performance. Neither Globe nor Blackfriars had much in the way of scenic effects, with portable stage objects such as thrones, rings and costume serving to create a sense of time, place and atmosphere. Yet notwithstanding these undoubted similarities, there were some significant differences between indoor and outdoor performance conditions. One of these was the audience demographic. The details printed on the title page of Q1 distinguish between performances given 'privatly' and 'publiquely', a somewhat misleading distinction in that it suggests that entry to the Blackfriars was by membership only. In principle it was open to all, though the high price of admission guaranteed its upmarket status, a place where well-heeled playgoers could parade their finery, untroubled by the changeability of the English weather. The theatre scholar Andrew Gurr supposes that the numerous erudite references in Webster's writing were carefully tuned to the 'more learned hearers at the Blackfriars' (Gurr, *Playgoing*, 99) and he and others have supposed that the playwright's foregrounding of female characters in his two tragedies took account of the increasing number of women frequenting indoor theatres.

The opening of the Wanamaker Playhouse on London's Bankside in January 2014 provided an exciting new space for researching the impact of venue on performance. Inspired by a seventeenth-century sketch discovered in Worcester College, Oxford, in the 1960s, the project was developed through a combination of expert research and not a little guesswork. The choice of *Malfi* as the theatre's inaugural production was an ideal means of underscoring the Globe's commitment to exploring original practices both indoors and outdoors. Moreover, Webster's tragedy launched a repertoire which extends well beyond the works of Shakespeare, featuring early modern dramas rarely staged in professional theatres, such as Beaumont and Fletcher's *The Knight of the Burning Pestle*, John Ford's *The Broken Heart* and John Marston's *The Malcontent*. The then artistic director of the Globe, Dominic Dromgoole, has described the new playhouse as an 'anti-Globe' (Dromgoole), a phrase that rings particularly true to visitors used to attending the outdoor theatre in the summer season. Housing only 340 spectators (about half the number thought to have been accommodated at the Blackfriars), the intimacy of this new space is in striking contrast to the lively bustle of the Globe. Once seated, audiences have only to focus on the stage and, should they so choose, their fellow playgoers, without the outdoor distractions of inclement weather and the noise of helicopters traversing the city.

While seeing *Malfi* performed in London's newest theatrical venue offered audiences some insight into how the Jacobeans might have experienced the play at the Blackfriars, these were limited by a number of factors. No gallants seated on stools graced the flanks of the stage as they would have done in Webster's day – a presence that would surely have added an extra perspective to the play's action – and the building offered no natural light through the windows as would have been the case at the Blackfriars. Rather, Dromgoole's 2014 *Malfi* made much of its opportunities to control lighting effects through total blackout, as one reviewer observed: 'A particularly memorable moment occurs when Ferdinand demands darkness in order to offer his hand to his sister in reconciliation but – in the darkness – gives her a dead man's severed hand instead' (Schafer, *THE*).

Such a moment of horror could not have been created so intensely in the broad daylight of the second Globe, nor even on the stage of the Blackfriars, which was illuminated by a mix of natural light and candlelight. Nonetheless, what the Globe Playhouse production vividly brought home was the impact of candlelight on the audience experience, its flickering chiaroscuro managing to both enhance the romance of the play's tender love scenes and its moments of Gothic nightmare. The actors' carrying of single candlesticks and candelabras had the effect of directing audience attention to focal points in the performance, as observed by theatre critic, Michael Billington: '[T]he image of this production I shall retain is of Dawson's [Ferdinand's] pale, pinched features glimpsed by a flickering candle as he vows to go hunt the badger by moonlight' (Billington, *Malfi*).

One other aspect of watching *Malfi* in the replica Jacobean playhouse which reviewers frequently highlight is the intimacy of the experience. The proximity of spectator to actor provoked a range of audience responses to Dromgoole's production: from feelings of voyeurism at the execution of the Duchess – heightened by the fact that audience members could watch each other watching acts of extreme cruelty – to tension as the consort of madmen threatened to spill out into the auditorium. That the playgoers are visible to the actors means that lines can be addressed directly to the audience, a practice usually confined to outdoor theatre. As Duchess, Gemma Arterton directed her complaint that those born great are 'forced to woo' (1.2.352) to the audience; likewise, Ferdinand pronounced his vision of his sister in bed with 'a strong-thighed bargeman' (2.5.42) to the spectators seated before him, provoking laughter and lessening as a result the impact of a speech loaded with perverse menace.

Though London's latest playhouse does not offer an entirely 'authentic' experience of Jacobean theatre – health and safety regulations if nothing else have made sure of that – it does illuminate ways in which venue might have shaped both performance and audience response in early modern London. Moreover, it offers theatre scholars exciting opportunities for promoting, in the words of Dromgoole, 'dynamic conversations between past and present' (Dromgoole).

Further reading

Roberta Barker, *Early Modern Tragedy, Gender and Performance, 1984–2000: The Destined Livery* (Basingstoke, 2007)

Christine Dymkowski and Christie Carson (eds), *Shakespeare in Stages: New Theatre Histories* (Cambridge, 2010)

Eve Keller, *Generating Bodies and Gendered Selves: The Rhetoric of Reproduction in Early Modern England* (Seattle, 2007)

Christina Luckyj (ed.), *The Duchess of Malfi: A Critical Guide* (London, 2011)

Gail Kern Paster, Katherine Rowe, Mary Floyd-Wilson (eds), *Reading the Early Modern Passions: Essays in the Cultural History of Emotion* (Philadelphia, 2004)

2

Money and the modern city:

The Merchant of Venice and *Volpone*

> [This] noble citie ... this incomparable city, this most beautifull Queene, this untainted virgine, this Paradise, this Tempe, this rich Diademe and most flourishing garland of Christendome.
>
> CORYATE, 290

The English traveller Thomas Coryate was spellbound by the opulent and extravagant world of Venice, its 'maruelous affluence and exuberancy of all things' (Coryate, 256). His travel journal (1611) describes in exhaustive detail the magnificence of its architecture and its people: he was particularly struck by the courtesans sumptuously arrayed in gold and 'orient pearl' and, famously, bare-breasted. Like Byron, 200 years later, Coryate found a city dedicated to pleasure:

The pleasant place of all festivity
The revel of the earth, the masque of Italy!

BYRON, *Childe Harold's
Pilgrimage*, 4.3.7–8

Travellers discovered a ceremonial world of ritual and display, much of which celebrated the city itself: in Carpaccio's early Renaissance paintings a crowded Venetian scene is engaged in elaborate processions, both religious and secular. Phillipe de Commynge, the French ambassador contemporary with Carpaccio, found Venice to be 'the most triumphant city that I have ever seen, and that gives most honor [*sic*] to ambassadors and foreigners' (cited in Fortini Brown, *Venetian*, 167). Coryate was impressed by the sober dignity of the Levantine Jews – 'goodly and proper men' – whom he viewed as men of learning, practising, with stoic endurance, the rituals and traditions of their Mosaic religion. Indeed, their strict sabbatarianism provoked him to comment that English Christians would benefit from following their example. The Jewish ghetto and its synagogue intrigued English visitors: Jews had been exiled from England in 1290 and although there were clearly Jews resident in London, there was then no sense of a discrete community with freedom of worship. Arguably the richest city of Renaissance Europe, Venice's wealth had always derived from its crucial situation commanding Mediterranean trade routes. As Antonio himself recognizes, 'the trade and profit of the city/Consisteth of all nations' (3.3.30–1): '[A] marketplace of the world not of the citie . . . Here you may see all manner of fashions of attire and heare all the languages of Christendom . . . each nation distinguished from another by their proper and peculiar habits' (Coryate, 173, 1, 5).

Venice welcomed foreign traders, it was a byword for religious tolerance and, as a republic and city state, it was entirely separate from its Italian neighbours. Religion itself was determined by political and commercial factors: Venice was at odds with the papacy because Rome was seen as a rival city. The legal processes of Venice were also remarkable: the city was governed by an elected Duke at a time when primogeniture and absolute monarchy was the prevailing norm across Europe. Shakespeare would have known of the city from traveller's tales – both oral and printed – and possibly from London's Italian expatriates, a sizeable community living and working in close proximity to the heart of London's merchant city. Two plays – *Othello* and *The Merchant of Venice* – are set in this urbane and sophisticated world, both dramatizing the confrontations between an indigenous elite and a foreign 'Other': Renaissance Venice was 'an excellent setting for presenting complex issues' (Levith, 15).

The merchants of Italian cities were financially and culturally highly influential. Historian Alison Brown makes a key connection between the wealth and trade of Italian merchants and the artistry of the Renaissance: 'It was the existence of so many merchants, traders and artisans that made the culture of Italian cities distinctive. And it was these men ... who created the consumer boom that stimulated the artistic revival; for they made and paid for the art and artefacts that adorned the new Renaissance palaces and chapels' (Brown, *Renaissance*, 14). Lisa Jardine shows how the rich fabrics depicted in paintings such as Bellini's *Doge Leonardo Loredan* 'symbolized Venetian access to wealth and goods in the East through its historic position as dominating maritime power in the Mediterranean' (Jardine, 19). Merchants, in other words, both created and supplied the desire for luxury commodities. Within Venice's 'marketplace of the world' Antonio is a 'royal merchant' (3.2.238), commanding respect among his peers. Yet advancing sums of money in the expectation of profit also defines the merchant's business: he lays out funds; he looks for a return. As Auden observes

> Venice does not produce anything itself, either raw materials or manufactured goods. Its existence depends upon financial profits which can be made by international trade ... that is to say, on buying cheaply here and selling dearly there.

> Money has ceased to be simply a convenient medium of exchange and become a form of social power which can be gained or lost.
>
> AUDEN, 219–20

Sea-trade is hazardous, however; cargoes and investments could be lost. For the Christian West, still wrestling with medieval attitudes towards usury, money presented moral and spiritual conflicts.

* * *

> 'yf you have care of your owne soules, for Christes sake abhorre thys ugly usury and lothe with all your hartes this this cursed limme of the devil'
>
> WILSON, *Discourse* 373

It is perhaps difficult now to grasp the extent to which riches were regarded with suspicion. Money was a cause of spiritual anxiety to the medieval Catholic church; it was invariably connected with the mortal sins of envy and covetousness and thereby regarded as ensnaring and corrupting. Biblical authority underpinned this: Jesus' parable of Dives and Lazarus, the rich man and the beggar, depicts the wealthy Dives agonizing in hell while the leprous beggar rests in heaven beside the patriarch Abraham; St Paul instructed that 'the love of money is the root of all evil' (1 Tim. 6.10). But if money was seen as either barren or a lure of the devil, then usury, making money only through money, was profoundly immoral, even impious. Contemporary writing establishes why, for moral and religious reasons, lending money for gain was unacceptable. Thomas Wilson's *A Discourse Upon Usury* (1572) expresses centuries of Christian preaching on the subject: '[The] woord of god is directley againste all usurie and usurers, and doth not onely forbid the same synne but threateneth deathe and dampnacion to them that use it' (Wilson, 279).

The central thinking behind this was the belief that money as a substance was inherently sterile and it was therefore 'against nature for money to beget money' (Bacon, 421). Loans had always existed, however, and financial exigencies could be pressing. The reality of the late Elizabethan period is that many of the Queen's chief courtiers died heavily in debt. In 1571 Elizabeth's government approved a statute which, on the one hand reiterated the prevailing thinking that usury was damnable and, on the other, legalized interest rates of 10 per cent or less thereby drawing attention to the contradictory attitudes of the time. Furthermore, 'money' was changing from a realizable physical entity – gold and coin – to the unseen and powerful commodity with which the modern world is familiar. The 1590s saw an emerging economy of insurance (the first modern life insurance policy in England was 1583) as well as business speculation: lending money in the hope of gain. So the early modern period saw the beginnings of modern banking practice while moral and religious argument thundered on, opposing the pursuit and acquisition of wealth by means other than honest diligence. Bacon's essay 'On Riches' articulates the Protestant viewpoint of 1625:

> The ways to enrich are many, and most of them foul. Parsimony is one of the best, and yet is not innocent; for it withholdeth men from works of liberality and charity. The improvement of the ground is the most natural obtaining of riches; for it is our great mother's blessing, the earth's; but it is slow ... Usury is the certainest means of gain, although one of the worst ... for that the scriveners and brokers do value unsound men, to serve their own turn.
>
> BACON, 410–11

* * *

While Shakespeare dramatizes Venice in all its fabled magnificence, the differences from and similarities with London repay exploration. In a discussion of the immediate popularity of the play, James Bulman identifies the concerns of 1590s' London as '[the] acquisition of wealth, weighed against the perils of trade, class antagonisms ... prejudice against minorities' (Bulman, 13). By the end of Elizabeth's reign the long-established, conservative world of England's trade in wool and cloth with the Low Countries had altered completely. Braudel's study of the Mediterranean establishes that, by the end of the sixteenth century, 'the English were everywhere in the Mediterranean, in Moslem, or Christian countries, and travelling along all the overland routes ... to Europe or the Indian Ocean' (Braudel, 628). Shakespeare's audience would have seen the many vessels entering the Pool of London; they would also have heard tales of the seafaring exploits of Drake, Hawkins and Raleigh. In a study of England's sea empire, historians Quinn and Ryan discuss the extensive nature of English trade in the early years of the seventeenth century and the activity of the port of London – between 1609 and 1612, 714 ships were recorded (Quinn and Ryan, 152). Great naval victories, the circumnavigation of the globe, the seizing of Spanish treasure ships, all contributed to Elizabeth's naval and mercantile maritime supremacy, while new trading routes and undreamed of new colonies were established under James I. The Levant Company prospered from its inception in 1581, merging with the 'Venice Company' founded in 1583; London's powerful East India Company was founded in 1600 by Royal Charter. The political reality of the time is that London had overtaken Venice in terms of expansionism and colonialism. Mulryne's study of Shakespeare's Venice argues that 'the irreversible decline of Venice as a maritime power can be convincingly dated to the mid-sixteenth century and after' (Mulryne, 91). The 'myth of Venice', however, would prove well-established and long-enduring.

As early modern London became a city dedicated to commerce and finance, theatres explored the tensions of an increasingly acquisitive world. This chapter examines Shakespeare's portrayal of the complex conflicts of money, race and love in *The Merchant of Venice* and Jonson's ebullient, troubling satire of the pursuit of wealth in *Volpone*.

The Merchant of Venice

Antonio: The melancholy Merchant

The Merchant of Venice begins with a conundrum: the unexplained melancholy of the eponymous protagonist. Antonio possesses all the arrogant confidence of the successful merchant trader who is wealthy enough to loan money gratis. His financial probity is unquestioned and he arrogates the right to spit upon the moneylenders who operate outside his privileged position. Of course, Antonio's proclaimed sadness could be a statement of his inordinate affection for Bassanio. If so, Bassanio's hearty opening, 'when shall we laugh? Say, when?' (1.1.66) seems crassly unfeeling. Alternatively, critic David McPherson suggests that Antonio's sombre pessimism symbolizes the decline of Venice itself (McPherson, 54). A troubled opening is not incompatible with comedy as a genre: both Orsino in *Twelfth Night* and Orlando in *As You Like It* express their sorrows in the opening words of the play. Their melancholy is not inexplicable, however; Orsino is love-sick, Orlando is dispossessed. Antonio cannot identify the cause of his world-weariness and evidently it is a cause of annoyance to his companions. As far as they are concerned, anxiety over money is the obvious cause, their elaborate flattery evoking both the ostentation of Venice and Antonio's privileged place within it.

📖 *Read the speeches of Salarino and Salanio in the opening scene, looking closely at the language used to describe the merchant ships.*

Shakespeare conflates two discrete images here (7–13): the confident affluence of the wealthy merchant and the magnificence of the ship in full sail. These opening exchanges pursue, in **euphuistic** compliments, ideas of Antonio's commerce without needing to reference money itself, as if the brutal exigencies of trade are too vulgar to be connected with 'the pageants of the sea'. The merchant is land-bound, his presence commands respect, even obsequiousness from his inferiors – he is 'portly'. The primary meaning of this in Shakespeare's time was majestic and dignified (OED a) but Shakespeare himself, in 1596, contributes the fuller connotation of 'a portly man ... and a corpulent' (*2H6*, OED b). The two speakers emphasize the physical substance of Antonio's wealth and their admiration of it yet, paradoxically, they draw attention to its vulnerability:

> Should I go to church
> And see the holy edifice of stone
> And not bethink me straight of dangerous rocks,
> Which, touching but my gentle vessel's side,
> Would scatter all her spices on the stream,
> Enrobe the roaring waters with my silks

1.1.28–33

The beauty of Salarino's language belies the disaster he describes – silks and spices, the traditional merchandise of the Venetians, scattered across the seas. To Salarino, everything in life would conspire to remind him of the fragility of his cargoes; the church itself is adamantine rather than consolatory. Odds are stacked against the seafarer who has no resources against rocks, sands and stormy waters. He cites a contemporary prize ship: the 'wealthy Andrew' was a richly laden Spanish galleon, the San Andrés, captured in 1596 in Cadiz harbour by the Earl of Essex. The allusion to the trophy ship connotes, equally, rich prizes but perilous seas. Later, when Antonio's ships have failed to return, Salarino reports that 'Antonio hath a ship of rich lading wracked on the narrow seas. The Goodwins ... they call the place' (3.1.2–4). The Elizabethan audience would certainly know the reference to the treacherous Goodwin sands, stretching some miles off the coast of Kent and the site of several wrecks in the early 1590s. Mercantile anxieties are brought close to home in these references. Antonio's unremitting malaise corresponds, interestingly, with the pathology of melancholy analysed by Burton for whom ambition, covetousness and love of money were potential causes of melancholy: 'Our *summum bonum* is commodity, and the Goddesse we adore *Dea Moneta*, Queene Mony to whom we daily offer sacrifice, which steers our hearts, hands, affections, all' (Burton, 36).

Throughout the action of the play, Antonio appears strangely passive, expressing no enthusiasm for life and ready to accept martyrdom in the trial scene, seeing himself as 'a tainted wether of the flock' (4.1.113). He certainly does not identify with his fellow Venetians, the masquers before Bassanio's feast. Rather, like Shylock who instructs his daughter 'Let not the sound of shallow foppery enter/My sober house' (2.5.34–5), he makes an unexpected appearance to stop further merrymaking, 'No masque tonight, the wind is come about' (2.6.65). Mulryne argues that Antonio's inertia is representative of Venice itself: 'fragile, anxiety-ridden and characterised by surface not substance' (Mulryne, 89). Antonio's reserve is all the more marked in comparison with the insistent gaiety of his fellow Venetians:

GRATIANO　　　　　　　　Let me play the fool.
With mirth and laughter let old wrinkles come,
And let my liver rather heat with wine
Than my heart cool with mortifying groans.

1.1.79–82

The 'magnificos' of the play pursue pleasure with single-mindedly dedication, but are they an attractive opposition to Antonio? To Auden, the play is one of the 'plays unpleasant' (Auden, 221) and Bassanio, Gratiano and Lorenzo are inherently dislikeable: '[For] all their beauty and charm [they] appear as frivolous members of a leisure class, whose carefree life is parasitic upon the labours of others, including usurers' (Auden, 234). Shakespeare's merchant cares less for his cargoes than for Bassanio: '[He] only loves the world for him' (2.8.50). The fact that Bassanio initially appears to be as superficial and frivolous as Gratiano makes Antonio's offer of '[my] purse, my person, my extremest means' (1.1.138) the more poignant, while also signalling the catastrophic confusion of love and money in this Venetian world.

As the ostensibly prudent businessman, Antonio contradicts himself from the beginning. He reassures Salarino that 'My ventures are not in one bottom trusted,/Nor to one place; nor is my whole estate/Upon the fortune of this present year' (1.1.41–3) but he later informs Bassanio, that 'all my fortunes are at sea' (1.1.177). He is unable to raise credit for Bassanio and, when his ships are lost, his creditors are pressing. Tubal refers to 'divers of Antonio's creditors' (3.1.102) and Antonio himself writes to Bassanio that 'my creditors grow cruel' (3.2.315). This raises a telling question: does Shakespeare intend his merchant to appear commercially inept? It is a subject that has been raised by a modern actuary (risk assessor) who queries why Antonio's ships are not insured. Insurance contracts were long established in medieval Genoa and, in London, there is evidence that underwriting voyages was common practice by the mid-sixteenth century (Admiralty Court decisions are recorded from 1524). So it could be expected that risky voyages would have been underwritten by wealthy individuals or groups of merchants. Antonio himself expects that 'twice three times' the value of the bond will arrive in Venice when his ships return but is his complacency justified? In 1596, an expedition of three ships, the *Bear*, the *Bear's Whelp* and the *Benjamin*, under the command of Captain Benjamin Wood, left London for a trading voyage to China, funded by Sir Robert Dudley. The expedition was never heard of again and not one of the mariners returned (records of the late East India Company). For all Antonio's bravado, Shylock knows well the risks of his enterprises:

> He hath an argosy bound for Tripoli, another to the Indies; I understand moreover upon the Rialto, he hath a third at Mexico, a fourth for England, and other ventures he hath squandered abroad. But ships are but boards, sailors but men; there be land rats, and water rats, water thieves and land thieves – I mean pirates – and then there is the peril of waters, winds and rocks.
>
> 1.3.16–23

From the mid-twentieth century critics began to discern similarities between Antonio and Shylock, extending far beyond the superficial fact of their respective financial endeavours. In a study dated 1964, Professor David Moody argued that Shylock the outsider resembles Antonio 'an alien *within* his society [who] may be seen as an image of the inoperancy of love in the hollow heart of Venice' (Moody, 26–7, original emphasis). Certainly, Shakespeare has created, in Antonio, a merchant who is morose as the action of the play commences and, like Shylock, is excluded from its final celebrations.

Belmont and the lottery

Belmont, as the name suggests, should be the unworldly **antithesis** to commercial Venice; the Arden, Athenian forest or green place central to the structure and resolution of Shakespeare's comedies. Here, though, Shakespeare undermines neat oppositions and implies similarities. Portia's opening words are the mirror image of Antonio's: 'By my troth, Nerissa, my little body is aweary of this great world' (1.2.1–2). Just as

Antonio's ships are at the mercy of the wind and waves, Portia's happiness depends on a 'lottery' whereby 'the will of a living daughter [is] curbed the by will of a dead father' (1.2.23–4). She is the prize to be sought by the bevy of international suitors vying for her hand, although she clearly despises all of them. The tone of her gossip with Nerissa is casually racist; she dismisses her suitors on the basis of every national stereotype, jokes that the horse-loving Neapolitan prince must be the illegitimate son of the blacksmith, and objects to the dark-skinned Prince of Morocco with his 'complexion of a devil' (1.2.125). Indeed, Portia's words are the first in the play to introduce the subject of racial difference. When Morocco has chosen the wrong casket, she dismisses him with a resounding couplet:

> A gentle riddance. Draw the curtains, go.
> Let all of his complexion choose me so.
>
> 2.7.78–9

Yet courtship in the multicultural society of Venice inevitably implies the possibility of miscegenation: Gratiano greets Lorenzo and Jessica, newly married, as 'Lorenzo and his infidel!' (3.2.217) while Lorenzo challenges Lancelet over his amorous relations, 'the Moor is with child by you, Lancelet!' (3.5.35–6). Bassanio's courtship of Portia is not initially depicted in the familiar terms of Shakespearean romance; it is explored through **metaphors** of wealth and trade: 'In Belmont is a lady richly left' (1.1.161). Appealing to Antonio for 'the means' to compete with his rivals, he makes his 'quest' analogous with the Argonauts setting sail to win gold and glory:

> For the four winds blow in from every coast
> Renowned suitors, and her sunny locks
> Hang on her temples like a golden fleece,
> Which makes her seat of Belmont Colchis' strand,
> And many Jasons come in quest of her.
>
> 1.1.168–72

Jason's pursuit of the fabled golden fleece is a model of adventurous bravery but also cunning and betrayal, so Bassanio's allusion is not altogether felicitous. He makes no secret of his chief motive, his rocky finances:

> my chief care
> Is to come fairly off from the great debts
> Wherein my time, something too prodigal,
> Hath left me gaged.
>
> 1.1.127–30

Bassanio's eulogy of Portia bristles with terms of material good fortune: 'nothing undervalued ... her worth ... such thrift.' Like the merchant adventurer, Bassanio is borrowing money to secure money and in true courtly style he must engage in magnificent display, his arrival is preceded by a messenger bringing 'gifts of rich value' (2.9.90).

Critics are divided as to whether Bassanio is ineluctably led to make the correct choice of casket. Clearly Portia knows the secret: 'I could teach you/How to choose right' (3.2.10–11) but she is bound by her oath to her father. Jessica, however, has already 'forsworn' all allegiance to patriarchal authority and is richly rewarded; Portia, later, will assume her own masculine authority when she appears as the lawyer Balthazar. Perhaps the model of the dutiful daughter is open to question here. She reveals her anxiety that Bassanio might choose wrongly at the beginning of the scene, 'Pause a day or two/Before you hazard ... Before you venture for me' (3.2.1–2, 10). Her choice of the word 'hazard' suggests both the unpredictable world of Antonio's merchant ventures and the correct casket: 'Who chooseth me must give and hazard all he hath' (2.7.9). She calls for music, the 'dulcet sounds' that summon the bridegroom to marriage. The song offers a hefty aural clue with its opening rhymes of 'bred/head/nourishèd' and the warning against external attraction ('fancy'). Bassanio clearly comprehends that golden caskets are not only potentially deceitful but fraught with danger: 'Ornament is but the guiled shore/To a most dangerous sea' (3.2.97–8). His imagery is also uncannily close to the world of Venetian mercantilism: '[to] venture all he has' is factually true of Bassanio's situation; if he loses, he is financially ruined. He has gambled everything. But he is richly rewarded: Portia is the 'golden fleece' associated with profusion and abundance. She wishes herself 'A thousand times more fair, ten thousand times more rich' (3.2.154) and her bounty is immediately called upon to restore Bassanio's happiness and rescue Antonio:

> Pay him six thousand and deface the bond.
> Double six thousand, and then treble that,
> [...]
> You shall have gold
> To pay the petty debt twenty times over.
>
> 3.2.298–9, 305–6

Belmont, then, is ambiguous: it offers the limitless gold of fairy tales but it is irretrievably linked with moneymaking Venice. Unlike Arden or Illyria, it cannot claim to be 'the Great Good Place, the Earthly Paradise' (Auden, 221).

Connections between Venice and Belmont complicate the relationship between Lorenzo and 'his Infidel.' Jessica is the apostate who has already chosen to abandon her father's authority and culture. She is mistress of the 'sober house' and directed to lock the doors and casements against the masquers and their 'shallow foppery' but she chooses to open the casement and fling out her father's fortune: 'Here, catch this casket; it is worth the pains' (2.6.34). Like Portia, she defines herself in terms of monetary value, 'I will . . . gild myself/With some moe ducats' (2.6.50–1), creating verbal links with Belmont and the casket lottery, just as her male disguise suggests a link with Portia in the trial scene. Jessica's love is certainly courageous: if Lorenzo were to be a false suitor then she would be despised alike by the Christian and Jewish communities of Venice – 'no mercy for me in heaven, because I am a Jew's daughter' (3.5.29–30). Intriguingly, Portia appoints Lorenzo and Jessica as her substitutes – 'In place of Lord Bassanio and myself' – while she makes her secret journey to Venice. It is, therefore, in Belmont that Lorenzo speaks his powerful and evocative lines on music and harmony, imagery that implies a symbolic reconciliation of differences. The scene itself is complex, however, and the exchanges at the opening of the Act – 'In such a night' – impenetrable. What should be a celebration of their joyous union is a list of unfaithful and disastrous lovers: Cressida, Thisbe, Dido, Medea are scarcely an advertisement for romantic attachment. At the climax of their **stichomythic** exchange, Lorenzo and Jessica fuse with the heroic lovers they have cited:

> In such a night
> Did Jessica steal from the wealthy Jew,
> And with an unthrift love did run from Venice
> As far as Belmont.

5.1.14–17

Lorenzo's words operate on different levels: Jessica did literally 'steal' from her father but in what respect is Lorenzo an 'unthrift' lover, 'stealing her soul with many vows of faith' (5.1.19)? He will certainly gain, financially, from the marriage. His catalogue of lovers foregrounds danger, possibly tragedy, in passionate love. But Lorenzo's musical imagery also connotes the neo-Platonic view of music as expressive of a cosmic and eternal harmony: discords blend to yield complex and beautiful resolutions. The couple do not belong in Belmont; they will return to Venice and married life based on the solid foundations of Shylock's financial 'thrift'. Unlike Othello and Desdemona, they demonstrate the possibilities of assimilation: Jessica enters the dominant Christian culture, bringing her father's wealth. Their children, born of a Jewish mother, will inherit the cosmopolitan realities of Venice and racial difference will be subsumed into the capitalist world. Ironically, Shylock's money can normalize their situation. Alternatively, the romance of Belmont could be fleeting and Jessica fated to be the 'prodigal' implied in Gratiano's words:

> The scarfed bark puts from her native bay,
> Hugged and embraced by the strumpet wind!
> How like the prodigal doth she return,
> With overweathered ribs and ragged sails,
> Lean, rent and beggared by the strumpet wind!
>
> 2.6.16–20

The structure of the play encloses Jessica's elopement between the two scenes of Morocco's unsuccessful courtship and Portia's rejection of his racial otherness – a juxtaposition which might suggest Venetian desire to preserve racial separateness.

'Which is the merchant here, and which the Jew?': The law and the alien

Audiences who had enjoyed the ribald farce that is Marlowe's *The Jew of Malta* (1592) would find in Shylock a radically different portrayal of the European Jew. Marlowe's eponymous hero is given the biblical name of the thief released instead of Jesus; the name alone symbolizing centuries of anti-Semitism. Barabas is the epitome of the pantomime villain, delighting in evil:

> [I] kill sick people groaning under walls:
> Sometimes I go about and poison wells.
>
> 2.3.174–5

Like Shylock he despises the Christians around him in whom he sees only 'malice, falsehood and excessive pride' (1.1.116). When the Governor of Malta, Ferneze, needs money to pay his tribute to the Turks, he appropriates all of Barabas's wealth, hypocritically observing that 'covetousness, oh 'tis a monstrous sin!' (1.2.125). The revenge of Barabas includes sacrificing his daughter, Abigail, and her suitors, and murdering an entire nunnery. He dies an unlamented death, falling into a boiling pot.

Shylock, too, speaks of his hatred for Christians but uses biblical authority against Antonio:

> When Jacob grazed his uncle Laban's sheep,
> This Jacob from our holy Abram was,
> As his wise mother wrought in his behalf,
> The third possessor; ay, he was the third.
>
> 1.3.67–70

The biblical stories of Jacob and Esau – well-known to Shakespeare's audience – are part of ancient Jewish history, as recounted in the book of Genesis. Jacob receives the father's blessing from the blind and dying Isaac because his mother, Rebecca, has adroitly substituted her favoured younger son. Shylock is establishing his credentials here: '*our* holy Abram'; he too is descended from the Patriarch. He might be implying that Christians also respect the fathers of the Hebrew religion –'our' Abraham is then a common bond between the two men. Jacob is indeed blessed by the deceit practised by his mother and later outmanoeuvres his uncle Laban, gaining further riches. His 'woolly breeders' produce parti-coloured lambs and thus an abundant flock for Jacob and his heirs:

> This was a way to thrive, and he was blest:
> And thrift is blessing, if men steal it not.
>
> 1.3.85–6

Shylock's parable suggests divine approval of Jacob's actions, and his means of consolidating his inheritance. Indeed, Antonio sees it as such: 'swayed and fashioned by the hand of heaven'; his interpretation is simply that God is pleased to favour Jacob's 'venture' and rewards him with prosperity. Biblical authority is provocative in this commercial context and undermines Antonio's moral high ground. The book of Genesis is emphatically not 'a knowledge no different in kind from ... Plutarch's Lives' (Mahood, 198); it is, for both Jews and Christians, the word of God. Arguably, Shylock's words here are more challenging to Shakespeare's audience than the later 'Hath not a Jew eyes ...?' (3.1.53) Antonio is the man who 'hates our sacred nation' (1.3.44); here, he is forced to confront his hypocrisy.

The tone and subject of this conversation before the sealing of the bond is, then, crucial to understanding the later scenes of Shylock's pursuit of revenge against Antonio. Clearly, although it is Bassanio who pursues the financial backing for his courtship, it is Antonio that provokes Shylock's hatred. The ludicrous nature of the bond – 'in a merry sport' – (1.3.141) follows Antonio's challenge that Shylock should lend the money as 'to thine enemy,' the better, if he defaults on the loan, to 'exact the penalty.' The Venetians expect a loan on the basis of the familiar terms of interest, or usury, with an exemplary penalty should the loan be defaulted upon. It is Antonio who insists on the gulf between them; 'I am as like .../To spit on thee again, to spurn thee too' (1.3.125-6). The blood forfeit draws on the prejudices of the Elizabethan audience who would be familiar with ancient stories of Jewish bloodlust, such as the fabled child crucifixion.

Shakespeare, through the structure of the play, emphasizes ideas of difference and prejudice: the scene between Antonio and Shylock is followed by a striking visual image: 'the Prince of Morocco, a tawny Moor, all in white ...' arriving in ceremonial fashion to woo Portia. His opening words demonstrate his consciousness of racial identity: 'Mislike me not for my complexion' (2.1.1) but, although he is greeted courteously, Portia is no Desdemona and her parting words reject him wholly for his colour. The lengthy and essentially undramatic scenes of Morocco and then Aragon engaging fruitlessly with the casket test are juxtaposed against Shylock's developing revenge. While Bassanio, bank-rolled by Shylock, moves towards romantic and financial success at Belmont,

Shylock struggles with the news of Jessica's elopement and betrayal. Like Morocco, he proclaims his alien identity: 'I am a Jew' (3.1.53), throwing back at the typically abusive Venetians the lessons learned from their Christian example:

> If a Christian wrong a Jew, what should his sufferance be by Christian example? Why, revenge! The villainy you teach me I shall execute, and it shall go hard but I will better the instruction.
>
> 3.1.63–6

As Kiernan Ryan argues, this is 'the monstrous, symmetrical logic of the terrorist: to inflict on the foe the mirror image of their own malignity, dramatizing the consequences of the cruelty they hypocritically disown' (Ryan, *Comedies*, 114). The play's emphasis upon financial transaction brings to the surface one of the most searching moral and emotional questions from Shylock:

> You have among you many a purchased slave,
> Which, like your asses, and your dogs and mules,
> You use in abject and in slavish parts,
> Because you bought them. Shall I say to you,
> 'Let them be free, marry them to your heirs,
> [. . .]
>   You will answer:
> 'The slaves are ours.' So do I answer you.
> The pound of flesh which I demand of him
> Is dearly bought; 'tis mine and I will have it.
>
> 4.1.89–99

The phrase 'dearly bought' is disturbing: Shylock does not refer to the loan – by this point Bassanio has offered to double the amount – he refers to the humiliation he has suffered and his anger against their hypocrisy. He echoes the very words Portia has used to Bassanio – 'you are dear bought' (3.2.312) where she alludes, presumably, to the expense of paying Antonio's forfeit. Romantic love is costly here: Bassanio has borrowed a large sum to win Portia and then must entreat the same from her to requite the loan. The echoed phrase emphasizes the wholesale commercialization of their world, ironically uniting Portia and Shylock.

The famed Venetian legal system initially appears to favour Shylock; the Duke and Portia know he is within his rights and will award the lawful judgement. Portia's arrival in the court introduces a degree of neutrality: 'Which is the merchant here, and which the Jew?' (4.1.170) is an intriguing question at a time when Jews would be recognized by their prescribed clothing. Her speech about mercy offers Shylock a democratized vision – it is above 'the dread and fear of kings' (4.1.188), offering him the possibility of breaking out of the restrictive hierarchical world he inhabits and transcending it. Her theology – that mercy is an attribute of God – is a Judaeo-Christian masterpiece. It recalls Shylock's own reference, earlier, to God's mercy towards Jacob. Mercy, however, will not be shown towards Shylock, once Portia has produced her trump card, the 'one drop of Christian blood' because this leads her inexorably to the statement that could have prevented the entire trial: his life and goods are forfeit because he is

> an alien
> That by direct, or indirect, attempts
> [To] seek the life of any citizen
>
> 4.1.345–7

With the word 'alien' Shakespeare incites Elizabethan prejudices; without a homeland Jews would always be 'strangers where they dwell and travellers where they reside' (Samuel Purchas, cited in Shapiro, 175). The trial scene is disturbing because a hideous disproportion takes over and the protagonists are all driven to extremes. Shylock prepares to sacrifice the man who spits on him thereby isolating himself from all social bonds; Patrick Stewart playing the role in 1978 found 'a bleak and terrible loneliness' in him – he will 'compromise no more' (Brockbank, 16, 19). Portia is not simply the bright girl, good at debating; she proceeds against Shylock with single-minded rigour, depriving him of the entirety of his means and forcing his conversion to Christianity. Modern audiences find the scene painful and disturbing. His *modus vivendi* in the city has been stripped from him: 'You take my life/When you do take the means whereby I live' (4.1.372–3). Here, too, there are connections with Antonio. When Portia reveals, in the final lines of the play, that Antonio's ships 'are richly come to harbour', his thanks suggest a form of resurrection, 'you have given me life and living' (5.1.287). For both Shylock and Antonio the mercantile world is life itself.

Playing the Jew: Al Pacino in Michael Radford's *The Merchant of Venice* (2004)

Anxiety about the anti-Semitism of *The Merchant of Venice* is perhaps more evident in the history of twentieth-century production and performance than in the world of scholarship. As recently as 2002, critic Charles Edelman argued that the sensitivity of the play's subject matter precluded the likelihood of a full-length feature film ever being made (Edelman, 86). It is not unusual to find North American writers arguing that 'the Holocaust has rendered 'traditional' *Merchant of Venice* productions so problematic as to make them virtually extinct everywhere but in the United Kingdom' (Horowitz, 8). The play is unmistakeably Shylock's: students encountering the text for the first time invariably assume that he *is* the eponymous 'Merchant', although he appears in only five scenes and speaks 13 per cent of the text. Inevitably, the most troubling accounts of the play occurred in Nazi Germany and in the immediate post-war period. Even here, the situation is not simple: in his major history, *Shakespeare on the German Stage*, Wilhelm Hortmann records a significant drop in the number of performances during the Nazi period, presumably because the play did not conform to Nazi ideology. The marriage of Lorenzo and Jessica would have been prohibited and Shylock's 'Hath not a Jew eyes?' hardly corresponds with Nazi demonization. However, the play was hijacked for propaganda purposes, notably in the Vienna Burgtheater's adaptation (May 1943) in which Shylock was caricatured on the lines of Streicher's virulent propaganda. Post-war productions have all been played in the shadow of the Holocaust, most radically in George Tabori's metadrama, *The Merchant of Venice as Performed in Theresienstadt* (performed Berkshire, MA, 1966). Tabori (1914–2007), Hungarian playwright and director, transformed Shakespeare's text into a play-within-a-play performed as part of the cultural programme of the Theresienstadt concentration camp. For Tabori, who had lost members of his family at Auschwitz, Shakespeare's play '[highlighted] the potential Holocaust lurking at the heart of the play' (cited in Edelman, 64). The performance opened with Nazi guards marching into the auditorium and the actors played their roles as traumatized and emaciated inmates of the camp. In Tabori's ending to the play, Shylock produces a 'real' knife and attacks one of the camp guards, only to be overwhelmed and murdered. Tabori exploited to full effect the irony of Jewish prisoners engaging in a cultural artefact which might have contributed to the anti-Semitism bent on destroying them.

Political and cultural tensions in the early years of the twenty-first century have shifted rather than abated: post-9/11 audiences are highly alert to the dangers of racial stereotyping. Michael Radford, in interview, has said of his filmed version, 'the whole thing is a rail against fundamentalism [this play] is about human complexity. And fundamentalism doesn't allow for human complexity' (Radford). The opening montage to the film presents contrasting vignettes of Christian and Jewish Venice, accompanied by an unrolling scroll describing aspects of the historical situation of Jews in the city. The contrasts establish a bitter divide fuelled by religious fanaticism; the Franciscan friar who denounces usury in the opening shots causes a young male

Jew (distinguished by his mandatory red hat) to be hurled from the Rialto bridge, possibly to his death. Religious apartness follows: the friar celebrates the Catholic Mass for Antonio and his worldly fellow Venetians; Shylock, Tubal and the Venetian Jews are seen worshipping in the synagogue. In these brief but intense contrasts, the detail that stands out dramatically is the degree of Antonio's racist antipathy: he spits directly at Shylock's face. The crowd is chaotic and unruly but this individual gesture of loathing is intimate and profoundly disturbing. The shot is followed by the romantic Lorenzo devotedly holding to his face Jessica's dropped handkerchief. His longing and desire is the antithesis of Antonio's revulsion.

Radford creates a well-established Jewish community, where Shylock is portrayed as a man of business, a father governing his domestic world and a devout follower of his religion. In this context the request from Bassanio and Antonio is unexpected and bizarrely hypocritical: they despise his moneylending yet come to borrow his money. He engages with them on their own terms and will not extract interest for the loan but – perhaps suggested by the freshly slaughtered goat-meat that lies beside him – a pound of Antonio's 'fair flesh' can act as forfeit. Radford's implication is that Shylock makes a deliberately irritating joke at their expense. Samuel Crowl, writing on filmed and academic interpretations of Shylock compares Greenblatt's account of the play (in *Will in the World*, 2004) and Radford's film and argues that Pacino offers a 'more complicated embodiment [of Shylock]' and 'conspicuously avoids bending his portrayal to catch at modern sensibilities' (Crowl, 'Shylock', 113). Shylock's 'Hath not a Jew eyes?' speech is, of course, the great speech that appeals for humanity and tolerance. Pacino himself saw the speech as an event, part of the currency of street life: '[It] was something that was happening on the street. It wasn't a speech anymore. It was an incident that was taking place ... You've got the whores looking at him and you've got those two guys that he's talking to and it just happened. It might not have happened. He might've just kept walking' (Pacino).

The trial scene effectively bears out Crowl's view, that Shylock 'transcends the sentimentality at the heart of ... Radford's designs' (Crowl, 'Shylock', 115). A full twenty-five minutes of film builds up to an emotionally highly charged climax, drawing the viewer close to the action with the use of handheld camera. The perspective shifts between Antonio's fear of the ordeal to come, the turbulent mood of the crowd and Portia's observant recognition of the affection between her husband and his mentor. As Shylock pursues his rights in a quietly implacable way, the tension is wound up to breaking point; he yields nothing to the authority of the Duke or the appeals of Balthazar. Pacino has described Shylock as being 'violated by the conditions of his life'; the trial is his way of 'standing up to the oppressors.' Radford underlines the political point when Shylock observes that they all keep slaves and the camera lingers on an enslaved Moor fanning his master. The point at which he is sharpening his knife and the clearly terrified Antonio is bound and gagged with leather bonds seems to move inevitably towards an unthinkable barbarism. Portia's cry of, 'Tarry!' comes as the knife approaches Antonio's bared breast; the emotion is then dispelled in the tearful embrace between Antonio and Bassanio. Radford made very few textual cuts in the pursuit and humiliation of Shylock that follows and he is reduced to a broken and pitiful figure after the Duke's final judgement. Meanwhile, in Gratiano's racist bullying and brawling, Radford also reveals that the 'civilized' values of Venice are no more than a veneer.

The triumphant return to Belmont, with Portia's subsequent victory over her husband and Antonio in the matter of her ring, establishes normative social and sexual bonds – to the evident exclusion of Antonio. But Radford's final frames suggest poignant struggle and pain. Shylock is viewed outside the locked synagogue, stripped of his yarmulke and the Hebrew symbol he has worn throughout. Meanwhile, dawn rises over the enchanted world of Belmont and in the morning light over the lagoon, a solitary figure gazes longingly over the water. Jessica, looking down at her father's turquoise ring – that she had evidently not exchanged for a monkey – seems isolated and despairing. Does she yearn for the identity she has cast aside, or mourn for her father? Jessica's precarious new identity suggests a subtle lack of resolution and the fabled world of Venice begins and ends in melancholy.

Further reading

John Gross, *Shylock: Four Hundred Years in the Life of a Legend* (London, 1992)

Graham Holderness, *Shakespeare and Venice* (Farnham, 2010)

John W. Mahon and Ellen Macleod Mahon (eds), *The Merchant of Venice: New Critical Essays* (London, 2002)

Katharine Eisaman Maus, *Inwardness and Theater in the English Renaissance* (Chicago, 1995)

Linda Woodbridge, *Money and the Age of Shakespeare: Essays in New Economic Criticism* (Basingstoke, 2003)

Volpone, or The Fox

Venice and genre

Jonson's satiric comedies could be described as relentlessly urban and firmly rooted in the society of his time. At the beginning of his career as a dramatist his (now lost) play *The Isle of Dogs* (1597) was judged by the Privy Council to be dangerously seditious as well as 'lewd'; Jonson, together with several members of the acting company, was duly imprisoned for some months. His first extant text, *Every Man in His Humour* (1590), commences with a Prologue which rejects plays where the Chorus 'wafts you o'er the seas', proposing

> Deeds and language, such as men do use
> And persons, such as Comedy would choose,

> When she would show an image of the times,
> And sport with human follies, not with crimes
>
> Prologue, 21–4

Jonson's Prologues and Epistles establish a significant difference between Shakespearean and Jonsonian dramatic and textual procedures. Shakespeare does not enter his texts in the way in which Jonson – argumentatively – does. The Epistle to *Volpone*, addressed to the universities of Oxford and Cambridge, is a case in point: Jonson reminds his academic addressees that they have approved his play; he observes his fidelity to classical conventions and emphasizes his didactic intention, 'to inform men in the best reason of living' (Epistle, 114–15). He draws on classical notions of satire as a means of exposing society's idiosyncrasies or depravities. Beneath the comic activity lies a darker purpose, effectively defined by Philip Sidney: '[The] Comedy is an imitation of the common errors of our life, which [the play-maker] representeth in the most ridiculous and scornful sort that may be, so as it is impossible that any beholder can be content to be such a one' (Sidney, 98).

Appeasing Puritan objections to comic theatre could well lie behind Jonson's defence of his art, especially where his comic villains emerge relatively unscathed at the end of the plot. His two great satires of London life, *The Alchemist* (1610) and *Bartholomew Fair* (1614) dramatize, respectively, the ebullient creativity of dedicated tricksters and the anarchic energies of carnivalesque festivity. For Jonson,

> Our scene is London, 'cause we would make known,
> No country's mirth is better than our own.
> No clime breeds better manners for your whore,
> Bawd, squire, imposter, many persons more,
> Whose manners, now call'd humours, feed the stage
>
> Prologue to
> *The Alchemist*, 5–10

Jonson plays to his appreciative London audience, secure in the knowledge that his very topicality will provoke humour. Why, then, is *Volpone*, performed by the King's Men in 1606, located with an unusual degree of specificity in the republic of Venice? Critics have established the thoroughness and accuracy of Jonson's detailed referencing: *Volpone* includes 'more details about Venice [than] any other play of the period' (McPherson, 91). Throughout the play place names, details of costume, and traditions exclusive to Venice demonstrate the extent to which Jonson had researched his subject. Brian Parker explores the Italian literary and musical milieu known to Jonson at the time, in particular John Florio, compiler of the first Italian–English dictionary and friend to Jonson (Florio was the dedicatee of the 1607 **quarto** text of *Volpone*). As Parker establishes, the vocabulary of Jonson's text 'ripples constantly with Venetian-Italian words from Florio's 1598 dictionary: a sforzato, scartoccios, canaglia' as well as precise geographical references (Parker, 102). The wealth of Jonson's detail differs significantly from many later Jacobean tragedies where a mere suggestion of Italian or Spanish court life suffices to create a threatening atmosphere; *Volpone* depicts a world of 'relentless particularity' (Barton, 108), crammed with desirable material goods and teeming with the social forms of everyday life as well as the politics and governance of Venice.

Volpone features two English tourists: Sir Politic and Lady Would-Be, satirized as the eager culture vultures of the play. Fashionable dress and decorum seems to be Lady Would-Be's motive for travel: 'a peculiar humour of my wife's ... to observe,/To quote, to learn the language, and so forth' (2.1.11–13). The suggestion that she models herself upon the famous courtesans of the city comically emphasizes her ignorance:

> Your lady
> Lies here in Venice for intelligence
> Of tires, and fashions, and behaviour,
> Among the courtesans? The fine Lady Would-Be?
>
> 2.1.26–9

Sir Pol cites 'Nick Machiavel' as though he were a personal friend and regales his fellow-countryman, Peregrine, with advice on fashionable etiquette, notably 'the use,/And handling of your silver fork' (4.1.27–8). He boasts that within a week of his arrival '[all] took me for a citizen of Venice;/I knew the forms so well' (4.1.37–8). He has done business with 'my Jews' for money and 'movables' and aspires to be a merchant of the city himself, with a far-fetched scheme to import red herrings from Rotterdam to Venice, via a Dutch cheesemonger. Lady Would-Be, meanwhile, has embarked on a comprehensive reading-list: from Dante to Aretine, 'I have read them all' (3.4.81). Her erudition, like her dress, is the object of mockery rather than admiration, though: Aretine's writings were notoriously pornographic. She mistakes the young traveller Peregrine for a cross-dressed Venetian prostitute with designs upon Sir Pol, reminding herself, however, that a public brawl would not be in the spirit of Castiglione's *The Courtier* (4.2.35). Jonson's satire is aimed at the ludicrous attempts of both Sir Pol and his Lady to inveigle themselves into high society while also taking a side-swipe at the mercenary attitudes of the Venetian tourist trade. The city has used and abused them and they make their eventual departure with their amour-propre thoroughly dented. Jonson draws on contemporary anxieties about travel here, and in particular the fear that seductive Catholic cities such as Venice might corrupt the innocent Englishman. Roger Ascham, Queen Elizabeth's tutor, attacked the Italianate Englishman for bringing home, 'The religion, the learning, the policy, the experience, the manners of Italy. That is to say, for religion, papistry, or worse; ... for policy, a factious heart, a discoursing head, a mind to meddle in all men's matters; for experience, plenty of new mischiefs never known in England before; for manners, variety of vanities and change of filthy living' (cited in Creaser, 49).

Venice, in other words, is alluring – but decidedly foreign. What, then, does Jonson wish to establish by anchoring the drama within the social world of Venice? A satire on cupidity and avarice could equally be set in London, particularly where the central characters are designated by names that connect them to the world of beast fable. MacPherson suggests that 'Volpone's passion for theatricality is more easily understood against the background of the extravagant theatricality prevalent ... in Renaissance Venice' (McPherson, 118). In *Volpone* the majority of characters are performing assumed roles, indeed when Celia and Bonario protest their genuine innocence, they are ridiculed and disbelieved. Volpone himself delights in his ability to play many parts, performing with enthusiasm his roles of invalid, mountebank, lover, commendatore before, finally, unmasking as himself in the final moments of the play. Venice is also key to the politics of the text: Brian Gibbons in his landmark study, *Jacobean City Comedy* (1965), sees *Volpone* as a cruel farce which reveals a society, analogous to London, dedicated to 'commerce, mercantile capitalism and ruthlessly unprincipled competition' (Gibbons, 94). Certainly, the sheer venality of the principal characters, and the play's concern with ludicrous and obsessive extremes of acquisitiveness, readily suggests Venetian extravagance and consumerism to the early modern mind while also flagging up a warning of the humiliating consequences of the single-minded pursuit of wealth. Lawrence Stone, in his analysis of the economics of the period, makes the connection between the stage and the conspicuous consumption of the early seventeenth century: 'As the playwrights never tired of telling their audience, this was an age of exceptionally prodigal living, made possible by the rising tide of luxury imports and stimulated by a desire to imitate the opulent Renaissance courts of Europe. Tastes which found favour with a Medici prince were sedulously copied by a less richly endowed English earl' (Stone, *Crisis*, 184).

In *Volpone*, then, a picturesque and exotic setting does not evoke the festive mood of Shakespearean romance (as in, say, *Twelfth Night* or *The Winter's Tale*); Jonson's tone is altogether more blackly comic and scatological. To Russ McDonald, Jonsonian comedy shares characteristics with Shakespeare's tragedies in a shared 'movement towards disillusionment' (McDonald, 100).

Money and the grotesque

> What should I do
> But cocker up my genius and live free
> To all delights my fortune calls me to?
>
> 1.1.70–2

Volpone as the narcissistic voluptuary is brilliantly captured in Aubrey Beardsley's highly stylized drawing, 'Volpone Adoring His Treasures' (1898); indeed Beardsley's stated 'If I am not grotesque, I am nothing' could be Volpone's house motto. The protagonist is designated by Jonson as 'a Magnifico', a Venetian plutocrat, wealthy and powerful; it is Corvino who is the 'merchant' of this Venetian scene. One of the recurrent ironies of the play is the extent to which Volpone denies himself the potential pleasures of his position in order to assume his mask of decrepitude. He is a man of egregious appetite who can never be satisfied, the hedonist whose desires cannot be fulfilled within the scope of the play. The nomenclature of the beast fable identifies Volpone as the crafty old fox, the sly, 'sneaking, lurking, wily deceiver' (Watson, *Volpone*, 2). His plots depend upon his cynicism and greed but in his perpetual restlessness there is a mockery of Renaissance idealism. As Alvin Kernan has argued: 'Jonson's characters are all satiric portraits of Renaissance aspiration, of the belief that man can make anything he will of himself and of his world' (Kernan, 180).

📖 *Now look at Volpone's opening speech, paying close attention to the syntax and imagery of this **apostrophe** to wealth.*

Famously, his waking invocation to his gold mirrors the Anglican church's Morning Prayer: praise and thanks for life, light and the new day. It is useful to identify first the language which is specifically biblical or liturgical. Replacing the worship of God with Mammon is provocatively idolatrous; Volpone's second, syntactically convoluted sentence compresses a number of breathtakingly hyperbolic analogues. '[The] day struck out of chaos' evokes the moment of creation as described in the opening verses of Genesis. For the early modern audience the 'price of souls' (1.1.24) is, however, a highly blasphemous reference, implying that Christ's sacrifice for mankind is 'worth' less than Volpone's gold. The room itself, the 'shrine' or holy place is overflowing with 'sacred treasure' and 'relics' for Volpone to adore and to kiss (relics suggesting holy and miraculous objects such as saints' bones). The scene recalls the opening of Marlowe's *The Jew of Malta* where Barabas appears surrounded by his 'infinite riches in a little room' (1.1.37) and Marlovian tragedy. When gold makes hell 'worth heaven,' Volpone is closer to Faustus than to the buoyant comic characters of *The Alchemist*. Clearly, Volpone would barter his soul for money. Is there, then, beneath the glittering surface of the **blank verse** and the exuberant, exclamatory rhetoric, a paradoxical darkness? Shrines and relics are associated with chantry chapels and tombs; it is essentially life-denying to assert that wealth

> far trans[cends]
> All style of joy, in children, parents, friends,
> Or any other waking dream on earth.
>
> 1.1.16–18

As Michael Neill argues, gold is 'the instrument and epitome of unnatural relationship; it is what, in the corrupted patriarchy of Jonson's Venice, effectually replaces the bonds of natural kinship' (Neill, *History*, 154). Gold was commonly regarded as possessing the highest values of aesthetic, even spiritual perfection; it was far more than a means of exchange. The Italian Renaissance writer Botero published his *Treatise Concerning the Causes of the Magnificencie and greatnes of Cities* [sic] in 1606; where, as well as lauding Venice, 'Lady of the Spiceries', for her 'gloriousness' and 'multitude of ships' (Botero, 256, 233) he proclaims that gold 'even through the very virtue thereof, containeth in it all greatness, all commodities, and all earthly good whatsoever' (Botero, 253).

Volpone is enamoured of his gold partly for its beauty and partly for its potency: it can 'do nought' yet 'makst men do all things' – a statement which recoils on the speaker as well as describing his suitors. He claims that 'I glory/More in the cunning purchase of my wealth' (1.1.31) but he transforms himself into a physically repulsive, emotionally sterile, sexually impotent carcase. He embarks on a bravura performance in both his speech and his play-acting but there is a hollowness at the centre: 'I have no wife, no parent, no child, ally, /To give my substance to' (1.1.73–4). His schemes to uncover the avarice and hypocrisy around him will only give him the final satisfaction of knowing that no one cares for him – 'they never think of me' (5.3.17). He is presumably trying to cheat death – gold will not accompany him to the next world – yet he performs the role of the dying man and witnesses the complete lack of feeling prompted by his 'death'. At the outset he is exposed to the contempt of those who woo him, shamelessly longing for his death, as well as the cynical playfulness of Mosca who exploits all the potential of his double-dealing:

> [*Aloud to* Volpone] The pox approach, and add to your diseases,
> If it would send you hence the sooner, sir.
> For, your incontinence, it hath deserved it
> Throughly, and throughly, and the plague to boot.
>
> 1.5.52–5

Volpone's soliloquy at the opening of Act 5 is expressive of a radically different mood; no longer ebullient but fearful of death. The trial of Act 4, in which he is displayed in court as an impotent old corpse frightens him to the point where he suffers psychosomatic symptoms: 'some power hath struck me/With a dead palsy' (5.1.6–7). 'Lusty wine' and the perverse determination to pursue his scheming to its limit result in his final, disastrous plot: to be dead. This is a fatal misjudgement because power is surrendered to Mosca. If his feigned sickness has a metaphoric dimension to it, then the grotesque imagery used by Mosca signifies an end to Volpone's play-acting:

> MOSCA   But, what, sir, if they ask
> After the body?
>   [...]
> I'll say it stunk, sir; and was fain t'have it
> Coffined up instantly, and sent away.
>
> 5.2.77–8

The court's final judgement on him is horrifyingly apposite. His wealth will go to the hospital of the *Incurabili* and Volpone himself will 'lie in prison, cramped with irons' until sick and lame.

The dupes calling on Volpone in the opening scenes are all defined through their extraordinary greed and their willingness to humiliate themselves and betray the love of those dearest to them. It is hard to judge whether Volpone or his victims are the more obsessed with money. They tend to be judged as a unit – wrongly because they are all in open competition with each other and are corrupt in different ways. As a concept they are modelled, initially, on the legacy hunters of Roman satire: Horace and Juvenal both attack 'captators' – the grasping will-chasers of imperial Rome. Lay siege to a rich dotard's will is the advice given in Horace's *Satire* 2. Jonson alludes also to Petronius' *Satyricon* where the wealthy Trimalchio pretends to be dead in order to solicit eulogies from his followers and where, more alarmingly, Eumolpus' will is read to his impatient legacy hunters with its clause that requires them to devour his dead flesh before succeeding to his vast wealth. Volpone himself uses cannibalistic imagery when gloating over his morning's acquisitions:

> Why this is better than rob churches, yet;
> Or fat, by eating, once a month, a man.
>
> 1.5.91–2

Volpone's gulls span youth and age and represent different professions within the city. Satire often questions how far folly will go, and Jonson's characters go to troubling extremes. Corbaccio is, in many ways, the most ridiculous fortune-hunter; he is old and infirm himself but, unlike Volpone, has the benefit of a noble and honest heir, his son Bonario. Clearly he is attempting to evade death; grasping with delight at Mosca's descriptions of Volpone's decrepitude, 'Excellent, excellent, sure I shall outlast him:/This makes me young again, a score of years' (1.4.55–6). Mosca's scheme; that Corbaccio should disinherit his son and remake his will in favour of Volpone, appears extreme – but Corbaccio confesses that he had already thought of it himself. Full of lively enthusiasm for betraying the innocent Bonario, he finds himself quite rejuvenated: 'I may ha' my youth restored to me, why not?' (1.4.128). Behind his passionate desire for gold is a quasi-religious belief that it is the philosopher's stone which can miraculously renew his youth.

Corvino, described as 'our spruce merchant' (1.4.161) is presumably intended to appear as the young and fashionable merchant of the city, rejoicing in the possession of an exceptionally beautiful wife. His opening gifts to Volpone are an orient pearl and a diamond, possibly symbolizing the alacrity with which he will offer Celia, his 'pearl of great price', to win advantage over his competitors. Corvino is easily betrayed by Mosca to launch into abusive verbal attacks on Volpone, believing him to be deaf, and seems troublingly close to complicity with Mosca's suggestion that they should stifle Volpone. His chief concern is his public image; the loss of Celia matters less to him than being named as a cuckold. On first appearance Voltore, clutching his antique silver plate, has little to say. He appears as a master of rhetoric in the court-scene where he defends Volpone as the impotent invalid, but he is betrayed by his cupidity which is clearly stronger than his professional judgement. Like Corvino, he cares for his public reputation and his final bitter comment that he has been 'outstripped thus, by a parasite? a slave?' (5.7.1) reveals his weakness in class terms. He simply did not expect to be bested by the servant, Mosca.

Mosca's soliloquy is as full of self-love and admiration as Volpone's opening speeches, although it is his talent for dexterity which delights him:

> O! Your parasite
> Is a most precious thing, dropped from above,
> Not bred 'mongst clods and clod-polls here on earth.
> [...]
> But your fine elegant rascal, that can rise
> And stoop, almost together, like an arrow;
> Shoot through the air, as nimbly as a star;
> Turn short as doth a swallow; and be here,
> And there, and here, and yonder all at once
>
> 3.1.7–9, 23–7

If Volpone resembles Milton's Mammon who prefers the false glitter of Hell, Mosca, too, lusts after a world of desirable 'things': the 'inventory scene' (5.3) is a masterpiece of comic irony where all three dupes plus Lady Would-Be are given the news that Volpone has bequeathed his entire wealth to Mosca, while the seemingly fortunate Mosca runs through the list of his new and precious acquisitions. For Anne Barton, the specificity of the things enumerated acts as a moral comment on both Venice and London: 'Things, in *Volpone*, the urban detritus of a civilization out of control, are perpetually on the verge of rising up to drown the people who wade and push their way through them' (Barton, 108).

Mosca's list draws attention to the rich world of material goods central to the play and to city comedy as a genre. Things – of value or rarity – abound, signifying a new commodity culture. In Jonson's city, whether London or Venice, 'all relationships are dictated by power and money, by the link between seller and client' (Parker, 109). It is worth considering whether this statement is true, also, of *The Merchant of Venice*.

Comparisons can be drawn with Shakespeare and Middleton's *Timon of Athens* (1606), a brutally cynical play about money where the eponymous hero discovers that he has been esteemed only for his wealth; those on whom he lavished his 'bounty' abandon him when he is in need. Timon, like Volpone, comments on the transforming power of gold: the 'yellow slave' that will destroy religions, make 'leprosy adored', ennoble thieves and transform the widow whom the 'spittle house and ulcerous sores' would retch at into an 'April day' (*Tim*, 4.3.34–42). Editors of the Arden 3 text find 'distinct affinities' between *Volpone* and *Timon of Athens*: '[both] plays deal prominently with the circulation of money and commodities, both display the manipulative trickery typical of city comedy and both feature an apostrophe to gold' (Dawson and Minton, 13).

Sex in the City: Erotic possibilities in *Volpone*

Volpone pursues his lascivious pleasures with the same avaricious enthusiasm he has for gold. The first reference to his prodigious sexual appetite comes from Mosca – and therefore might have no validity at all. The early modern audience would certainly find Mosca's account of Volpone's paternity aberrant:

CORVINO   Has he children?

MOSCA   Bastards,
Some dozen, or more, that he begot on beggars,
Gypsies, and Jews, and black-moors, when he was drunk.
Knew you not that, sir? 'Tis the common fable.
The dwarf, the fool, the eunuch are all his:
He's the true father of his family.

1.5.43–7

Volpone himself concludes the highly satisfactory scenes with his dupes by calling for 'all delights'; 'the Turk is not more sensual, in his pleasures/Than will Volpone' (1.5.88–9) as if he were the sultan of a harem. Mosca certainly knows Volpone's susceptibility when he dangles before him the image of Celia as luscious grapes or cherries. Her beauty is 'ripe, as harvest' to tempt the voluptuary but, more significantly, she is equated with Volpone's material treasure: 'Bright as your gold, and lovely as your gold!' (1.5.114). Her 'value' is further enhanced by the fact that she is locked up and kept away from the public eye, 'kept as warily as is your gold' (1.5.118). In other words, Celia is the archetypal wife-as-prisoner – a **trope** that features frequently in Jacobean plays set in Spain or Italy. According to Coryate, Venetian Gentlemen 'coope up their wives' and they are seldom seen publicly with the exception of 'the solemnization of a great marriage, or at the Christening of a Jew' (Coryate, 265). The appearance of Celia at her window is arguably ambiguous, then; she exposes herself to the public gaze, dropping her handkerchief by way of token. Is she simply the innocent who is swayed by the mountebank's promises or is her gesture flirtatious? To the frantic and violent Corvino there is no doubt that his merchandise is at risk. He threatens her with sexual disgrace; murder; imprisonment and sodomy but is almost immediately importuned by Mosca to yield up his wife to Volpone. The uncertain promise of Volpone's fortune ranks higher than his jealous possessiveness and he instructs her to make ready with her 'best attire, [and] choicest jewels' (2.7.14). Jonson depicts Corvino as the quintessential merchant here; he intends Celia to be the investment that will secure his fortune: 'if you be/Loyal, and mine, be won, respect my venture' (3.7.36–7). He is a man hysterical about the possibility of cuckoldry but has persuaded himself that his gold is not 'the worse for touching' (3.7.41). He assumes, also, that Celia operates at his own base level, attempting to bribe her with clothes and jewels if she will be complicit.

Volpone, too, offers Celia ropes of pearl and priceless rarities. Clearly, both men expect Celia to find exotic and glamorous objects irresistible. Volpone's lengthy seduction scene is intriguing for the dichotomy between what he promises and the reality of what he is. In his elaborate speeches, he is attempting to model himself on the classical models of Roman love poetry: he woos Celia with music and a 'carpe diem' song derived from Catullus' sublime 'Vivamus, mea Lesbia' but the debauched world of Roman excess soon supplants romance. With aristocratic insouciance, he offers untold wealth which she is at liberty simply to discard – 'a rope of pearl; and each more orient/Than the brave Egyptian queen caroused:/Dissolve, and drink 'em' (3.7.190–2). He describes a disturbingly decadent feast – they might eat the phoenix if she were for sale. And sexually, they can enact the aberrant loves of Ovid's *Metamorphoses*:

> Thou, like Europa now, and I like Jove,
> Then I like Mars, and thou like Erycine,
> So, of the rest, till we have quite run through
> And wearied all the fables of the gods.
> Then will I have thee, in more modern forms
>
> 3.7.221–6

Volpone invents a world of elaborate role-playing but the brutal reality is that when Celia resists his overtures, his language is immediately more direct: 'Yield, or I'll force thee' (3.7.265). Celia's refusal connects her with the virtuous women of Jacobean tragedy but recent critics have argued that Celia's desire for martyrdom is suspect; to Sean McEvoy, her conventional classical chastity is the expression of a 'repressed perverse desire' (McEvoy, 60).

The comically clichéd rescue by Bonario might, in other dramas, signify a happy conclusion but Jonson's city world is dark and corrupt; in the first of the two court scenes, Celia is judged as a whore and publicly humiliated. Her own faith that heaven 'never fails the innocent' appears unjustified. The final resolution fails to compensate Celia with any romantic possibility: part of Corvino's punishment is that he must return his wife to her father with her dowry tripled, yet she is hardly escaping the confinements of the patriarchal world if she cannot remarry. As Alvin Kernan observes in his analysis of satiric comedy, 'That the victory is a sterile one is suggested by the fate of Celia. In a true comedy she would marry some younger, more vital member of the society and her marriage would signalize the restoration of the city to a condition of healthy vitality' (Kernan, 190).

Venice offers a highly sexualized backdrop to the play yet there is not a single romantic encounter or declaration of love. The subplot introduces Lady Would-Be's pursuit of Volpone – 'How does my Volp?' (3.4.39) but Volpone ridicules her and despairs that her visit might 'expel his appetite' for Celia (3.3.29). Volpone is capable of spontaneous affection but only for Mosca when the latter has performed a particularly virtuosic manipulation of one of the gulls – 'Let me embrace thee. O, that I could now/Transform thee to a Venus' (5.3.103–4). The character who should be the romantic heroine is objectified, abused and sentenced to a life of chastity. Coleridge, in his judgement of the play, opined that a 'most delightful comedy might be produced, by making Celia the ward or niece of Corvino, instead of his wife, and Bonario her lover' (cited in Steggle, 49) but this would distort the 'brutality [and] lack of sentiment' of Jonson's play (Eliot, 159). As the play ends, the only suggestion of marriage has come from the 4th Avocatore who believes that Mosca, if inheriting Volpone's wealth, might be a 'fit match for my daughter' (5.12.51), a notion that mocks the conventions of romantic comedy. Stefan Zweig, in his 1926 adaptation of the play, subtitled it appropriately: 'a loveless comedy.'

Volpone as beast fable

Volpone is a play featuring a fox, a fly, three carrion-eating birds (crow, raven and vulture), a peregrine hawk, a parrot and his mate, and, finally, a tortoise. The second scene is a verse and musical interlude performed by Nano the dwarf, Castrone the eunuch and Androgyno the hermaphrodite, tracing the soul of Androgyno through various cross-species reincarnations; Jonson introduces a fantastical world of carnivalesque revelry from the opening. For all the classical antecedents of Jonson's principal theme of will-chasing, the familiar tales of Reynard the fox and Aesop's fables underlie *Volpone*, informing the structure of the play and dominating the language. To John Creaser, the pattern of images and allusions connecting with the play's animal imagery, adds to the play's 'feeling of savagery and perversion' (Creaser, 40). Modern sensibilities differ from those of Jonson's audience: today's readers are accustomed to anthropomorphizing animal figures. The UK now has anti-fox-hunting legislation – a wholly different picture from the bear-baiting world that existed alongside Jacobean theatres. In the medieval bestiary and the tales of Aesop, two **motifs** emerge from the popular fox-lore: first, the craftiness of the fox (where the fox succeeds in stealing cheese from the crow by flattering the bird.) *Volpone* refers specifically to Aesop's tale 'The Fox and the Crow' in the final Act when the disguised Volpone, believing that his plans are victorious, mocks Corvino:

> A witty merchant, the fine bird, Corvino,
> That have such moral emblems on your name,
> Should not have sung your shame, and dropped your cheese,
> To let the fox laugh at your emptiness.

5.8.11–14

The specific reference hammers home the mockery of Corvino's empty vanity and superficiality: he is a victim of trickery but there can be little sympathy for his succumbing to the fox's blandishments. The second strand of fox-lore, found frequently in medieval bestiaries, featured stories of the fox lying apparently dead waiting for carrion birds to be attracted by the dead flesh and land upon his body. The fox would then open his jaws and seize his prey. At best, the bird would escape with the fox snapping at its feathers – as perhaps Voltore and Corbaccio do. To the medieval mind, the fox operated as an analogue of the devil: deceiving his victims in order to lure them to damnation. The balance of sympathy is unmistakeable, the fox is witty and ingenious; the carrion birds arouse only disgust for feeding on dead flesh. The combination of beast fable with the sophisticated world of Venice is unique to *Volpone*: Jonson emphasizes the parasitism at the heart of the city: 'Almost/All the wise world is little else, in nature,/But parasites, or sub-parasites' (3.1.11–13). The didacticism in unmissable; the final moral from the Avocatore is that wickedness is like a fat beast, ripe for slaughter. However, the animalia undoubtedly contributes to the energy and verve of the play: Volpone identifies himself as 'a fox/Stretched on the earth, with fine delusive sleights/Mocking a gaping crow' (1.2.94–6) and transforms himself into a beast as he welcomes the gulls by putting on his furs:

> Now, now, my clients
> Begin their visitation! Vulture, kite,
> Raven, and gorcrow, all my birds of prey,
> That think me turning carcass, now they come
>
> 1.2.87–90

In this respect, Jonson is true to the tone of the Reynard stories, where the fox invariably outwits all around him, including courts of law; usually escaping from the death penalty by adroit arguments. Indeed, the beast fables add a final twist to Volpone's final appearance, still unscathed, at the end of the play. In theory, he is about to undergo hideous punishment; yet he appeals for applause with his customary aplomb. Will he, like Reynard, escape his fate? In the French film based on *Volpone* (2003, directed Auburtin), comic duo Gérard Depardieu and Daniel Prévost escape to new adventures, the final frames showing their amicable bickering before the final surprise – Celia, concealed in a trunk (Hatchuel and Vienne-Guerrin, 2011).

Volpone's bizarre household – Nano, Castrone, Androgyno – contribute to the play's carnivalesque appeal as well as implying the play's 'carnival concupiscence' (4.2.60). Critics of animal and species theory draw attention to the fact that the early modern period debated the distinction between man and beast, as well as the challenging question of 'human-ness' in a newly expanding world that introduced native peoples to European thinking. Erica Fudge cites William Perkins for whom the difference between man and beast is the operation of conscience (Fudge, 34). For Fudge, the opening two scenes introduce the audience to 'a world without God and without species difference' (Fudge, 83). The play is subversive because it suggests that Volpone willingly assumes the guise of the fox – putting on his furs to do so – whereas Corvino, Corbaccio and Voltore are limited to being only what they seem – birds who consume dead flesh. This is particularly disturbing to Puritan objectors to theatre, such as Prynne: his objection to cross-dressed boys is notorious but transformation into the beast is infinitely worse: 'between [Beasts] and man there is no Analogie or proportion, as is between men and women': 'God, who prohibits, the making or likenesse of any beast, or fish, or fowle, or creeping thing, whether male or female ... must certainely condemne the putting on of such brutish Vizards, the changing of the glory, the shape of reasonable men, into the likenesse of unreasonable beasts and creatures, to act a bestiall part in a lascivious Enterlude' (cited in Fudge, 88–9).

Corvino might not recognize himself as the crow but he identifies with the stock characters of the *commedia dell'arte*; the world of improvisatory Italian farce, when he upbraids his wife for appearing at her window:

What, Is my wife your Franciscina? Sir?
    [...]
Heart! ere tomorrow, I shall be new christened,
And called the *Pantalone di Bersogniosi*,
About the town.

2.3.4–8

His rage is slanderous: Celia is far from the 'Franciscina' stereotype; a notoriously coquettish servant girl. The two worlds of beast fable and *commedia dell'arte* combine effectively in *Volpone*, where the action often depends upon Volpone's and Mosca's improvisatory skills. As a form of theatre it had developed in the early sixteenth century and revolved around stock characters (Pantalone, the Venetian merchant and miser; Arlecchino, the cheeky servant; Pierrot the Clown; the innamorati or young lovers are perhaps some of the better known). Plots were fluid and operated around thematic subjects such as love, jealousy, old age and miserliness. Within static plot-lines there was then ample opportunity for improvisation, music and dance. Essentially performative, there are close connections with *Volpone*, notably with the principal character himself, 'performing' as the mountebank Scoto as well as playing his role of *magnifico* and seducer. Jonson relies on his audience's knowledge of *commedia* traditions to exploit comic and satiric effects. Actors – both male and female – were masked, an effect often duplicated in modern productions of *Volpone* where the chief characters of the beast fable perform in stylized half-masks (illustrated Watson, *Volpone*, xxix).

Sir Politic Would-Be attempting to escape Venice beneath a giant tortoise shell is the comic climax to this art of caricature: his risible plots and schemes have come to nothing and Peregrine frightens him with the news that a spy has revealed Sir Pol's intention '[to] sell the state of Venice to the Turk' (5.4.38). He is completely humiliated and desires only to leave Venice and 'shrink my poor head, in my politic shell' (5.4.89). Jonson's dramatic use of beast fable is, ultimately, ambivalent: grotesque bestiality signals human depravity but, theatrically, is close to the folkloric and carnivalesque: 'the farce of the old English humour, the terribly serious, even savage comic humour [of] *Volpone*' (Eliot, 123).

Further reading

Jonathan Goldberg, *James I and the Politics of Literature: Jonson, Shakespeare, Donne, and Their Contemporaries* (London, 1983)

Alexander Leggatt, 'The Suicide of Volpone', *University of Toronto Quarterly*, 39 (1969–70), 19–32

James Loxley, *The Complete Critical Guide to Ben Jonson* (London, 2002)

Julie Sanders (ed.), *Ben Jonson in Context* (Cambridge, 2010)

Robert Watson, *Ben Jonson's Parodic Strategy: Literary Imperialism in the Comedies* (London, 1987)

3

Performance and performativity:

The Taming of the Shrew and *The Tragedy of Mariam*

It might be helpful to distinguish between the different types of Performance Studies, and the critical and sociological concepts of Performativity. To the Shakespeare scholar 'Performance Studies' probably suggests research into conditions and practice in the early modern theatre, together with production and reception history. This is in itself a widely divergent field: on the one hand critics such as Andrew Gurr (*The Shakespearean Stage, 1574–1642*, 2009; *The Shakespearian Playing Companies*, 1996) have researched the records of early modern London and its theatres; as a result far more precise information, as well as original documentation, is now widely available. 'Performance' could also be taken to mean any adaptation or spin-off from the original, however, so 'Performance Studies' could equally suggest the discussion of cross-cultural productions. It might seem ironical that, at a time, when every effort can be expended on performing 'Shakespeare' with scrupulous historical accuracy – extending to original pronunciation (Globe theatre, 2004) – Performance Studies also accommodates, say, Vishal Bhardwaj's *Haider* (2014) a film based on *Hamlet* which depicts the struggle of Kashmiri separatists in the 1990s. Cross-genre adaptations raise fascinating questions of the relationship between original text and creative response in different media. This can be a contested field: some recent theorists of performance have argued that 'theatre studies' engaging with the relationship between text and production operates in ways which are discrete from, even opposed to, performance discourse. Foremost critic in this field, W.B. Worthen, identifies this as a 'conceptual crisis in drama studies', arguing that the combination of post-structural theory and late 1960s' experimental theatre had the effect of 'dismantling textual authority, illusionism and the canonical actor' (Worthen, 1093). To the cultural theorist Richard Schechner, the history of Shakespeare production is one of undue reverence to textual authority, and the traditions of past productions. To Schechner, the world of conventional theatre is no more than a niche interest within the wider world of performance: 'Theatre as we have known and practiced it [*sic*] – the staging of written dramas – will be the string quartet of the 21st century: a beloved but extremely limited genre, a subdivision of performance' (cited in Worthen, 1094).

'Performance studies' is also an area of critical analysis that extends beyond literary and theatre studies to embrace a wide range of sociocultural disciplines. Anthropology and ethnography engage with 'Performance' as social and cultural phenomena, the analysis of societies and their respective modes of expressiveness – the 'performance' of shopping, for example, or the group dynamic of social gatherings, say for sport or for political demonstrations. Linguistics and semiotics – the study of both verbal and non-verbal signs – also theorize ways in which 'performance' can be decoded.

Performativity is, first, a term defined by the linguistic philosopher, J.A. Austin (1911–60). In his *How To Do Things with Words* (1962) he identifies **performative** words and phrases that enact, rather than simply describe, their function.

In linguistic terms, such verbs are seen as executive in that they possess inherent agency. Obvious examples are verbs with a specifically formal function: 'I sentence you to two months in gaol' or 'I baptize you in the name of the Father . . .' Everyday rather than religious or legal versions might include 'I promise I'll be there' or 'I congratulate you!' From this linguistic connection between utterance and action, and the concomitant analysis of what language can effect, a wider exploration has developed, focusing on ways in which the individual performs versions of the self. In terms of the psychology of behaviour, it could be argued that 'all performance involves a consciousness of doubleness, according to which the actual execution of an action is placed in mental comparison with a potential, an ideal, or a remembered original model' (Carlson, 5). For a gender theorist like Judith Butler, gender identity is not inherent within the self but created and enforced through the performance of ritualized repetitions of stereotypically gendered acts: 'an identity instituted through a *stylized repetition of acts*' (Butler, 'Performative' 519). '[G]ender is an act which has been rehearsed, much as a script survives the particular actors who make use of it, but which requires individual actors to be actualized and reproduced as reality once again' (Butler, 'Performative', 526).

For Butler, the theatrical **metaphor** of performativity offers ways of expressing the temporality and instability of gender; just as a script may be enacted in different ways and a performance requires both text and interpretation, 'so the gendered body acts its part in a culturally restricted corporeal space and enacts interpretations within the confines of already existing directives' (Butler, 'Performative', 526). Butler's theories of 'acting' selfhood are readily transferable to the superficialities of class, whereas the question of 'race' and performativity is both complex and contested. In terms of Renaissance theatre, performance and performativity offer important perspectives on the relationships between text and dramatic realization and also the functions of performativity in a highly ritualized age. As Phyllis Rackin observes, the stage 'was an important site of cultural transformation – a place where cultural change was not simply reflected but also rehearsed and enacted' (Rackin, 'Androgyny', 29). Shakespeare often draws attention to the boy actor playing the female role, creating metatheatrical comedy from the situation. On the modern stage, the performativity of gender is interrogated through all-female casting or the playing of the eponymous hero by a female actor. Beyond the theatre, the early modern world within walking distance of the Globe displayed complex variants on the performative: the medieval cathedrals of Southwark and St Paul's; a monarchy displaying power through stylized processions; the grotesque rituals of state executions. The performance of class hierarchy, and contemporary awareness of social mobility, became a major theme of the city comedies of the day.

Middleton and Dekker's *The Roaring Girl* (1608) is unique in dramatizing a living character and thereby addressing contemporary concerns over performance and gender. Whereas male disguise is invariably a **trope** offering the heroine a means of survival, Moll's britches, boots and weaponry are her own preference. Further, the play does not deal in an invented fantasy but adapts the story of the notorious Mary Frith (*c.*1584–1659), a woman arraigned more than once for unseemly behaviour – masculine clothing, swearing, smoking, blaspheming, and frequenting low-life establishments. The Prologue alludes to the city's many 'roaring girls':

> For of that tribe are many: one is she
> That roars at midnight in deep tavern bowls,
> That beats the watch, and constables controls;
> Another roars i'th'daytime, swears, stabs, gives braves,
> Yet sells her soul to the lust of fools and slaves.
> Both these are suburb-roarers. Then there's beside
> A civil, city-roaring girl . . .
>
> *The Roaring Girl*, Prol., 16–22

Mary Frith was evidently not alone; the 'masculine woman' encompassed all classes and had spread to the suburbs. From the 1580s to the late 1620s, male writers protested against the 'masculine woman'; Philip Stubbes was among the first to identify women sporting 'dubblets and Jerkins . . . buttoned up the brest . . . as mannes apparel is . . . yet thei blushe not to weare it' (Stubbes, 37). London's 'Amazonian women' were clearly seen as performing masculine roles as well as adopting male fashions; an anonymous tract entitled *Hic Mulier: or, The Man-Woman* (1620) objected that 'since the daies of *Adam* women were never so Masculine . . . Masculine in Moode from bold speech, to impudent action' (*Hic Mulier*, n.p.). By Jacobean times, the king himself weighed in with instructions to the clergy of London to preach against cross-dressing and 'the insolencie of our women' (Cook, xxxiii). Moll displays fearless 'masculinity'; she fights her would-be seducer, Laxton, until he is reduced to begging for his life and boasts, at the end of the play, that she can guarantee safety from the city's pickpockets and cheats. While *The Roaring Girl* threatens normative assumptions – Moll simply enjoys dressing and behaving as a man – Jonson's *Epicoene or The Silent Woman* (1609) could be seen as infinitely more subversive. Here, the bride Morose has chosen for her modesty and reticence is, in fact, male. Unusually, the unmasking of Epicoene takes place in the final scenes of the play; no one among Morose's household or acquaintances is privy to the secret except for the instigator of the plot, Dauphine. Gender is performed as an entirely artificial construct throughout the play; Captain Otter complains that his wife 'takes herself asunder when she goes to bed, into some twenty boxes, and about next day noon is put together again, like a great German clock' (4.2.88–90). The city wives or 'collegiate ladies' of society assume their own 'hermaphroditical authority' (1.1.77), rejecting marriage and childbirth and openly discussing contraception and abortion. The play's foppish young men claim falsely to have slept with Epicoene as a woman, presumably to conceal their sexual preferences, and Clerimont, whose levee opens the play, has 'his mistress abroad and his ingle (catamite) at home' (1.1.22–3). Early modern comedies frequently exploit metatheatrical effects but these two plays go further in drawing attention to the inherent instability of gendered identities.

The analysis of performance and performativity is grounded in the study of societal expectations – whether of gender, class or race. As such, its significance for Shakespeare scholars is to move discussion decisively away from the essentialism of character criticism. Cultural assumptions are inevitably shifting and ephemeral; it is no longer possible to argue that Cleopatra is 'woman everlasting' with an expectation that such a phrase possesses a single, irreducible meaning.

> This discussion focuses on the ways in which levels of illusion foreground ideas of performativity in *The Taming of the Shrew* thereby drawing attention to the role-playing of Petruccio and Katherina. Cary's closet drama, *The Tragedy of Mariam*, highlights ideas of female speech and performativity within a highly stylized Senecan framework.

The Taming of the Shrew

The Induction

> My Lord this is but the play, theyre but in iest
>
> *A Shrew*, in Hodgdon, Appendix 3,
> line 1330

The key textual difficulty of Shakespeare's *The Taming of the Shrew* (1594) is its relationship with the anonymous play, *The Taming of a Shrew* (hereafter *A Shrew*). Which of the two plays was the original; whether both might have been written in part or substantially by Shakespeare; whether both derive from a lost original is a matter for scholarly conjecture. Ann Thompson suggests that the **Folio** text of Shakespeare's play is incomplete, the result of cuts and revisions from the early

1590s (Thompson, *Shrew*, 181–2). Barbara Hodgdon in Arden 3 draws attention to the complex circumstances surrounding the ownership of playscripts given the unstable nature of the different acting companies. Recent research into theatre practices and printing history has opened up a complicated world where plays were 'open to penetration and alteration not only by Shakespeare himself and by his fellow players but also by multiple theatrical and extra-theatrical scriveners, by theatrical annotators, adapters and revisers (who might cut or add), by censors, and by compositors and proofreaders' (Werstine, cited in Hodgdon, 28).

The Christopher Sly Induction raises contested textual and performance issues; should Sly be present on stage throughout and should the framing device reappear as an epilogue to the Paduan plot? The Induction functions as a complex metatheatrical device, just as the Pyramus and Thisbe play concluding *A Midsummer Night's Dream* mirrors and ironizes the narratives and emotions of the play's protagonists. The attempts to persuade Sly that he is an amnesiac aristocrat introduce more than a farcical joke at his expense, they raise questions of class, gender and performativity that resonate with the play that follows. The drunken Sly is thrown out of the tavern for disorderly behaviour and threatened with the stocks and the constable by the indignant alewife. The **motif** of the commanding female voice is thereby introduced through a familiar comic figure. Chris Fitter suggests that Sly is part of a carnival mood where the audience would identify with his 'visceral vitality in execrating authority' (Fitter, 131). At the same time, the bossy and intractable woman had always been a popular theatrical figure from medieval depictions of Noah's wife. Class inflections bubble up even here; when Sly is humiliated by the alewife, he protests ancestral status, 'we came in with Richard Conqueror' (Ind. 1.4). When he is confused by the Lord's retinue, however, he takes refuge in a modest lineage:

> Am I not Christopher Sly, old Sly's son of Burton Heath, by birth a pedlar, by education a cardmaker, by transmutation a

bear-herd and now by present profession a tinker? Ask Marian
Hacket, the fat ale-wife of Wincot if she knows me not.

Ind. 2.16–21

Anchoring Sly firmly in the Warwickshire countryside is
doubtless a good joke; it has the added effect of distancing the
ensuing drama of 'fair Padua'. To the passing Lord returning
from his hunting, Sly is, 'a monstrous beast' ripe for comic
exploitation (Ind. 1 33). His scheme to 'practise' on Sly raises
questions about identity relevant to the embedded Paduan
plot: can external trappings and modes of address achieve
internal transformations?

> What think you, if he were conveyed to bed,
> Wrapped in sweet clothes, rings put upon his fingers,
> A most delicious banquet by his bed
> And brave attendants near him when he wakes,
> Would not the beggar then forget himself?
>
> Ind. 1. 36–40

The Lord's household is, in fact, about to engage with two
discrete sets of 'performances'. As Bartholomew the page is
instructed to act the part of Sly's Lady, the travelling players
are welcomed.

📖 *Now read Ind. 1. 104–37.*

- *Think about the implications of the Lord's confidence
  that his Page can effectively 'usurp the grace,/Voice, gait
  and action of a gentlewoman' (130–1). Is the playwright
  drawing attention to the fact the 'gentlewomen' of the
  play are all played by boys?*
- *The speech is expansive in terms of physical expressiveness:
  'kind embracements . . . tempting kisses' (117). Why does
  the Lord choreograph the physical intimacy of the scene
  in such detail?*

- *The Lord anticipates uncontrolled merriment from the role reversals set up here: does his carnivalesque scheme complicate gender relations in the play as a whole?*

The duping of Sly, then, involves the 'performance' of both class and gender. As Lena Cowen Orlin argues, the play deals in a world of 'things' that themselves have a role in the performance of gender and class identity (Orlin, 171 and onwards). The bewildered tinker is bombarded with the courtly and exotic: beautiful music, the voluptuous couch of Semiramis, finely decorated horses, hawks that will 'soar / Above the morning lark' (Ind. 2. 41–2). For further piquant delights, he is offered the illustrated stories of Venus and Adonis, Jupiter and Io, Daphne and Apollo. Like Sebastian in *Twelfth Night*, he cannot believe that he is not dreaming and needs to affirm reality: 'I do not sleep. I see, I hear, I speak, / I smell sweet savours and I feel soft things' (Ind. 2. 68). To Jonathan Bate the opening scenes offer 'an induction . . . to the whole phenomenon of Shakespearian comedy' (Bate, *Ovid*, 118). The motif of Ovidian transformation is intriguing in this context: the tales from *Metamorphoses* are all tragic tales of sexual brutality and female suffering, an uneasy backcloth to the later story. Or, does Shakespeare want to draw attention to a wider motif of transformation: Sly into a Lord, Bartholomew the page into a gracious lady, the English players into a merchant's household in Padua – and Katherina Minola into a submissive wife? The emphasis on performance as a temporary state underlines the provisional and transient nature of all performances. Equally, the play metaphor 'demonstrates [how] elements of illusion can insinuate themselves into life, and be mistaken for reality' (Righter, 95). Sly greets his new 'wife' enthusiastically; he has, after all, been thoroughly humiliated by the alewife. His masculinity is affirmed by the promise of marital delights:

My husband and my lord, my lord and husband,
I am your wife in all obedience.

Ind. 2. 103–4

The formal device of **antimetabole** emphasizes Sly's change of status, provoking laughter from the onstage audience and, more importantly, anticipating Katherina's final speech. Further interruptions from Sly – or even his continuing presence on stage – complicate and disrupt the dramatic illusion, reminding the audience that the story of the Minola daughters is an entertainment for a lord's household and a joke at the expense of Christopher Sly. The Induction is both elaborate and extended; it seems consistent that Shakespeare would have reintroduced Sly at the end of the play, as in *A Shrew*. The latter concludes with poor Sly dumped outside in his everyday clothing and woken by the tapster to the cold light of day. His illusions of grandeur linger in his mind and he questions, 'am I not a Lord?' Like Caliban he has dreamed the 'bravest dream' he ever knew; like Caliban he might weep to dream it again because he is about to return to a harsher reality. The tapster predicts, 'your wife will course you for dreming here to night' (Hodgdon, 394, l. 1618); in the Sly household, 'taming' is the stuff of fantasy.

Courtship and marriage in the *Taming of the Shrew*

From his first sight of Bianca, Lucentio expresses himself in stereotypical **Petrarchan** clichés, 'I burn, I pine, I perish' (1.1.154), establishing his courtship as the conventional opposite of Petruccio's. He sees perfection in Bianca because she is not her sister:

> In the other's silence I do see
> Maids' mild behaviour and sobriety.

1.1.70–1

The pursuit of Bianca is ludicrously complicated; pretence and performance becoming a trope that dominates the courtship rituals. This farcical complexity derives, in part, from Shakespeare's source material, *Supposes* (1566), an English prose drama by George Gascoigne, translated from Ariosto's *Gli Suppositi*. Gascoigne's Prologue establishes the motif of changed identities: 'For you shall see the master supposed for the servant, the servant for the master: the freeman for a slave and the bondslave for a freeman: the stranger for a well-known friend, and the familiar for a stranger' (cited, Hodgdon, 64).

Bianca's suitors constantly adopt new identities to pursue love: Lucentio's plan is to woo Bianca in the disguise of a schoolmaster; Tranio, his servant, can therefore impersonate him:

> We have not yet been seen in any house,
> Nor can we be distinguished by our faces
> For man and master. Then it follows thus:
> Thou shalt be master, Tranio, in my stead,
> Keep house and port and servants as I should;
> I will some other be – some Florentine,
> Some Neapolitan, or meaner man of Pisa.
> [...]
> [*They exchange outer clothing*]
>
> 1.1.198–204, 207

Here, as in the Induction, superficialities such as clothing symbolize class and status: Lucentio's words suggest that there is no discernible class difference in their speech or demeanour. Where Petruccio appears simply as himself, 'I come to wive it wealthily in Padua' (1.2.74), Bianca's lovers adopt a vertiginously complex series of identities. Tranio is disguised as Lucentio, his master; Lucentio is disguised first as Tranio and then as the tutor, Cambio. Hortensio, his rival, is disguised as Licio, the music master. Later, a passing Merchant is persuaded to enact the role of Vincentio in order to validate Tranio's story. There is carnivalesque comedy in the sheer dexterity of multiple disguises. But is identity any more than performativity? To Jean Howard the comedies raise a profound question: is there 'a "real self", or is personhood a succession of social roles adopted because of coercion, social expectation, material circumstances?' (Howard, 176). The structure of the drama makes a point here too: before Bianca is wooed by the disguised Lucentio and Hortensio, Baptista negotiates the marriage settlement with Tranio and Gremio who attempt to out-argue each other in terms of possessions. Baptista is only concerned to secure the wealthiest suitor: 'he/That can assure my daughter greatest dower/Shall have my Bianca's love' (2.1.347–8). Gremio's list of moveable goods sounds appropriate to a great Italian merchant; costly tapestries and Turkish fabrics as well as valuable fat oxen. But Tranio plays his part by offering 'three great argosies, besides two galliases,/And twelve tight galleys' (2.1.382–3) at which point the auction is concluded: 'I must confess your offer is the best ... She is your own' (2.1.390, 392). At no point does Baptista contemplate whether Bianca has an opinion on the subject, not least about whom she might choose to love. The negotiations are farcical: Gremio is the foolish old *pantaloon*, a stock figure of the *commedia dell'arte*; Tranio is the disguised servant. Two points emerge: first that money is the only significant factor to Baptista; secondly that the outward appearance of the 'gentleman' is quite enough to secure social recognition and a fair bride.

The actual wooing of Bianca, by the disguised Lucentio and Hortensio (3.1) is ironically at odds with the fact that her father believes that he has just sealed the marriage contract on her behalf. Equally, Bianca's confident assumption of authority in this scene belies Lucentio's earlier vision of the obedient and docile maiden. As her rival suitors wrangle with each other, she is quite certain of her governing role, 'I am no breeching scholar in the schools:/... But learn my lessons as I please myself' (3.1.18, 20). In her willingness to match Lucentio's game over the Latin 'translation' she is both encouraging and flirtatious. Lucentio proceeds to Ovid's *Ars Amatoria* (a classical text regarded as dangerously 'lewd' at the time) with Bianca's approval, 'may you prove, sir, master of your art' (4.2.9). Her rejection of Hortensio is not as violent as Katherina's but it is certainly perfunctory. Yet, Hortensio's apparent devotion is questionable; when he sees Lucentio and Bianca 'kiss and court' (4.2.27) he rejects her as 'unworthy' of his favours and proceeds speedily to an alternative: 'I will be married to a wealthy widow/Ere three days pass' (4.2.37–8). There is undoubtedly an element of comic farce in the bevy of disguised suitors wooing Bianca – the 'counterfeit supposes' (5.1.108) revealed by Lucentio to his own father and to Baptista when he confesses that he and Bianca are secretly married. Because the docile Bianca has, of course, entirely rejected patriarchal authority and eloped.

Courtship and Katherina

> Faith, gentlemen, now I play a merchant's part
> And venture madly on a desperate mart
>
> 2.1.330

To Baptista the marriage of his daughters is essentially an unpredictable commercial affair and Tranio, pursuing the mercantile metaphor further, emphasizes the perishability of Baptista's goods: 'a commodity lay fretting by you;/Twill bring you gain, or perish on the seas' (2.1.332–3). Here, Katherina is the 'commodity' and 'fretting' does not have modern connotations of worrying but connotes rotting or decaying (OED 3). Women, as goods, lose their value quickly. Baptista's opening words offer his elder daughter to either suitor, one of whom is an elderly buffoon. Katherina's response might express indignation or could be seen as an appeal to the one person who should be defending her interests:

> I pray you, sir, is it your will
> To make a stale of me among these mates?
>
> 1.1.57–8

'Stale' invariably suggests prostitute as well as a laughing stock; she fears that her father is capable of securing any degraded or ridiculous match for her. Equally, Baptista's favouritism evokes not fury but despair from her:

> She is your treasure, she must have a husband,
> I must dance barefoot on her wedding day
> And, for your love to her, lead apes in hell.
> Talk not to me, I will go sit and weep
>
> 2.1.32–5

The proverbial phrase 'that women dying maids lead apes in hell' is cited by Beatrice in *Much Ado About Nothing* (2.1.41) in reply to Leonato's 'thou wilt never get thee a husband' – like Katherina, she is 'curst'. Beatrice, though, turns the joke against Leonato rather than against herself whereas Katherina appears anguished and self-despising. The proverb almost certainly originated in the post-Reformation opposition to monasticism and priestly celibacy. In Protestant terms marriage and childbearing was seen as the ideal state and the unmarried woman could be too easily designated as unnatural. In Lyly's *Euphues* (1578) a concerned father urges his daughter to marry anyone at all rather than 'to thy great torments lead apes in Hell' (Lyly, 74). In medieval lore apes symbolized male lasciviousness so the virgin is mated for eternity with bestial lusts. But Katherina is not simply the unhappy maiden, she is, according to the male characters around her, the shrew. Their exaggeration is intriguing: Tranio comments that Katherina 'raise[d] up such a storm/That mortal ears might hardly endure the din' (1.1.171–2). She has, in fact, said very little at this point although she strenuously reacts against Hortensio's rudeness. Coppélia Kahn suggests that Katherine's famed 'shrewishness' is a male construct: 'Kate is called devil, hell, curst, shrewd (shrewish), and wildcat ... because, powerless to change her situation, she *talks* about it' (Kahn, 108, original emphasis). Petruccio mocks their fear of Katherina's 'scolding tongue' (1.2.99) with some masculine bragging and delights in

Hortensio's story that Katherina has broken a lute over his head: 'Now, by the world, it is a lusty wench;/I love her ten times more than e'er I did' (2.1.159–60).

Petruccio's courtship is a performance from the outset: he declares he will 'woo her with some spirit' (2.1.168). The **stichomythic** exchanges that begin the scene establish how well matched the two are verbally: their language resembles the sparring between Beatrice and Benedick in *Much Ado*. In his opening gambit he insistently repeats her name as if offering her a spectrum of potential personalities: 'plain Kate/And bonny Kate, and sometimes 'Kate the Curst'; /But Kate, the prettiest Kate in Christendom' (2.1.184–6). Unlike Lucentio he has no need to hide behind classical texts but seizes the opportunity to cap her words with sexual innuendo: 'my tongue in your tail' (2.1.219). Her violent response betrays her consciousness of his meaning but when she responds with violence he describes her behaviour as 'pleasant, gamesome, passing courteous' (2.1.247). The motif of performativity here offers both characters licence to create new personae, his disorientating tactics bewildering or liberating.

'of all mad matches never was the like'

The 'performance' of the wedding is, simply, too radical to be acted in front of the early modern audience (although film productions enjoy the challenge). Shakespeare's comedies invariably conclude with weddings and where marriage takes place at an earlier stage in the drama, it is a broken nuptial. *Much Ado* and *All's Well That Ends Well* are notable examples where the ceremony is destroyed by the bridegroom. Katherina is humiliated from the outset when Petruccio fails to arrive, and her first words express her shame and despair: 'Would Katherina had never seen him though' (3.2.26). The appearance of the bridegroom is scarcely reassuring; in his patched and ill-assorted clothes and broken-down old horse, he is not a romantic or desirable prospect. Yet he refuses the offer of more seemly attire observing, 'To me she's married, not unto my clothes' (3.2.116). Petruccio goes on to trivialize and mock the sacrament and the priest, blasphemously swearing, cuffing the priest himself, and carousing with the communion wine. He concludes with a 'clamorous smack' on the lips of Katherina '[that] all the church did echo' (3.2.178). Performance is everything in this scene, with Petruccio acting the part of a crazed or impious fool, belittling 'matrimony' as an event, violating the sacrament and offending both Baptista and Katherina. The initial exchanges between husband and wife are equally contradictory: when the bride cannot prevail with her new husband, Petruccio produces perhaps the most misogynist lines in literature, but as if he is defending Katherina:

> She is my goods, my chattels; she is my house,
> My household-stuff, my field, my barn,
> My horse, my ox, my ass, my anything,
> And here she stands. Touch her whoever dare,
> I'll bring mine action on the proudest he
> That stops my way in Padua.
>   [...]
> – Fear not, sweet wench, they shall not touch thee, Kate;
> I'll buckler thee against a million.
>
>   3.2.231–6, 239–40

His performance of these two discrete roles characterizes the marriage scenes that follow. Petruccio is violently enraged against his household servants whom Katherina attempts to protect. When she falls off her horse and into the mire, she is left to struggle while Petruccio beats Grumio who later recounts how 'she waded through the dirt to pluck him off me' (4.1.69–70). Onlookers clearly regard them as well matched, using interchangeable terms to describe their relationship: 'being mad herself, she's madly mated./I warrant him, Petruccio is Kated!' (3.2.245–6). The punchline to Grumio's narrative – 'he is more shrew than she' (4.12.76) – being particularly significant.

The married Petruccio is confident that his method of 'kill[ing] a wife with kindness' (4.1.197) will be effective; his metaphor of falcon and haggard theorizes his vision of control. How far his method is successful, is arguable. When the tailor visits with new and fashionable clothing, Katherina's opening bid is uncompromising:

> Why, sir, I trust I may have leave to speak,
> And speak I will. I am no child, no babe;
> Your betters have endured me say my mind,
> And if you cannot, best you stop your ears.
> My tongue will tell the anger of my heart,
> Or else my heart concealing it will break,
> And, rather than it shall, I will be free
> Even to the uttermost, as I please, in words.
>
> 4.3.75–82

The notion of Katherina as 'free . . . in words' is worth bearing in mind when considering her final speech. Nuances of language govern these scenes between Katherina and Petruccio: he expects victory over his wife in terms of verbal assent. But does Katherina yield in the exchanges over the sun and moon or does she mock his, by now, familiar excursions into twisting words and meanings? She appears to adopt Petruccio's own methods and repeat his linguistic demands hyperbolically: sun, moon or rush-candle 'it shall be so for me' (4.5.14–15). The lowly rush-candle makes a mockery of her reversal. Similarly, she slips in a subtle insult while apparently agreeing that the sun is the moon, because the moon changes 'even as your mind' (4.5.21). She is performing in exactly the same way when she greets Vincentio as a 'young budding virgin' (38), moving far beyond a modest greeting to speculate on the happiness of the bridegroom that will possess this 'lovely bedfellow'. Her studied apology similarly turns the verbal play back against Petruccio, excusing herself for being 'bedazzled with the sun' (47) which looks back at the beginning of the scene and her robust 'I say it is the sun that shines so bright.' In these exchanges, then, both Katherina and Petruccio are engaged in the performance of wit and contradiction; there is no real evidence of 'taming' here, they are evenly matched. Their return to Padua occurs as the deceptions and false identities of the 'Bianca plot' have reached a climax. The theme of playing a part is all-pervasive at this point; identity can be altered as easily as changing clothes.

The submission speech (5.2.142–85)

'To her, Kate!/To her, widow!' (5.2.34–5). The famous speech begins as a comic wager between the two men; Petruccio happily confident in his wife's superior wit. It is by far the longest speech in the play and undoubtedly the most controversial – and not just for modern audiences. Bernard Shaw objected to it as a Victorian playwright and for many actors of the role it remains a difficulty. Understanding the speech demands a thorough consideration of the language, obviously, but audience perception is ultimately directed by the individual performer or director. Katherina's final gesture must be performative; in the absence of stage directions Shakespeare offers no clues. As early as 1929 Mary Pickford famously delivered the speech with a knowing wink to Bianca – one small gesture that renders the words entirely ironic. To Sinead Cusack (1982) the speech 'is really about how her spirit has been allowed to soar free' (Rutter, *Voices*, 1). The darkest vision is doubtless Charles Marowitz's brutally sadistic adaptation (1974) where the violently abused Kate appears as 'a mesmerized or drugged victim droning the words her tormentors could not make her speak' (Marowitz, 19).

📖 *Turning to the speech itself:*

- *To whom are the different questions and **apostrophes** addressed?*
- *What is implied by the contract with the husband?*

- *How does the metaphor of the Prince and subject function?*

In *A Shrew* the parallel speech includes a blast of theology: the 'King of Kings [and] glorious God of heauen' made first Adam and then the 'woe of man', the cause of sin and death (Hodgdon, 392, 1559, 1565). Woman must atone for her primal sin by obedience and submission. Katherina's speech is both more personally and more politically inflected: her opening lines are clearly intended as an insult to the Widow who has mocked her. The second significant statement is transactional: the husband 'commits his body/To painful labour both by sea and land' requiring only 'love, fair looks and true obedience' in recompense. Clearly, neither Baptista nor Petruccio fits the bill here. Both have married for money and owe their material comforts to their respective dowries. Is Katherina therefore implying that 'true obedience' might be won in gratitude for heroic labours? A contract is implied. The political reasoning that follows is familiar to the early modern audience: to revolt against the ruling prince is treason – but what if the prince is a tyrannical despot? Katherina pursues her metaphor in terms of the wife's obedience to the 'honest will' of the husband where the analogy might suggest that the absence of such honesty renders the obedience superfluous. And her final comments to the listening women – 'you forward and unable worms' – depends on a cryptically placed 'seeming', reminding the viewer that the gracious speaker is of course the boy actor, at which point the continuing presence on stage of Sly and his 'lady', Bartholomew, casts the entire scene in an ironical and metatheatrical light, reminding the audience of the Page's identical words in the Induction. There are no certainties in this final scene: Bianca, the new bride, scarcely exhibits the silent modesty Lucentio has first admired in her – 'more fool you for laying on my duty' (5.2.135) – and it is clear that the Widow is the commanding figure in her marriage with Hortensio. Writing about Zeffirelli's film and Elizabeth Taylor's passionate delivery of the speech, Jorgens suggests that

Katherina reacts against 'the meanness and vulgarity of the widow and Bianca' (Jorgens, 70). Status in these different marriages seems questionable: are all three new bridegrooms destined to find the balance of power more complex than they had initially imagined? Katherina's speech expresses the orthodox views of the Anglican marriage service while suggesting that 'obedience' is provisional, transactional, even theoretical. She has deflected Petruccio's verbal dominance with a satirical performance that mocks the fantasy of male supremacy. Returning to old traditions of shrew fables, it might be worth considering, also, that traditionally, the shrew triumphs.

The tamer tamed

Speculation over Katherina's possible submission is complicated by the unique existence of a comic sequel, *The Woman's Prize; or, The Tamer Tamed* (1609–11) by John Fletcher, Shakespeare's successor with the King's Company and occasional co-author. As the play opens, the bereaved Petruchio is about to remarry, and his companions express concern for the fate of his new wife. Clearly, he had failed to tame Katherina – 'she was a rebel' (1.1.19) – and is reported to wake at night from nightmares that make him hide his breeches unless she should appear as a ghost and wear them. His new wife, Maria, however, has every intention of becoming a 'tempest' until she has 'wrought a miracle upon him' (1.2.69) and thoroughly tamed him into submission, aided by her female companions. A subplot features the bride's sister, Livia, who refuses to marry her father's choice of husband, the elderly Moroso. The women are a significant part of the comedy – they launch enthusiastically into the scheme – 'let's all wear breeches' – and they crack bawdy jokes about the sexual potency of their men. Petruchio is locked out of the bridal chamber on his wedding night and is forced to parley through 'Colonel' Bianca; the 'race of Amazon' imposes martial law on the men and a total impasse is reached. Petruchio is driven to despair over the situation and feigns illness, then announces he is leaving for foreign parts before, finally, pretending to be dead. Maria is unimpressed by all of these ruses and delivers a speech over his coffin where she regrets his wasted life – 'his poor, unmanly, wretched, foolish life' (5.4.19). When he leaps from the coffin protesting his misery, Maria relents: 'I have tamed ye' (5.4.45). On this basis they kiss and he vows he will never give her occasion to regret her marriage. Livia confesses that she has married her own choice of husband, Roland; victory lies with the women.

Shakespeare goes to Hollywood: Burton and Taylor (1966)

The Taming of the Shrew was Hollywood's first full-length non-silent Shakespearean film: Mary Pickford and Douglas Fairbanks starred in Sam Taylor's popular 1929 adaptation. The action remains firmly in the tradition of the highly stylized gesture of silent film; the pair fight each with whips and in the entirely non-verbal bedroom scene push and shove at each other in equal measure until finally Katherina flings a stool at Petruccio and he is knocked down and wounded. As he staggers around, concussed, she flings his whip on the fire and the scene concludes with her gently cradling his head. Petruccio appears far more 'tamed' than his bride. The following morning she delivers part of the submission speech while winking broadly at her sister. Zeffirelli's achievement is to transform Shakespeare into a Hollywood 'battle of the sexes' movie starring the Western world's favourite screen personalities. The idea of the 'Liz Taylor' of the 1960s being in any way submissive would be unthinkable. She had already appeared with Burton in Joseph Mankiewicz's *Cleopatra* (1963) and in Mike Nichols' film version of Edward Albee's *Who's Afraid of Virginia Woolf?* (1966). Taylor had acquired celebrity status for her extravagant lifestyle and her marriages (five husbands by the time that *Shrew* appeared); the love affair between Burton and Taylor had flourished on the filmset of *Cleopatra*, eliciting papal denunciation and, by the standards of the day, a media frenzy of prurient fascination (both were already married). So Zeffirelli's choice of stars suggests his interpretation of the text before the opening sequences roll. He invites and exploits intertextual links throughout; comparisons with Bianca or with the Sly Induction are irrelevant as the focus of the film is entirely on the central couple and the potent sexual charge between them (they first married in 1964). Performativity lies at the heart of the constructed image of 'Liz Taylor': a wilful and strikingly beautiful actress is expected to rage and storm and, indeed, is admired for it.

The extended opening sequences are wholly carnivalesque: Renaissance Padua in all its glorious and subversive energy. As Deborah Cartmell observes, 'Shakespeare is for Zeffirelli a "frustrated traveller" with a desire to take his audience on a sight-seeing tour of Italy' (Cartmell, 216). The opening frame displays Lucentio journeying through a background which is exaggeratedly false – clearly aiming to resemble a painted quattrocento background. The succeeding chaos of the arrival in Padua is all the more pronounced as the camera pans across a crowded city scene with jostling crowd, abundant merchandise, a caged prisoner. A vast blonde woman gazes coquettishly from a window, to Tranio's delight. Lucentio's pursuit of Bianca, in the film's favoured motif, dominates the arrival in Padua; as yet, Katherina is invisible. Petruccio's arrival is marked by triumphal music and his characteristic robust laughter. Katherina's first appearance is, famously, a watchful – and unmistakeable – eye through a key hole followed by an explosion of violence against her sister. The first scene between the protagonists is filmed as a lengthy and dangerous chase; balancing uneasily on the rooftop, they both fall through the ceiling and land on mountainous heaps of stored feathers. Both pursuit and its climax are energetically physical; Katherina is finally panting and exhausted, lying among the feathers as in a bed. All is suggestive of the sexual pleasures to come – the text itself seems an irrelevance.

Petruccio's humiliation of Katherina in his ill-fitting bridal clothes and the treacherous journey back to his home is not underplayed; she is angry and vengeful. Zeffirelli's resolution of the wedding-night stalemate reveals contradictions typical of the age. Taylor is the undoubted bully of the scene, thwacking her bridegroom firmly on the head with a warming pan after seeming to woo him with an alluring smile. Left alone, she sheds a few unconvincing tears before waking to a bright new morning in which she features as the epitome of the perfect housewife, scarf around her head, directing the cleaning. Untamed, but domesticated. Or, perhaps, a mutual taming? Jorgens suggests that Petruccio is 'crass, drunken, self-serving and materialistic' where Kate is the 'spoiled, egotistical, well-fed rich girl' (Jorgens, 68) and that both require civilizing. In the final scenes Zeffirelli emphasizes a maternal quality in her, and a shared affection between the couple who emerge as infinitely better suited than Bianca and Lucentio or Hortensio and his Widow. Her final speech certainly attacks them before gazing adoringly at Petruccio – but then she disappears and the chase begins again with Petruccio as the willing pursuer. The film cannot be seen as making a feminist claim for Katherina, but dwells rather on a highly charged sexual attraction between two notorious lovers. As Jorgens argues, they are well suited as the 'Lord and Lady of Misrule' launching a 'thorough assault on Padua and Paduan values' (Jorgens, 72).

Hollywood returned to the fundamental *donnée* of the text with teen romcom *Ten Things I Hate About You*, 1999. Gil Junger's film translates Kate and Bianca to modern Seattle and the sexual rivalries of the school prom. The female protagonist Kat Stratford (Julia Stiles) is the class feminist and reviled for her notably anti-male attitudes. There can be no equivalent to the 'submission' speech in this context so Kate produces a tearful statement of affection for her Petruccio, Patrick Verona (Heath Ledger), by performing her own version of a Shakespearean sonnet in front of the class. It has been argued that Kat exemplifies the Girl Power of 1990s' pop culture in identifying with the alternative rock scene of the American north-west. Certainly, she desires freedom from the constraints of her home and her father, and has won a place at an east-coast college. But the 'feel-good' conclusion could also be judged as materialist bathos: Kat is humiliated when she discovers that she has been the butt of a wager between the boys, but swiftly recovers when a smart new guitar appears in her car. The BBC *Shakespeare Retold* version by Sally Wainwright (2006) is arguably more faithful to the text; Kate (Shirley Henderson) is thoroughly diminished by the wedding and believes that the publicity will destroy her stellar political career. Yet Kate is to be the next prime minister so Wainwright neatly resolves the problem of inequality. Like Zeffirelli, this adaptation also suggests a strong sexual bond between the pair; they are equally unconventional and the fiercely feminist and brutally ambitious Kate is seen in the closing frames outside 10 Downing Street with her faithful family – it is, of course, Petruccio (Rufus Sewell) who stays at home to look after their triplets.

Further reading

Pamela Allen Brown, *Better a Shrew Than a Sheep: Women, Drama, and the Culture of Jest in Early Modern England* (Ithaca, 2003)

John O'Connor, 'Kate', in *Shakespearean Afterlives: Ten Characters With a Life of Their Own* (Cambridge, 2003)

Frances E. Dolan (ed.), *The Taming of the Shrew: Texts and Contexts* (Boston, 1996)

Graham Holderness and David Wootton, *Gender and Power in Shrew-Taming Narratives* (Basingstoke, 2010)

Kiernan Ryan, '"A Kind of History": *The Taming of the Shrew*', in *Shakespeare's Comedies* (Basingstoke, 2009)

The Tragedy of Mariam, The Fair Queen of Jewry

Elizabeth Cary, Lady Falkland (1585/6–1639) was the only child of Elizabeth Symondes and Sir Lawrence Tanfield, lawyer and judge. She benefited from the humanist educational ideas of her time; home-schooled, she was widely read and proficient in several languages, including Hebrew. In her teenage years she was married to Sir Henry Cary; he possessed the superior title, she brought the abundant dowry. Because Cary was engaged in military campaigns and then a prisoner of war, his young wife remained with her parents and continued her life of reading and translation, until her mother-in-law deemed it more suitable for her to join the Cary household in London. Her attachment to her scholarly pursuits was clearly viewed as anomalous: her own mother tried to prevent her reading at night and her mother-in-law sought to deny her any books at all – a restriction which simply encouraged her to write. On the surface her marriage appears conventional: once reunited with her husband, in 1609, her first child was born, succeeded by ten further living children. She commanded her household and, when her husband was Lord Deputy of Ireland, not only accompanied him but engaged herself vigorously with the troubles of those around her, learning Gaelic and attempting to alleviate the poverty and distress of Dublin's poor. But in 1626 she announced her conversion to Roman Catholicism, and instantly became estranged from her husband and ostracized by his social milieu. She suffered a brief period of imprisonment and continuing financial hardship. By the time of her death, in 1639, she had converted four of her daughters, all of whom were received into the Benedictine convent at Cambrai. Her biography was written by one of her daughters (*The Lady Falkland: Her Life*) and offers an intriguing insight into the feelings and opinions of a highly independent woman. Needless to say, it is hardly an impartial account and concentrates almost entirely on Cary's religious convictions. Her verse drama, *The Tragedy of Mariam*, printed in 1613, but probably written 1603–10 and thereafter in manuscript circulation, has the distinction of being the first tragic drama published by a woman. Her other writings – some now lost – include translations, poetry and possibly a historical work, *The History of the Life, Reign, and Death of Edward II* (authorship disputed).

According to Cary's biography, she enjoyed theatrical performances and frequently attended plays. The fact of authoring a play is not, in itself, unique, as recent editions of Renaissance plays by women demonstrate (Purkiss, 1998; Cerasano and Wynne-Davies, 1996) but it is a radical step to move from the private world of closet drama (or, simply, writing for personal pleasure) to publicly printing the work under her own name: 'that learned, virtuous, and truly noble Ladie, E.C.' is the appellation given on the frontispiece of the text. The first known dramatic text by a woman is Lady Jane Lumley's *Iphigenia at Aulis* (*c.*1555), probably the first translation of Euripides in England and a text she cut and adapted but did not publish. Lady Mary Sidney's translation of a French classical tragedy, *Antonie*, was published in 1592 and 1595, perhaps inspiring Cary with the possibility of publication. The subject matter chosen by these earliest female writers is startling: the sacrifice of Iphigenia; the death of Cleopatra; the murder of Mariam by her husband. All three engage with the ways in which political circumstances destroy women's lives. Iphigenia, Cleopatra and Mariam are all figures of rank and status, born to expectations of a noble life, a powerful dynastic marriage and a commanding sphere of influence. Iphigenia and Cleopatra are victims of war and military ambition; Mariam's fate is also tied up with the colonizing power of Rome. Connections can also be made with the ruthlessness of Tudor history: Lady Jane Lumley translated *Iphigenia* contemporaneously with the execution of her cousin, the young Lady Jane Grey; Cary's Herod clearly mirrors the brutal paranoia of Henry VIII. All three writers, then, embrace classical subjects treating powerful themes of politics and individual destiny. Cary's subject matter is derived from classical and biblical sources: she had read Josephus' *History of the Jews* in Lodge's translation (1602) and extracted from a lengthy history the dramatic events between Herod's return from Rome and the execution of Mariam. Compressing and contracting her material to fit the classical unities of time and place, Cary connects the macrocosmic world of power politics with the factional struggles within Herod's court. The play is highly stylized with lengthy speeches which depend on poetic and rhetorical effects. The role of the Chorus, commenting on the drama and adding moral **sententiae**, shows the influence of Senecan tragedy; dramatically, it could not be further from the riotous, scurrilous world of London's city comedies. A considerable number of verbal echoes from Shakespeare, however, whether conscious or not, establish the play within the canon of its day.

The play opens with the responses of the major female characters to the (false) news of Herod's death in Rome. Mariam expresses a degree of conflict – she has been loved by Herod and returned his passion – but she also knows that Herod left orders to have her killed in the event of his own death. Her mother, Alexandra, reminds her of the murders of her brother, Aristobolus, and her grandfather, Hyrcanus, and urges her to rejoice at Herod's death. Herod's sister, Salome, pursues her own desire to divorce her (second) husband, Constabarus, and marry Silleus. Herod's brother, Pheroras, seizes the opportunity to marry Graphina, the woman he loves, rather than his young niece, as Herod has commanded. Constabarus has concealed the two sons of Babas, safeguarding them from Herod's death sentence; he believes they can now be freed. Herod's divorced wife, Doris sees this as the opportunity for revenge against Mariam and the rightful advancement of her own son. It is only at the beginning of Act 4 that Herod returns, rejoicing that he will be reunited with Mariam. He instantly orders the deaths of Constabarus and the sons of Babas. Mariam appears in black, upbraids him for the murder of her brother, and refuses to offer the welcome he expects. The Butler brings a drink Herod suspects to be poisoned; he accuses his queen of adultery with Sohemus, the servant who confided Herod's secret orders to kill Mariam. Salome persuades him to proceed with the execution and he gives the command but instantly regrets his words, attempting, unsuccessfully, to countermand his order. His final speech praises Mariam's lost beauty, characterizing himself as worse than Cain. The drama ends with the Chorus pointing the moral that his 'lunatic' raving should be a 'warning to posterity'.

Herod: Playing the tyrant

> Herod, the king, in his raging
> Chargid he hath this day
> His men of might, in his owne sight
> All yonge children to slay.
>
> *The Coventry Plays*, 110–11

Herod the Great, King of Judaea, would have been familiar to Cary's contemporaries as the iconic figure of infanticide and tyranny, forever associated with the Slaughter of the Innocents – the murder of all male babies under two years old (Mt. 2.16). The anonymous creators of the Mystery cycles created a vividly evil figure from the brief biblical references to Herod, and the Slaughter of the Innocents was a popular subject in medieval and Renaissance iconography. In the Coventry cycle, Herod is the pantomime villain, ranting and raging:

> [The] myghttyst conquerowre that euer walkid on grownd:
> [. . .]
> And prince am I of purgatorre and cheff capten of hell
>
> KING and DAVIDSON, 96, line 437 and 97, line 453

The bombastic Herod was evidently a familiar dramatic figure – Hamlet tells Elsinore's visiting players not to 'out-Herod Herod' (*Hamlet*, 3.2.13–14). As Helen Cooper has shown, in

Shakespeare and the Medieval World, records reveal 'the continuing widespread performance of various kinds of religious play after Elizabeth's accession' (Cooper, 56). Rewriting, to accommodate post-Reformation doctrinal changes, was not uncommon and Coventry staged Corpus Christi plays as late as 1579. This would be a day's walk for Shakespeare, at fifteen years of age, but obviously too early for Elizabeth Cary, although she may well have heard oral accounts of the plays. Cary's play is set before the notorious massacre but references from the opening of the play clearly foreshadow this dark future. To Alexandra, he is 'heir of hell' (1.2.22), already guilty of the murder of her son, Aristobolus, described by Mariam as an innocent martyr: 'the loveliest youth/That ever did in angel's shape appear' (1.1.35–6). Cary's prose Argument, prefacing the play, links Herod with the Machiavellian villains of contemporary drama, implying that he is a usurping ruler who has 'crept by the favour of the Romans into the Jewish monarchy' (Argument, 2). Cary also chooses to highlight the crucial detail that Herod's 'violent affection' for Mariam means that he is 'unwilling that any should enjoy her after him' (Argument, 18–19) – if he is slain, she must also die. The opening scenes between Mariam and her mother, Alexandra, focus on Herod as the archetypal tyrant. 'Base Edomite . . . vile wretch . . . a toad' are the terms used by Alexandra in a speech that recalls the lamenting queens in *Richard III* (1592) – a play Cary may well have read or seen. As Weller and Ferguson have established, Thomas Creede, the original printer and publisher of *The Tragedy of Mariam* also produced the first and third **Quartos** of *Richard III* (Weller and Ferguson, 43–5).

Cary's structure, whereby the opening scenes enumerate Herod's atrocities and the many grudges against him, demonstrates her knowledge of the dramatic traditions of her day, in particular the Queen's courtly masques. Hodgson-Wright suggests that Cary consciously 'inverts Anna's innovative masque and antimasque structure' where, conventionally, a longed-for arrival brings joy. Here, Herod's arrival 'transforms the liberated Judea into a site of misery and destruction' (Hodgson-Wright,

55). Despite the lengthy perorations and the static nature of the drama, suspense is built up by the fact that every member of Herod's household rejoices at the news of his death. The possessive and narcissistic nature of his love is immediately apparent when he objects to Mariam's appearance – she has chosen to dress in mourning. Like Hamlet, her mourning is a performative statement signifying her integrity and refusal to conform to expectation:

> My lord, I suit my garment to my mind,
> And there no cheerful colours I can find.
>
> 4.3.5–6

Herod offers her unlimited power and wealth by way of wooing her favour, but in doing so is alarmingly sacrilegious: 'I'll rob the holy David's sepulchre/To give thee wealth if thou for wealth do care' (4.3.19–20). Herod's despotism, then, is revealed as soon as he appears on stage. Within minutes he has proceeded through annoyance at Mariam's lack of joy and deference to a conviction of her infidelity. His performance is marked by veering rapidly from extremes of uxorious devotion to vilifying his wife as a 'white enchantress' (4.4.18):

> Oh, thou art so foul
> That hyssop cannot cleanse thee, worst of evil.
> A beauteous body hides a loathsome soul.
>
> 4.4.17–19

He argues, bizarrely, that had she planned his death in order to secure her son's succession, it would have been preferable to her 'defilement'. Like Othello he believes that she must die, 'else she'll betray more men' (*Oth*, 5.2.6). Unlike Othello, Herod's swiftness in ordering her death is not subject to the persuasions of others; Salome's Iago-like role is performed later when Herod cannot decide the method of her execution. Dympna Callaghan observes that Herod is racialized in the play in a way that emphasizes difference; as 'the Edomite' he is 'both more Jewish than Mariam and racially debased' where Mariam is the 'pure' Jew (Callaghan, 172). Intriguingly, the Beverley Mystery plays record a 'black Herod' – possibly indicating a painted face or mask to underline Herod's wicked otherness. Despite the fact that Cary's Herod spends the final act of the play repenting Mariam's death, it would seem that she desires to create a character immediately recognizable from medieval traditions – the bloodthirsty tyrant driven by egotism.

Salome the 'custom-breaker'

Impudency on my forehead sits

1.4.34

Salome is a name that resonates with performative associations. The biblical Salome, invariably depicted in Western art as the archetypal temptress, is, in fact, a later generation. She infamously, 'danced, and pleased Herod' – and was rewarded with the head of John the Baptist 'on a charger'. Cary's Salome is a composite figure, largely based on Josephus' account of Herod's sister Salome where Salome emerges as a determined opportunist, willing to murder her perceived enemies. Cary elaborates the role by emphasizing Salome's lascivious appetites and, more significantly, her arguments in favour of divorce. Her subject is thereby political as well as biblical: the denunciation of Herod by John the Baptist (for marrying Herodias, his brother's wife) had contemporary relevance in terms of the arguments over Henry VIII's secession from Rome. Roman Catholics defended Henry's marriage to Catherine of Aragon where Protestants had found a loophole in the fact that Henry had married his brother Arthur's widow. (The topicality of the subject matter is discussed in Weller and Ferguson's text, 30–5).

Cary's Salome is certainly a determined and powerful villain, arguably unique at the time of writing. As a woman who plans and carries out the murder of her husband she has something in common with the early play *Arden of Faversham* (White); in terms of revenge tragedy she compares with Beatrice-Joanna in Middleton's *The Changeling*. In terms of her plotting and opportunism, she resembles Iago or Richard III; she controls and drives events throughout the drama and her ruthless machinations stand out as exceptional for a female character on the early modern stage. Here, the debate over closet drama and the possibilities of performance are key and the telling – and fascinating – question must be whether female members of the household could have articulated Salome's words. Liz Schafer, producer of the play in 1995, suggests that a household performance of the play (as opposed to a reading or readings) would have been wholly disruptive: 'Cary becomes ... a director, cajoling her friends into declaiming her lines with aplomb, and organising the traffic of the stage. And a performance would have to have an audience. Who might have been in the audience listening to Cary's extraordinary rhetoric?' (Schafer, *Witch*, 42–3).

📖 *Now read Salome's soliloquy, 1.4, thinking about its inherent performativity.*

- *Bearing in mind Schafer's speculation as to Salome's listeners, consider the radicalism of the ideas expressed.*
- *Examine her use of rhetorical questions: these accumulate throughout as a way of exploring the reality of her situation and challenging biblical and social convention.*
- *What is gained by her extraordinary candour about her 'tainted' reputation and lack of honour?*
- *Why does she remind her hearers of the ideal of the dutiful wife, 'blush[ing] at motion of the least disgrace' (32)?*
- *Salome knows how transgressive her thoughts are: is she persuasive or, ultimately, only villainous?*

Schafer's speculation about the nature of domestic performances is most telling when Salome articulates the radical position that women, as well as men, should be entitled to divorce:

> Why should such privilege to man be given?
> Or, given to them, why barred from women then?
> Are men than we in greater grace with heaven?
> Or cannot women hate as well as men?
> I'll be the custom-breaker and begin
> To show my sex the way to freedom's door
>
> 1.4.45–50

This is an outstandingly radical statement in the early years of the seventeenth century and the modern feminist is tempted to applaud Salome's desire for equality within the law. Divorce barely existed in Cary's age and could not be initiated by a woman. William Gouge cites the Mosaic law where 'divorce was suffered to be made between a man and his wife, in case he hated her' (Gouge, 352) but he does not offer the corresponding possibility that the wife might hate the husband. However, it is dangerous to regard Salome as a spokesperson for women's rights in marriage and, equally, 'simplistic connections with Cary's personal circumstances should be avoided' (Callaghan, 165).

Salome enacts the part of the Machiavellian manipulator to perfection: she informs her new love, Silleus, that she will 'wrest' divorce from the law and dismisses the attempts of Constabarus to remind her of the worth of the virtuous woman. Ironically, Constabarus later yields her to Silleus on the grounds that he now hates her as a 'painted sepulchre' (2.4.41); a serpent, that 'poisons where it kisses' (2.4.50). Herod's return, however, expedites action on the part of Salome and she blackmails Pheroras to reveal the secret that Constabarus had hidden the sons of Babas, thus securing the deaths of all three. Marriage to Silleus will not content her entirely, though: she wants revenge on Mariam and her motive here is racial. Just as Alexandra dismisses Herod as 'the

Edomite', a descendent from Esau, rather than Jacob, so too Mariam greets Salome as 'parti-Jew and parti-Edomite', a 'mongrel, issued from rejected race!' (1.3.29–30). Given that Mariam, the rightful Jewish queen, is the undisputed heroine and martyr of the play, this cannot be seen as casual anti-Semitism on Cary's part. Callaghan explores the text through its complex racial referencing and argues that Salome's evil is 'specifically racialized' as, throughout, she is 'conspicuously dark and morally tarnished' while Mariam appears to become 'blanched and purified' as the action develops (Callaghan, 175). Even Herod himself describes his sister as a 'sunburnt blackamoor' in comparison with Mariam (4.7.106). Salome's revenge on Mariam is complete: she sends a poisoned drink to Herod with a message that it has come from the Queen; she bribes the butler to reveal that Sohemus had told Mariam about Herod's decree to have her put to death. In terms of an 'unfeminine' performance, her role in ensuring the execution of Mariam is highly dramatic. She breaks into Herod's **hyperbole** over his wife with brutally simple lines: 'Let her be beheaded'; 'drown her then'; 'let the fire devour her' (4.7.4, 14, 21). She undermines his praise of Mariam's beauty and ensures that the command for the execution is given. At no point in the drama does she correspond with early modern prescriptions of female behaviour; Salome, more than any character of the drama, is the consummate performer. And, contrary to the conventions of revenge tragedy, she is unpunished at the end of the play.

Mariam and 'unbridled speech'

If Salome is an anomalous presence on account of her remorseless villainy, Mariam is also an atypical heroine. Indeed, the play is structured around contrasts and comparisons, particularly in terms of marriage and the female characters. Mariam is not identified with Salome's wilful sexual abandon – she prides herself on her chastity and fidelity – but, like her sister-in-law, she refuses to conform to societal expectations.

Normative, conservative views chime regularly through the play in the words of the Chorus, an intriguing use of the classical tradition which leaves the play's contradictory voices unresolved at the end of the drama. In Mariam, Cary presents a heroine who transgresses through her speech and her failure to act in the expected fashion. Her withholding of the performance Herod expects ensures her death. Yet female speech is questioned throughout the play and it is difficult to find a viable female role: Graphina is the innocent and modest woman who might marry for love if Herod is dead but Pheroras finds her very silence untrustworthy: 'Move thy tongue,/For silence is a sign of discontent' (2.1.41–2). The fact of Mariam's lengthy opening soliloquy is remarkable: there is no play in the canon which opens with a female character introducing the action. Furthermore, her very life is a rejection of monarchical authority as Sohemus has been instructed to kill her in the event of Herod's death. Cary displays her poetic skills here: the speech is written in **blank verse**, generally with alternate rhyming lines. She opens with fourteen lines in sonnet form, concluding with a rhyming couplet which draws attention to the paradox Mariam has been exploring. Her opening line claims rights of speech and political comment; she does not present herself as a domestic woman: 'How oft have I with public voice run on/To censure Rome's last hero [?]' In other words she expects to opine on the politics of the Roman world, and to find fault with the great Julius Caesar for hypocrisy.

📖 *Look closely at the language of the opening scene.*

- *The verse is formal and stylized throughout with characteristic use of apostrophe, **anaphora** and rhetorical questioning. What is the effect of Mariam's appropriation of these Senecan devices?*
- *Why might Cary choose to commence with the contradictory nature of Mariam's feelings about Herod's apparent death?*

- *What is suggested in her rejection of Herod's attempts to control her? ('barring me from liberty', 25–6)*
- *Consider how far the rhetorical structure of the speech is performative, ranging through Herod's cruelty to Aristobolus and Hyrcanus, before introducing the subject of her own death*
- *The speech introduces the first of many Shakespearean echoes when Mariam states that she would rather 'a milkmaid be' than 'the monarch of Judaea's queen' (1.1.57–8). After Antony's death, Cleopatra describes herself as 'commanded/By such poor passion as the maid that milks' (AC, 4.15.75). If Shakespeare's play was written c.1606, Cary could have seen early performances at the Blackfriars. Does this verbal identification with Cleopatra suggest female power – or a tragic destiny? Compare Mariam's later distancing of herself from Cleopatra's reputation as the 'wanton queen that never loved for love' (4.8.13).*

Lisa Hopkins, in exploring the 'prejudices and difficulties surrounding a woman's right to speak' suggests that Mariam and Cleopatra are 'repeatedly counterpointed' in the play: '[They] emblematise two competing traditions, Judaeo-Christian and classical, each of which is connected to a myth of origins which possessed considerable cultural capital in Jacobean England' (Hopkins, *Hero*, 150).

Mariam certainly knows, in theory, that her role is to enchant Herod on his return. Her outburst at Sohemus' news is spontaneous and heartfelt: 'Foretell the ruin of my family;/Tell me that I shall see our city burned;/... But tell me not that Herod is returned!' (3.3.9–12). Sohemus offers both advice and a warning 'for your issue's sake more temperate be' (3.3.31) but Mariam has sworn her own vow that she will not be reconciled to Herod; her acknowledgement of the performance that is expected of her and her rejection of the role, is decisive:

> I know I could enchain him with a smile
> And lead him captive with a gentle word.
> I scorn my look should ever man beguile,
> Or other speech than meaning to afford.
>
> 3.3.45–8

The third Chorus that follows offers the conventional view of the time, that a wife must be spotless, free from suspicion and, furthermore, deny herself any rights of liberty: 'When to their husbands they themselves do bind, /Do they not wholly give themselves away?' (Chorus 3, 19–20). This implied rebuke of Mariam cannot be seen as authoritative: Salome, Alexandra and the rejected Doris are all women who perform roles wholly in opposition to these views. Indeed, in terms of the plot, it is Salome who has agency. Andrew Hiscock suggests that Cary consciously uses the genre to set up an irreconcilable dialectic: 'exploit[ing] the dynamic, multivocal nature of dramatic discourse in order to probe in particular the irresolvable inconsistencies in cultural expectations of female experience' (cited in Britland, xv). The function of the Chorus is to produce sententiae, moralizing observations on human behaviour with warnings of the retribution of the gods and dire consequences that can befall.

Mariam, however, is consistent: she greets Herod dressed in black and transforms Herod's welcome into an accusatory reminder of his actions in usurping and murdering Hyrcanus and the youthful Aristobolus. Herod, like Sohemus, offers Mariam her cue: 'smile, my dearest Mariam, do but smile' (4.3.57) but, again, the prescribed performance is one she cannot enact:

> I cannot frame disguise, not ever taught
> My face a look dissenting from my thought.
>
> 4.4.59–60

Herod's response that she should 'let your look declare a milder thought' (4.1.67) establishes his despotism and psychological tyranny. Mariam must adapt her feelings and demeanour to suit his fancy. As Catherine Belsey observes, 'A wife's right to speak, to subjectivity, to a position from which to protest, is among the central questions of [*Mariam*]' (Belsey, 171). Mariam's final soliloquy (4.8.1–50) establishes her performance as Christian martyr: part of her self-recognition before death lies in her understanding that her beauty and chastity did not suffice to placate her husband. A performance of humility, on the other hand, would have saved her life. She is extraordinarily clear-sighted about the value of female 'allurements' and the fact that she is being punished for her verbal protestations. As she draws to a close, however, her language has shifted to a different plane of reference – martyrology. In common with both Catholic and Protestant martyrs of the post-Reformation period, she can proclaim that, while her physical body is destroyed, her soul 'is free from adversaries' power' (46). She anticipates the glory of heavenly reward 'in Sarah's lap'. A number of textual details connect her with the death of Christ: the Butler who lied to Herod has hanged himself, like Judas Iscariot; she is reviled on the journey to death by Doris and Alexandra; Mariam herself comments that Herod would be pleased to see her restored to life in three days. The Nuntio, reporting Mariam's death to Herod, alludes to the 'sun-admiring phoenix' (5.1.24), the mythological bird associated with the resurrection of Christ. He also reveres Mariam for her acceptance of martyrdom, '[her] look did seem to keep the world in awe' (5.1.27). Elaine Beilin suggests that the idealization of Mariam at the end of the play 'foreshadows redemption from the old law' transforming Mariam into 'a prophet of Christianity' (Beilin, 171, 2). Cary is, of course, influenced by Josephus whose account of the execution is brief and concentrates on Mariam's performance on the scaffold, 'going to her death without change of colour, so that those who beheld her, perceiued in her a kind of manifest courage and nobilitie, euen in her vtmost extremitie' (Wray, 213). The source material makes no reference to beheading, though, and Cary's emphatic repetition of this detail links Mariam with the

Tudor dynasties' execution of queens: Anne Boleyn, Katherine Howard, Mary Queen of Scots – women regarded as transgressive for their religion or for their behaviour.

In terms of domestic closet drama, Cary's text is powerfully subversive, silencing Mariam through the paranoia of Herod and the intrusive and destructive voice of Salome. In worlds where women are expected to perform a public role, Cary reveals the consequences of female desire for integrity and an individual self beyond performativity.

Closet drama

Closet drama is a term used to describe plays intended to be read in private homes rather than acted in the commercial theatre; it was not defined as a discrete category in the early modern period and was first used to denote the verse dramas of the Romantic poets. It is not synonymous with 'coterie drama' which refers to the masques and plays performed at the court of the reigning monarch (or his consort). The practice of reciting a lengthy playscript within a small and elite group probably derived from the sixteenth-century discovery of Seneca's plays. These melodramatic and bloodthirsty texts were immensely popular, translated by young scholars, and 'performed' at Oxford and Cambridge colleges (from around 1550). Seneca's texts were eminently suited to dramatic readings: lacking in plot or character development, they were characterized by long declamatory speeches with abundant use of rhetorical devices such as apostrophe and anaphora. Scenes concluded with moralizing sententiae spoken by a Chorus. Renaissance humanist attention to classical texts, however, meant that young women educated in households with a strong belief in the values of classical learning were also enabled – and often encouraged – to translate key texts. Thus the plays authored by women in the Tudor period derived from this new interest in scholarly closet drama. The earliest surviving manuscript is Lady Jane Lumley's *The Tragedy of*

Iphigenia (1555–7), translated either from Euripides' original Greek or from a later Latin version; the first published text is Mary Sidney, Countess of Pembroke's, *Tragedie of Antonie* (1592–4), a translation of a French contemporary play (by Robert Garnier, 1578). The authoring of closet drama is a matter of class as well as gender: playwrights were the journeymen of the theatre; aristocrats might act as patrons and commissioners of the acting companies but did not engage artistically with the theatre world. The literary circle associated with Sir Philip Sidney and later his sister (Countess of Pembroke) numbered several male writers who wrote closet dramas – Sir Fulke Greville is a typical example, as the author of poetic treatises, a sonnet sequence, a biography of Sir Philip Sidney and two closet tragedies, *Mustapha* and *Alaham*. Politically, this amounted to more than a gesture of aristocratic elitism, however: Albert Tricomi sees this as 'a profound indictment of Jacobean political life' (Tricomi, 67). Greville and Daniel had found a means to express their disillusionment with James I and his court without attracting the attention of the censor. Mary Sidney was the epitome of the aristocratic patron of the arts; as well as publishing her own translations of French and Italian texts, she rewrote the biblical Psalms as Elizabethan lyrics and edited and published her brother's writings after his death. She was also responsible for the flourishing of Wilton House as a cultural 'college' dedicated to literary pursuits and where she encouraged and enabled dramatic production.

Closet plays, then, formed a part of the country house entertainment of Elizabethan and Jacobean households, raising two significant questions: what distinguishes a 'reading' from a 'performance' and, secondly, to what extent did female members of the household actively participate? The world of the commercial London theatres was still 'fundamentally incompatible with the conception of female virtue as domestic' (Straznicky, 247). The most famous surviving example of the genre is probably Milton's *A Masque Presented at Ludlow Castle* (1634, better known as *Comus*) where the role of the

Lady was performed by the fifteen-year-old daughter of the household, Lady Alice Egerton. The role was a challenging one and, as the performance was supervised by Henry Lawes, court musician and composer, amateur and professional distinctions are blurred. The parents of Lady Alice clearly had no objections to the display of her musical and acting talents in the context of the Ludlow masque. A number of factors indicate that the idea of the female performer was becoming more acceptable in the early seventeenth century; undoubtedly the private world of closet drama and the courtly world of the masque facilitated this development. Recent debate over a Jacobean portrait might shed interesting light: the unknown noblewoman is attired as Cleopatra, complete with asp and basket of figs, and holding an inscription from Samuel Daniel's closet drama, *Tragedie of Cleopatra* (1594, revised 1607, and commissioned by Lady Mary Sidney). Art historian Yasmin Arshad suggests that the costumed figure could be identified as Lady Anne Clifford and the painting might be the record of a performance of the play, probably at Wilton House or Penshurst, in which Anne Clifford acted the part of Cleopatra. An alternative possibility is that Anne Clifford might have 'struck the pose of Cleopatra during the performance while, as in masques, professional players or the sons of gentlemen ... spoke the lines' (Arshad, 35).

The masques of the Jacobean court were more than expensive and frivolous entertainments; they established the Queen's sphere of autonomous influence and authority; '[in] the masques, Anna and her ladies displayed their unity as an elite coterie and their independence from the king and his supporters' (Curran, 6). David Bergeron's study of female involvement in courtly entertainment reveals that women appeared regularly in private performances of masques, 'impersonating some of the symbolic and mythological figures' of the drama as well as executing the concluding dances (Bergeron, 76). The list of masque 'actresses' (the term was first used – pejoratively – of Queen Henrietta Maria) is startling, enumerating forty-six in Jonson's masques alone, including Queens Anne and Henrietta

Maria, Lady Anne Clifford and the writer Lady Mary Wroth. These were the theatrical performances that prompted Prynne's hyperbolic outburst against the court's entertainments and, in particular, the involvement of the queen in a speaking role. Prynne lost his ears for describing female actors as 'notorious whores'. Meanwhile, in 1629, a French acting company with female performers appeared at the Blackfriars Theatre to act an 'unchaste' comedy in French. According to contemporary accounts, they were 'hissed and booed and pippin-pelted' from the stage; an unpromising reception. But did the audience object to the female players or the fact of the French company performing in their own language? Moll Frith appeared on stage at the Fortune Theatre in 1612, singing and playing, in male dress, and became the eponymous heroine of *The Roaring Girl*. In the early Jacobean years, attitudes to female performance can only be summed up as various and contradictory.

In the theatres of France and Italy, however, female actors were commonplace by the early seventeenth century; the prolific writer and correspondent Margaret Cavendish (1623–73) recorded her enthusiasm for seeing female players, despite the fact that she could not understand the language: 'I took such delight to see them Act upon the Stage, as I caused a Room to be hired in the next House to the Stage, and went every day to See them . . . & their Actions did much delight my Sight' (*Sociable Letters*, cited Raber, 31). Cavendish herself published a number of plays in her own lifetime and wrote lengthy prefaces discoursing on styles of performance. Clearly, she expected the play-reading to function as a dramatic event: 'Playes must be read to the nature of those several humours, or passions, as are exprest by Writing: for they must not read a scene as they would read a Chapter; for scenes must be read as if they were spoke or Acted . . . Tragedies or Tragick Scenes [in] a sad serious Voice, as deploring or complaining' (cited in Fitzmaurice, 36).

Closet drama, then, offered women the opportunity to engage with drama, the quintessentially new and vibrant genre of the day. While the plays themselves derived from and contributed to the wider theatrical world, the relative privacy of private drama proved intellectually enabling.

Further reading

Alexandra G. Bennett, 'Female Performativity in *The Tragedy of Mariam*', *Studies in English Literature, 1500–1900*, 40 (2000), 293–309

S.P. Cerasano and Marion Wynne-Davies, *Renaissance Drama by Women: Texts and Documents* (London, 1996)

Marta Straznicky, *Privacy, Playreading, and Women's Closet Drama, 1550–1700* (Cambridge, 2004)

Sophie Tomlinson, *Women on Stage in Stuart Drama* (Cambridge, 2006)

Heather Wolfe (ed.), *Elizabeth Cary Lady Falkland: Life and Letters* (Cambridge, 2001)

4

Servants, masters and service:

Othello and *The Changeling*

The figure of the servant is considerably less familiar today than it was in early modern England. The development of Western democratic thought and government, coupled with increasingly sophisticated technologies, has meant that the state of servitude is now generally regarded as ethically undesirable and, practically speaking, unnecessary. And while it would not be true to say that servants no longer exist – the well-off still employ people to look after their children, clean their houses and chauffeur them around – the status, living conditions and experiences of the servant in the sixteenth and seventeenth centuries are now radically unfamiliar, at least in the developed world. Mark Thornton Burnett in his survey of master–servant relationships and prevailing ideas of authority and obedience, begins from the premise that, unlike modern society '[f]rom apprentices learning a trade to the officials of the great noble households, servants were perhaps the most distinctive socio-economic feature of sixteenth- and seventeenth-century society' (Burnett, *Servants*, 1).

It was the norm for English households of the early modern period to include servants and, where there was a craft to be learned, apprentices. A large percentage of young Britons formed part of a shifting and moving class of servants, at any one time. Wrightson's study estimates that 'perhaps 60 per cent of the English population aged between fifteen and twenty-four lived as servants' in wealthier households (Wrightson, 33). In economic terms, service at this time could improve the prospects of young adults, supplying them with both wages and skills – the means of establishing themselves independently. There was, however, no single 'servant class' as such but differing degrees of social standing, entitlement and authority: from the labouring journeyman, to the 'Groom of the Stool' (a much sought-after office which involved assisting the king with his bodily functions).

There is consensus that the late sixteenth and early seventeenth century was a period of unprecedented social change; indeed, one recent historical study refers to 'the widespread experience of social dislocation' during the 1590s (Cust, 16). At this time, the social model of the 'three estates' (those who fight, those who pray and those who labour) which had held fast in the Middle Ages was unrecognizable. In a time of relative peace, knights no longer rode off to fight for their lord and Christendom as depicted in Chaucer's *Canterbury Tales*; the Reformation and Counter-Reformation had brought about a reconfiguration of the role and status of the clergy; and the working man – or at least those belonging to the professions – had some prospect of rising up the social ladder. The perception and practice of service had also undergone significant change. Michael Neill's study clarifies the difference between an older, more feudal aristocratic order where numbers of apparently idle servants (Lear's retinue of knights, for example) existed simply to demonstrate 'their master's liberality and magnificence' (Neill, *History*, 29). In physical terms, new architectural fashions in grand establishments removed servants from participation in the life of the castle to the servants' hall and backstairs. Rather than a 'highly visible hierarchy of honour, itself conferring honour upon the householder' the servant body had become 'an invisible machinery sustaining the visible and exclusive social world of the householder' (Bryson, 143). The organic world of the large household had altered completely.

In William Harrison's *The Description of England* ([1577] 1994), an encyclopaedic account of sixteenth-century England and its people, the author emphasizes how distinctions of social types are by no means fixed, especially at the line between those who are 'simply called gentlemen' (Harrison, 94) and the two ranks beneath them. While those born into the gentleman class rise through titles and honours conferred on them by the monarch, it is through commerce that merchants 'often change estate with gentlemen' (Harrison, 115). Also included in this climb up the socio-economic ladder are yeomen farmers who 'buy the lands of unthrifty gentlemen, and often, setting their sons to the schools, to the universities, and to the Inns of the Court, or otherwise leaving them sufficient lands whereupon they may live without labor, do make them by those means to become gentlemen' (Harrison, 118).

What is clear from Harrison's invaluable (though far from impartial) account of the country is that land sales and foreign trade were enabling more and more men to improve their status in life. Predictably, such social mobility was accompanied by anxiety and conservative attempts to resist or protest against any unsettling of the status quo. Early modern writing about the role of servants testifies to a desire to maintain a strictly stratified society. Conduct books emphasized biblical correctness of rank as God-given and sermons and homilies drew on church authority to reinforce hierarchical norms; St Paul's instruction to slaves to 'be obedient to those who are your earthly masters, with fear and trembling, in singleness of heart, as to Christ' (Eph. 6.5–6) proved a particularly popular text in this respect. According to Cleaver, in 1598, servants should 'chearefully, and willingly, performe the[ir] labours' (Cleaver, 385) and William Gouge, in *Of Domesticall Duties* (1622), urges the need for servants to submerge their personal identity in light of the fact that 'they are not their owne, neither ought the things which they doe, to be for themselves' (Gouge, 604). Protestant theology with its emphasis on biblical authority argued, paradoxically, in favour of an ethos of deference or, alternatively, claimed that servitude must be incompatible with the teaching of the New Testament. The Puritan Gouge, cited above, states dogmatically that servants must *not* obey their masters if required to commit unlawful deeds, including attendance at Roman Catholic Mass. Protestant conscience can, then, outweigh duty to the employer.

Two intriguing questions can be raised in terms of the social dynamic of the time: first, to what extent the literature of the period expresses concern or even awareness of change; secondly, whether the theatre played a part in challenging the status quo, or experimenting with new ideas. For some literary critics, the link between the stage and political unrest is inevitable: McRae argues that writers such as Middleton 'helped to make the confrontations of the 1640s thinkable' (McRae, 120). Linda Woodbridge's 2010 study of English revenge drama identifies the genre as peculiarly suited to the enactment of violent opposition, both fuelled by and expressive of the anger of class resentment: 'All species of Renaissance radicalism – resistance to tyranny; social, legal and economic egalitarianism – appear in revenge plays' (Woodbridge, *Revenge*, 252). Certainly, the early modern stage was a dynamic medium for exploring shifting class structures and power relations, though state censorship of the theatre meant that any social or political criticism tended to be found at below-surface level. However, as Chris Fitter argues in *Radical Shakespeare* (2012), subtext could be brought to the fore by 'on-stage activation in the public theatres' (Fitter, 32). After all, Elizabethan and Jacobean playhouses were in themselves spaces of transgression, where boys could play girls and commoners could play kings. At a time when increasing numbers of people could purchase the external signs of gentility such as land, clothing, leisure pursuits and service, a theatre which suggested that rank was little more than performative was, for some, deeply troubling.

> It is only since the end of the 1990s that the topic of servants and service has received any sustained attention from scholars. This chapter draws on some of the most recent writings in this field to explore the dramatic representation of the servant–master relationship in two early modern texts: Shakespeare's *Othello* and Middleton and Rowley's *The Changeling*.

Othello

Othello is one of Shakespeare's most popular plays, both from the perspective of its performance history and the scholarly interest it has attracted. From the late 1960s, critical readings of the drama have tended to focus on issues of race and gender, informed and influenced by the political and social changes of the second half of the twentieth century. Largely based on postcolonial and feminist theoretical paradigms, such readings have moved the play away from character criticism and, in particular, from a preoccupation with Iago's 'motive-less Malignity' (Coleridge, 2, 315). Coleridge's oft-quoted phrase provided the focus for debates which yielded numerous different theories. Revisiting these interpretations in the Introduction to Arden 3, E.A.J. Honigmann argues persuasively for taking each one of Iago's stated grievances seriously: 'His motives, like his roles, interpenetrate one another, somewhat like the different instruments that play together in a symphony' (Honigmann, 41). In resisting the critical desire to discount some of Iago's motives in order to clear the path for a consistent reading of a single one, Honigmann acknowledges the degree of complexity in Shakespeare's construction of character, as well as leaving open the possibility of privileging one motive over another – of allowing one instrument in the orchestra to dominate.

Commencing with Ralph Berry's *Shakespeare and Social Class* (1988), there have been a number of studies foregrounding

Iago's preoccupation with status and placing it squarely in the contexts of the early modern period. Michael Neill, for example, considers the 'lost lieutenancy . . . an essential *donnée* of the action' (Neill, *History*, 216), noting Iago's failed promotion as a major variation on Shakespeare's source text, Cinthio's *Hecatommithi*, wherein the villain is 'ardently in love with Disdemona' (Honigmann, 373). Linda Woodbridge, too, sees Iago's revenge as fuelled by 'intense resentment of his social status' (Woodbridge, *Revenge*, 241). As with these examples, critical interest in Shakespeare's engagement with class politics often rests on the interactions between master and servant. The tragedies include a broad range of servant types of differing social degrees – courtier, soldier, nurse, fool, gravedigger, attendant, doctor, gardener – to name but some. The extent to which relationships between master and servant are developed varies from play to play. In *Antony and Cleopatra*, the regular exchanges between the play's hero and Enobarbus contribute significantly to its dramatic tenor and meaning, as do those between Lear and his Fool, or Juliet and the Nurse. In other instances, communication between the ruler and the ruled can be fleeting: Hamlet's sardonic dialogue with the sycophantic Osric; the extraordinary moment when an unnamed servant in *King Lear* attempts to prevent the Duke of Cornwall from gouging out Gloucester's eye; the touching meeting between the imprisoned Richard II and his loyal former Groom of the Stable. For all their brevity, such interchanges have a considerable impact on the dramatic texture of the plays, as well as provoking some controversial social questions.

Yet if Shakespeare's presentation of servants raises some vital questions about the social system, the rich diversity of servant characters found both across and within plays inhibits easy answers. Some servants are unerringly loyal; some duplicitous and self-serving; some are afforded lines of devastating clarity and wisdom, while others are confined to common bawdy, malapropism or the choric. Exchanges between servants and masters are equally diverse, with the plays offering ample evidence to support the argument that Shakespeare was an opponent of the hierarchies of his day – or to refute it. That a playwright avoided making didactic or incendiary statements about his nation is, on a practical level at least, hardly surprising, given that the Master of the Revels had the power to prevent plays from being performed (and, from 1610, published) if they posed a direct challenge to the ruling powers. Moreover, the royal patronage which authors such as Shakespeare enjoyed meant that plays were often performed at court: not an ideal arena for searing indictments of social inequality.

Iago and the 'curse of service'

Othello offers the most sustained and perhaps the most subversive portrayal of the servant in the entire Shakespearean canon. The servant Iago has substantially more lines than the master-hero, the greater share of soliloquy, and gains mastery over three of his social superiors (Roderigo, Cassio and Othello). Moreover, despite his villainy being eventually disclosed, he remains alive, with the audience offered no guarantee that torture *will* break his vow of silence: an unsettling reminder to masters that thought is free – even for servants. What would have been likewise unsettling for early modern playgoers is the instability of Othello's status as an authority figure. While the idea of a black leader is now familiar, this was certainly not the case in the England of the 1600s. Thomas Rymer, whose 1693 response to *Othello* is one of the most splenetic in the play's history, regarded a Moorish general as belonging to the realm of fantasy: 'The character of that state is to employ strangers in their wars; but shall a poet thence fancy that they will set a Negro to be their general, or trust a Moor to defend them against the Turk? With us a blackamoor might rise to be a trumpeter, but Shakespeare would not have less than a lieutenant-general' (*A Short View of Tragedy*, in Vickers, 29). It is views such as Rymer's that the play seems intent on interrogating, with Iago serving as the dark voice of racial prejudice, spurred into agency by thwarted ambition.

From the outset, Iago raises Othello's awareness of his precarious status in Venetian society, warning him that Brabantio has 'a voice potential/As double as the duke's' (1.2.13–14). At this stage of events, with a Turkish invasion pending, Othello's past military honours ensure that merit will win over bloodline; however, once the threat of invasion is removed, so too is Othello's chief *raison d'être*, leaving his servant both the time and opportunity to play on his master's consciousness of being 'the Moor of Venice'. By midway through the drama, Iago has succeeded in destroying the confidence of a man who, initially at least, seemed quite secure in his authority. That Iago could so easily bring about such a transformation could be put down to his understanding of the workings of class consciousness, gained through his own experience of social injustice.

📖 *In the opening scene of the play, Iago fulminates against a system which has allowed the 'bookish theoric' (1.1.23), Cassio, to gain the lieutenant's post that he feels should be his by right of merit.*

Look closely at 1.1.1–56 and think about:

- *how a Globe audience of the early 1600s might have responded to this scene*
- *the significance of Roderigo as the listener here*
- *which words or phrases hold the greatest potential for an actor to express Iago's contempt for authority*
- *how Iago's speech (1.1.40–56) compares to the following stanza from William Basse's verse poem* Sword and Buckler, or, Serving-man's Defence *(1602):*

This man [servant] of all things must abandon pride,
Chieflie in gestures, and in acts exteriour
For greater states can by no meanes abide

Ambition in a person so inferiour
  Yet in his private thoughts no whit dismist
  To prize his reputation as he list.

> BASSE, stanza 6

An original Globe audience would have been socially diverse, accommodating the aristocrat who had paid sixpence for his seat in a lord's room along with the workman who had paid a penny to stand. From the very first lines of *Othello* there is plenty to alarm the gentlemen present. While certain linguistic denotations of status hold firm (Iago addresses Roderigo with the polite form 'you' and Roderigo addresses Iago as 'thou'), it soon becomes evident that the servant controls the master. Iago is shown to have access to Roderigo's money and to be the better informed of the two and, from the moment the servant interrupts the gentleman's complaint at line 6, the floor is his. And it is not only Iago's mastery of the conversation which would have proved disconcerting to the higher classes: the sentiments he expresses run entirely counter to traditional Christian thinking about the nature of service. Gentlemen listening to Iago might well have nodded in agreement on his declaration that 'We cannot all be masters', only to have had the rug pulled from under their feet when he follows it with 'nor all masters/Cannot be truly followed'. The ensuing lines destroy any notion that servitude is a natural state; rather, they imply that it is purely performative, made up of 'forms and visages'. For Iago, the word 'soul' signifies the energy of class rebellion – not the spiritual part of the human that needs to be prepared for the world beyond. Servant responses to such talk are unlikely to have been uniform, though it is safe to assume that some in the audience would have felt uplifted by Iago's railing against authority. Older playgoers, especially ex-soldiers, might well have sympathized with Iago's mockery of the 'fast-track' route to lieutenancy; while ageing servants might have identified with what the ensign sees as the inevitable trajectory of service: years of 'knee-crooking', followed by summary dismissal.

*   *   *

The ostensible reason for Iago's invective is to demonstrate to Roderigo how much he hates his master. In performance, a director has to decide how far the splenetic tenor of Iago's language is all part of a rhetorical strategy to convince the thwarted lover that he despises Othello and how far it is charged with genuine resentment. Opening the scene *in medias res* leaves an audience to wonder just how long Roderigo's petulant outburst has been in progress and thus how much further energy Iago needs to put into his defence. Perhaps the speed with which Iago takes charge of the conversation suggests that Roderigo is easily mollified. Iago's invitation to Roderigo to 'abhor' and 'despise' him seems sufficient to restore peace, with the swift shift of focus from the gentleman's anger to his own seeming to come more from animus than the need to persuade his listener. In Oliver Parker's 1995 film version of *Othello*, the scene is cut to about a quarter of its original length and Iago, played by Kenneth Branagh, delivers his lines with barely a glance at Roderigo; instead, he stares into the middle distance as if envisaging his revenge, making it clear to the viewer that his attack on servitude comes from the heart.

*   *   *

In performance, the physicalizing of a script through gesture and speech can substantially alter its signification. Iago's debut on stage offers ample opportunity for 'voicing': taking on inflections and accents not necessarily the character's own – in this instance to mock and ridicule them. An actor could convey Iago's scorn for the well-educated Cassio through his pronunciation of the richly **polysyllabic** word 'arithmetician'; likewise he could project his anger at a black man gaining rank in Venice through his delivery of the invented honorific '*Moor*ship', the primary vowel sound of which could be drawn out for full sarcastic effect. And the word 'cashiered', dangling at the end of a **hypermetrical** line, helps an actor evoke the sudden casting off of the servant, the late **caesura** preceding it adding extra force. Iago's reporting of the moment of his rejection in a snippet of reported speech (15–16) lends it a vivid immediacy, as well as allowing an actor playing Iago to voice Othello in a way that belittles or burlesques him. The upper-class term 'Certes', for example, with its strong **sibilance** and syllabic balance, could be pronounced in a self-conscious and ponderous manner to mimic Othello's 'bombast circumstance' (1.1.12).

* * *

It is an inescapable truth that early modern class-consciousness can only be recovered through the extant texts and artefacts of the period, and that what is gleaned from these is inevitably partial and prone to anachronistic interpretation. Nonetheless, circumspect attention to a play's co-texts can prove illuminating. Basse's seventy-five stanza poem, *Sword and Buckler*, published two years before the first known performance of *Othello*, is a spirited defence of servants from a servant's perspective (Basse claims to be a page, though the wealth of classical allusions in the work suggests that he may have been of higher status). Its author challenges the stereotype of servants as drunken whoremongers, asserting their right to be treated fairly by masters. In the lines quoted above, Basse underlines the necessity for servants to perform their roles through 'gestures' and 'acts exteriour', advice that, superficially at least, chimes with Iago's depiction of the servant as 'trimmed in forms and visages of duty'. Yet while the poet recommends the demonstration of servility as a means of keeping on the right side of the master (who is wont to feel threatened by any hint of ambition), Shakespeare's villain sees it as the means to a very different end: if those in authority are sufficiently flattered, they will not notice their servants lining their own pockets. Iago, then, seems to be a radicalized and malicious version of Basse's relatively moderate speaker-servant, who assures the reader that he recommends only a 'speaking fight' (Basse, stanza 24).

From ensign to lieutenant

Iago's role as Othello's '*ancient or ensign*' is not detailed in the cast list supplied in the **Folio** edition of the play. It is a role that an audience never sees him carry out: the Turkish attack fails to materialize, and the Venetian military is left stationed in Cyprus, with no battle to fight. The crisis averted, Iago is required to carry out tasks more in keeping with a manservant than a battle-hardened soldier, such as unloading luggage (2.1.207) and delivering letters (3.2.1), a shift in labour that mirrors in miniature the general move away from military to domestic service that took place over the second half of the sixteenth century. Yet if being required to carry out relatively menial tasks might appear as a form of humiliation to someone already full of class hatred, it also offers him the opportunity to disrupt – albeit temporarily – the social system he so despises. Iago's eventual appointment as lieutenant comes about ostensibly from what he himself terms 'old gradation' (1.1.36) though, as the audience is keenly aware, the promotion is actually achieved through his nimble opportunism and adroitness with language. No longer on military alert, the battle-ready troops find themselves in a foreign land with plenty of leisure time – a lull in action that enables Iago to engage his superiors in private conversations that eventually lead to their downfalls. Just as today's players of computer games move through levels of difficulty, so Iago moves from the easily gulled Roderigo, to the more intelligent and self-aware Cassio, to his direct master, the admired and 'valiant' Othello (1.3.48). As levels of challenge rise, so too does the degree of subtlety with which Iago negotiates the codes of servant behaviour and disrupts established signifiers of status.

In the case of Roderigo, Iago siphons off his money, before delegating to him the job of murdering Cassio: a task more usually reserved for the henchman, a figure at the lowest end of the socio-economic scale. His manipulation of Cassio has much more of a sense of personal jealousy about it. Cassio's first words to Iago are 'Good ancient' (2.1.96), immediately establishing the power relation between the two. While the address is not in itself unusual in a military situation, it recalls for the audience Iago's bitter pronouncement of the title in the opening moments of the play (1.1.32), a pronouncement made all the more prominent by being placed at the very end of a lengthy speech recalling his failed promotion. Thus Cassio's initial address to Iago has the effect of rubbing salt into wounds and, as events unfold, so the audience becomes increasingly aware of Iago's contempt for the Florentine's 'daily beauty' (5.1.19). The opening scene of Act 2 sees Cassio in the new environment of Cyprus and equally intent on asserting his position. Before kissing Emilia, he delivers a somewhat self-conscious speech, underlining his social superiority:

> Let it not gall your patience, good Iago,
> That I extend my manners; 'tis my breeding
> That gives me this bold show of courtesy.
>
> 2.1.97–9

Yet the kiss clearly does 'gall' Iago, as is evident from his aside later in the scene, in which he vows to 'gyve' Cassio in his 'own courtesies' (2.1.170) and conjures up the foul image of kissing 'clyster-pipes' (2.1.176) instead of Desdemona's fingers. While the transformation from the courtly to the vulgar is here confined to words, later in the play such a shift is evidenced in material terms, as Cassio's inebriation, urged on by Iago, changes him from an upright man of rank to a violent, swearing drunkard: behaviour more traditionally associated with the servant classes.

While Roderigo proves highly susceptible to Iago's linguistic manipulations, Cassio's greater awareness of the process enables him to resist it. When the ancient approaches the lieutenant in a spirit of male familiarity, hoping to draw him into a lubricious discussion of Desdemona's sexual desirability,

Cassio is quick to rebuff him, refusing to exchange his own decorous descriptions of Desdemona as 'exquisite' (2.3.18) and 'right modest' (2.3.23) for the soldier's terms 'sport for Jove' (2.3.17) and 'full of game' (2.3.19). Sensing the need for an alternative method of attack, Iago soon manages to 'fasten but one cup upon him' (2.3.45) and it is not long before the eloquent lieutenant is threatening to knock the Governor of Cyprus 'o'er the mazzard' (2.3.149–50). Dismissed from office, the newly vulnerable Cassio no longer finds the ancient's manner overfamiliar; rather, he listens intently to his advice, telling him, 'You advise me well' (2.3.321), the shift to the polite pronoun of address signalling the power shift between the two men. But Cassio's loss of status, like the effects of the strong drink which brought it about, is not permanent. As the play reaches its climax and the extent of Iago's villainy becomes apparent, so it appears that Cassio has regained the reputation whose loss he so plangently lamented after his drunken episode. No longer the disgraced lieutenant, he sits on stage (his wounds necessitating a chair) a trusted witness to events. It seems, then, that the assurance that comes from a classical education is not so easily stripped away. In this respect, Cassio provides a telling contrast to Othello, whose confidence and power come more from military prowess than class privilege. If Cassio's tongue can be temporarily coarsened by strong drink, Othello's can be brought to virtual incoherence by the servant's astute grasp of his master's social and psychosexual insecurities. Iago's relentless manipulation of Othello in the middle section of the play removes from him all the prime qualities of his earlier leadership: eloquence, control and a sense of perspective. That the power relation between master and servant has become inverted is represented on stage with visual clarity and force as the master kneels to the servant to make a 'sacred vow' (3.3.464) of vengeance, a performative act which marks a point of no return.

One of the ironic features of Iago's destruction of Othello is that he rarely steps outside of the linguistic conventions which govern master–servant discourse. One of the most obvious markers of status in early modern times were the pronouns 'you' and 'thou'. For a modern audience, 'thou' and its relations (thee, thy, thine) sound quite formal and elevated, probably because they are encountered only infrequently in texts such as the Bible; yet 'thou' was, in fact, the informal subject pronoun, used by parents to children, masters to servants and between intimates. Shakespeare's audiences would doubtless have been more attuned to 'thou-you' shifts in stage dialogue than modern ones – though any non-native speaker of French who has made the error of 'tutoying' someone they should have 'vouvoyed' will have some idea of the effects that such shifts can have. Certainly, any thorough study of the social politics of *Othello* requires close attention to the use of pronominal forms as key indicators of status and power. As Penelope Freedman observes in her extensive study of Shakespeare's use of pronouns: 'Norms of T/V use and the breaking of those norms are highly significant in the play as a whole' (Freedman, 146).

Iago is fully aware of the power that resides in pronouns. Even when the content of his conversations with Othello flagrantly transgresses what would have been proper for a humble ensign, he is careful to preserve the linguistic signs of the master–servant relationship and maintain his reputation as 'honest'. It is only in his dealings with the feeble-minded Roderigo that he allows the boundary between 'you' and 'thou' to loosen. Addressing the gentleman consistently as 'you' in the first scene of the play, he soon moves into a more confiding, intimate register, responding to the lovelorn suitor's announcement that he will drown himself with 'Why, **thou** silly gentlemen?' (1.3.307–8) and only reverting back to the respectful 'you' as they go their separate ways. From this point on, Iago moves swiftly between the two pronouns as a means of controlling his victim.

Read the dialogue between Iago and Roderigo (4.2.175–246), taking note of the two men's use of the 'you/thou' forms of address. How might the shifts from one to the other affect the way the scene is interpreted?

This scene demonstrates the importance of context when considering 'you/thou' usage. In Roderigo's first two speeches, he addresses Iago as 'thou' and it appears that the usual demarcation of social status has been restored – the gentleman is aggrieved and is putting an inferior back in his place. However, as his exasperation mounts, he starts to address Iago as 'you', a shift that suggests his initial use of 'thou' was a continuation of former intimacy, now withdrawn, rather than an assertion of rank. Iago responds accordingly, mirroring Roderigo's use of the less intimate pronoun and reverting to the traditional form for addressing a superior. It seems from Iago's terse responses that he is unperturbed by Roderigo's threat of asking Desdemona for his jewels back and seeking 'satisfaction'; it is only at line 206 that he starts to expend some rhetorical energy to take Roderigo back into his control. Attempting to recreate the intimacy of previous conversations, Iago asks for Roderigo's hand and returns to addressing him as 'thou'. However, it soon becomes apparent that the gull is less easily won over than previously and Iago is forced to move back to the deferential 'you' (234).

* * *

Of the eight treatises which make up William Gouge's *Of Domesticall Duties*, the seventh is devoted to 'Duties of Servants'. Iago would seem to fit securely into Gouge's category of servants who 'have *a heart, and a heart*, making shew of one heart outwardly, and have another, even a cleane contrary heart within them' (Gouge, 617). These 'eye-serving servants' (Gouge, 617) posed a far more unnerving threat to masters than the flagrantly disobedient. Indeed, what would have been most disturbing for the masters sitting in original audiences of the play was the way it draws attention to the performative nature of service. Iago's assiduous observation of the rules of speaking and behaving to his betters never falters and he plays the part of the bluff, forthright common soldier with consummate skill. However, as Lynne Magnusson points out in her illuminating essay 'Voice potential: language and symbolic capital in *Othello*', '[o]ne striking feature of Iago's performance is his preference for private conversation as the scene of his verbal virtuosity' (Magnusson, 172). It is through one-to-one encounters with his betters that Iago succeeds in subverting the codes of servant behaviour and, more precisely, it is his skill as a rhetorician of both prose and verse – usually deemed the preserve of the ruling classes – that help him rise from ancient to lieutenant without even setting foot on the battlefield.

Performing *Othello* in the twenty-first century

The narrative of *Othello* in performance is in itself the stuff of drama, full of conflict and controversy. Tracking the history of the tragedy on stage with its cast of unforgettable players – Richard Burbage, Edmund Kean, Ira Aldridge, Paul Robeson and Laurence Olivier, to name but a few – is also to trace the profound shifts in attitudes to race which have happened over the past 400 years. The shock evinced by some at the sight of the black actor, Paul Robeson, kissing the white actress, Peggy Ashcroft, in the 1930 Savoy Theatre production of *Othello* and, some fifty years later, the outrage expressed at Jonathan Miller's decision to cast a white actor, Anthony Hopkins, in the 1981 BBC Shakespeare series are responses that capture how far British society's thinking about race changed in just fifty years. Contemplating these changes is to realize just how unamenable *Othello* is to liberal humanist notions of a transhistorical Shakespeare: responses of audiences viewing the play at the height of the slave trade were surely far removed from those of theatregoers today.

Much of the controversy surrounding the performance of *Othello* in the nineteenth and twentieth centuries tended to focus on the casting of the play's protagonist. It is now taken as read that a black actor will play the role of Othello and the once common practice of white actors 'blacking up' for the part is generally regarded as aberrant. However, that is not to say that past controversies have entirely faded away, nor that there is unanimous agreement that a black stage Othello is something to be celebrated. In a survey of *Othello* in performance, published in the early years of the twenty-first century, Lois Potter observed that black actors are likely to turn down the titular role 'because they do not want to be considered stupid or animal-like' (Potter, *Othello*, 216), a perspective on the role that has been memorably and influentially explored by the acclaimed black British actor, Hugh Quarshie. In 1998, Quarshie gave a lecture (later published as *Second Thoughts About Othello*), expressing his misgivings about black actors taking on the role of Othello, fearing that it might encourage 'the white way, or rather the wrong way, of looking at black men, namely that black men, or "Moors", are over-emotional, excitable and unstable' (Quarshie, 5). His comments were quickly taken up by academics and, after frequent quotation in critical writings, hardened into a definitive statement, rather than a provocation to debate. Almost two decades later, Quarshie appears to have made up his mind about the question, taking on the part of Othello in the RSC's 2015 production in Stratford. Indeed, the majority view among the acting community nowadays appears to be that the role of Othello *should* be played by a black performer. Nicholas Hytner's 2013 production of *Othello* for the National Theatre starred the black actor Adrian Lester in the title role. Appearing on the stage of the Olivier, Lester was doubtless aware of appearing in a grand theatrical space which takes its name from an actor who, back in the 1960s, performed the role of Othello in layers of thick brown make-up. In a published interview, Lester rejects Laurence Olivier's conception of the character as a mighty leader who 'regresses in violence to an earlier form which was to do with blackness colour, heat, temperament', believing that 'We have come a long way since then' (National Theatre, 20). Many in the performing arts world would say that the progress that Lester notes here has come about largely thanks to the liberalizing of casting practices and, in particular, colour-blind casting. Pioneered by the theatre producer and director, Joseph Papp, in his 1955 New York Shakespeare Festival, the casting of black performers in traditionally white Shakespearean roles has enabled actors to extend their repertoire into areas of 'high culture' hitherto out of their reach.

Colour-blind casting continues to be warmly supported by actors across the globe, with British actors such as Meera Syal calling for more black and Asian performers to be cast in Shakespeare productions to help 'create a shared sense of heritage' among immigrant children (Griffiths). Yet while this casting principle might have gained majority approval, with playgoers growing increasingly used to seeing black actors play English kings, Italian noblemen and Viennese novitiates, it has also come up against some powerful opposition. In a rousing address, entitled *The Ground on Which I Stand*, the African-American playwright, August Wilson, told his audience at Princeton University: 'Colorblind casting is an aberrant idea that has never had any validity other than as a tool of the Cultural Imperialists who view their American culture, rooted in the icons of European culture, as beyond reproach in its perfection' (Wilson, *Ground*, 29). For Wilson, black performers should not be looking to 'assimilate' into the very culture which has, for centuries, oppressed them; rather, they should be putting their creative energies into black American theatre – an aspiration held back by unequal opportunities in national arts funding.

Controversy over casting Othello could explain why it has not appeared as frequently as other major tragedies in the repertoires of mainstream theatre companies. Since 1980 the RSC has put on four productions of *Othello* compared with nine of *Hamlet* and six of both *King Lear* and *Macbeth*; however, it has continued to thrive on screen and in smaller theatre spaces and there has been no shortage of innovatory staging. One notable characteristic of recent stage productions of *Othello* is the updating of the play to the here-and-now. In 2008, Frantic Assembly, a company noted for its physical theatre, reworked the tragedy to take place in a working-class community in West Yorkshire (a production reprised in 2014/15), while audiences at the Globe had the opportunity of seeing it transformed into the rhythms of hip-hop in *Othello: The Remix*, performed by the Q Brothers (Chicago Shakespeare Theater) as part of the 2012 'Globe to Globe' festival of world Shakespeare. Hytner's production at the National, while sticking closer to Shakespeare's original location of a military camp in Cyprus, brought the time forward to 2013. In these contemporary settings, Othello is imagined respectively as a football hopeful, a celebrity MC and a general in a modern-day army.

One other recent trend in productions of *Othello* is a move away from the issue of race. In the case of the National Theatre production, the Staff Director wrote in a diary documenting the rehearsal period that Hytner 'does not want the play to focus on race' (National Theatre, 5) and reviews of the production suggest that the director's vision was realized, one reviewer commenting that '[u]pdating the work ... means Othello's race is not at the forefront' (Carpenter). *Othello: the Remix* also seemed to circumvent the race question by placing emphasis on broad themes such as power, jealousy and ambition (the protagonist's colour is barely mentioned in a summary of the play included in the teacher resources accompanying performances at the Unicorn Theatre, London). Of the productions discussed here, Frantic Assembly's was the most alert to the play's racial issues, presenting a predominantly white working-class community which, while happy to embrace and replicate black culture through its fashion and music, was less prepared to accept a mixed-race relationship. Setting this updating in a region that had witnessed violent disorder sparked by racial tensions (most specifically in the Harehills area of Leeds in 2001), and which held vivid memories of the trial of Leeds United footballers Jonathan Woodgate and Lee Bowyer for what was seen by some as a racially motivated attack on an Asian student, ensured that colour would not be pushed into the background. Yet while one reviewer sensed that 'racism bubbles away with toxic intensity' (Cavendish), the majority agreed with *The Times* critic that the 'adaptation goes for the core of the text: no political background and no emphasis on race, but a sense of danger, anger, violence' (Peter). According to this reviewer, then, race is not at the 'core' of the play – a statement that would have surprised those involved in some of the more politically engaged productions of former decades, such as that directed by Janet Suzman at the Market Theatre, Johannesburg, in the final decade of apartheid.

One possible explanation for the subduing of the race question in recent productions is that colour prejudice is now considered a thing of the past, an anachronism. Such a straightforwardly optimistic view of today's Britain is expressed by the theatre critic, Quentin Letts, in his review of the 2007 Shakespeare's Globe production: '*Othello* is a play that has changed with our country. Twenty-five years ago it was hard to avoid the shock of the race difference, of alabaster-skinned Desdemona ... eloping with the 'monkey' Moor ... Today it feels like a secondary issue, if that' (Letts, 'Globe').

A rather less sanguine explanation is that directorial decisions to make the text more racially neutral are influenced by perceptions of the 'typical' audience. The white middle-class that makes up the majority of today's Shakespeare audiences may feel easier with a stage interpretation that cleanses the tragedy of the racist insinuations that are undoubtedly present in the original.

Broadly speaking, the theatrical community continues to cleave to the notion of a universal Shakespeare, a habit of mind that is often at odds with the historicist approaches that prevail in today's Shakespearean scholarship. Even theatres committed to 'original practices', such as London's Globe, only go so far in their quest for early modern verisimilitude. One reviewer of the aforementioned Globe production of *Othello* described it as '[s]crupulously authentic' (Mountford), an observation that overlooks a glaringly *in*authentic feature of the casting: Othello was played by a black man and not a white man in 'blackface'. As the leading Shakespearean scholar Marjorie Garber points out in *Shakespeare and Modern Culture*, '[w]hen we cast a black actor in the protagonist's role, we are "modernizing" the play' (Garber, *Culture*, 171). It is perhaps a statement of the historically obvious, but it is also one that underscores the inescapability of present values and perspectives: current disquiet at the prospect of a blacked-up white actor playing Othello trumps a desire to reconstruct a former age.

There is no doubt that the elision of high and popular cultures in twenty-first century productions of *Othello* has made for exciting and gripping theatre, well received by audiences and critics alike. However, there remains the question of how far the analogic approach, committed as it is to finding modern equivalences to early modern tragedy, has allowed potentially explosive questions about race to be turned down to a low simmer.

Further reading

Linda Anderson, *A Place in the Story: Servants and Service in Shakespeare's Plays* (Newark, DE, 2005)

Ralph Berry, *Shakespeare and Social Class* (Atlantic Highlands, 1988)

David Evett, *Discourses of Service in Shakespeare's England* (London, 2005)

Ayanna Thompson (ed.), *Colorblind Shakespeare: New Perspectives on Race and Performance* (London, 2006)

Judith Weil, *Service and Dependency in Shakespeare's Plays* (Cambridge, 2005)

The Changeling

'It is the false steward that stole his master's daughter'

Hamlet 4.5.166–7

Ideas of substitution, suggested by the title, pervade this drama from the opening scene to the final exchanges, linking the main plot and the subplot, and providing a means by which ideas of both 'service' and sexuality can be brought into sharp focus. Within the two discrete worlds of the play issues of rank are foregrounded and the key servants – Deflores, Lollio, Diaphanta – are resourceful, ambitious and willing to be unscrupulous. At a time of 'unprecedented social mobility' (Cust, 7) plays depicting issues of class might be reflecting the realities of a changing world or consciously engaging with and promoting dissident attitudes.

The social world of Alicante

On the surface, it would seem that the *ancien régime* exemplified in Vermandero's castle, and the bourgeois commercial world of Alibius' madhouse, typify all that is conservative and patriarchal. In the opening scene, Vermandero reserves his hospitality until he can assure himself of Alsemero's credentials:

> We use not to give survey
> Of our chief strengths to strangers; our citadels
> Are placed conspicuous to outward view,
> On promonts' tops, but within are secrets.
>
> 1.1.156–9

But it seems that Alsemero can be warmly received; his father was known to Vermandero in early youth and in Spain's warfare against Holland. It is significant that this exchange, establishing status and historic links, is followed immediately by Vermandero's boasting about the betrothal he has sealed between his daughter and Piracquo:

> I tell you, sir, the gentleman's complete,
> A courtier and a gallant, enriched
> With many fair and noble ornaments
>
> 1.1.205–7

He commands his daughter to prepare herself to marry within a week and follows this up with a display of aristocratic mastery over Deflores who is summoned to pick up Beatrice's dropped glove. Vermandero is unmistakably the autocratic ruler over his household, his daughter and, by implication, the potential suitors who woo her. He perceives no threat to his hierarchical and masculinist universe. Deflores' role is that of the trusted gentleman-servant: he is frequently referred to as 'honest Deflores', knows all the castle's architectural secrets and is the guardian of its keys. His situation has been tellingly altered from the source material, however, in ways which highlight issues of class. The story derives from a didactic and highly sensational prose work by John Reynolds, entitled *The Triumphs of Gods Revenge Against the Crying and Execrable Sinne of Wilfull and Premeditated Murther* (1621), a collection of moralizing tales where sin leads inexorably to violent death and damnation. In this original version, Deflores is a 'Gallant young Gentleman, of the Garison of the Castle, who followes [Vermandero]'; he is 'caught and intangled in the snares of [Beatrice-Joanna's] beautie' (Bawcutt, 122, 3). There is no suggestion of his physical ugliness nor her intense dislike. Middleton and Rowley retain Deflores' status to the extent that Beatrice describes him as 'a gentleman/In good respect with my father' (1.1.129–30). But they make a subtle alteration, one which Deflores himself draws attention to: despite his gentlemanly birth, he has suffered subsequent misfortune: 'my hard fate has thrust me out to servitude' (2.1.48). Like Bosola in *The Duchess of Malfi*, he pronounces himself a Malcontent, bearing a grudge against the class-dominated society that has seen him suffer, and desiring revenge. Gabriel Rieger suggests classifying the play as 'satiric tragedy' because of the 'class and gender tensions that drive the [plot]' (Rieger, 78). *The Changeling*, then, by focusing on Deflores' physical ugliness and social inferiority, suggests an erotic attraction that is infinitely more subversive than the source material.

Beatrice-Joanna, at the beginning of the play, is entirely unquestioning of the hierarchical status quo, if determined to defy her father's authority over her body and her choice of husband. When Vermandero dismisses her reluctance to surrender her virginity to Piracquo, and insists upon his paternal rights over her: 'I'll want my will else', Beatrice's 'aside' is an immediate challenge, 'I shall want mine if you do it' (1.1.212–13). She assumes class superiority over Deflores with her insults and commands – 'Who sent thee? What's thy errand? Leave my sight ... Slave, when wilt make an end?' (2.1.59, 68). Troubled by his attentions, she is determined to exploit her privileged position and be rid of him:

> The next good mood I find my father in,
> I'll get him quite discarded
>
> 2.1.92–3

Her language here reduces Deflores to the level of the glove she petulantly rejects because he has touched it. Indeed Beatrice unthinkingly regards both her trusted gentlewoman, Diaphanta, and Deflores as tools that can be useful to her schemes. When Alsemero suggests an honourable challenge to Piracquo to decide their fates, Beatrice passionately rejects the idea as too dangerous. She immediately makes a connection with Deflores, however, assuming his very existence is for the sole purpose of ridding her of an inconvenient suitor, 'the ugliest creature / Creation framed for some use' (2.2.43–4). She makes a similar assumption with Diaphanta, persisting in her belief that her servants will perform any task for financial reward:

> Seeing that wench now,
> A trick comes in my mind: 'tis a nice piece
> Gold cannot purchase
>
> 4.1.53–5

Later, she is indignant that Diaphanta should be enjoying her wedding night and 'never minds my honour or my peace'

(5.1.4). Her instinctive class awareness is intact and her rebelliousness contradictory: she ignores her father's authority over her and indulges sexual desires that are, in her world, unthinkable, while still assuming that her servants exist only to fulfil her wishes. The story of the servant as substitute bride was possibly drawn from a popular prose tale, *Gerardo the Unfortunate Spaniard*, translated by Leonard Digges in 1622, from a collection by the Spanish writer Cespedes y Menses. Here too the female protagonist, Isdaura, needs to conceal the fact that she is no longer a virgin. Isdaura, like Beatrice, deals ruthlessly with her maid: she persuades her to take her place in the bridal bed, proceeds to endanger the household with fire and kills her by pushing her down a well. Interestingly, Isdaura is dishonoured because she has been raped by the family's trusty servant, 'the Biscayner', who is passionately in love with her. Unlike Beatrice, though, she murders him as he sleeps and disposes of his body.

'servant obedience[changed]/To a master sin'

In terms of literary models, Deflores might be seen as aspirational: in *Twelfth Night* (1602) the steward Malvolio harbours a secret ambition 'to be Count Malvolio' and believes that there is precedent for such a marriage between classes. In Beaumont's *The Knight of the Burning Pestle* (1607/8) the apprentice Jasper succeeds in winning the hand of his master's daughter, Luce, when her father, a prosperous Merchant, has already decided on her future prospects. Both texts employ comic strategies to dramatize changing nuances of class and courtship. Deflores, though, is unambiguously pursuing a policy of class warfare: he desires Beatrice-Joanna but he also aspires to the role of courtly lover. He knowingly reverses the tradition of the *droit de seigneur* whereby a feudal lord can lay claim to the wedding-night 'deflowering' of a female servant. Deflores, here, is the servant assuming rights over Beatrice and, furthermore, ensuring that Alsemero knows this. From the opening scene Deflores expresses his obsession with Beatrice and his determination to win her; he will 'endure all storms' and absorbs her insults passively. Indeed, he sees himself in the light of the 'common Garden-bull' baited by dogs as a form of entertainment. Because of the intensity of his watchfulness of her, he is a witness to the secret meeting between Beatrice and Alsemero. When he suspects that she intends to betray her official betrothal to Piracquo, he assumes that she will therefore willingly prostitute herself to 'an army royal' (2.2.64). The key scene that confirms a change of status in Deflores' mind is Beatrice's appealing for his 'service' – a crucially ambivalent word in this context. In the mind of the noble Alsemero, 'One good service/Would strike off both your fears' – to challenge Piracquo to a duel is an act of valour, 'the honourablest piece about man' (2.2.27). Deflores is only responding in the same light in his response to her dilemma: 'O blest occasion! ... Claim so much man in me' (2.2.112–14). When he kneels to solicit the 'service' Beatrice desires, his gesture suggests the conventional scene of the courtly lover kneeling to his lady. And he further protests that her employment of him is so 'sweet' that he cannot express 'reverence enough' in claiming the privilege. His imagery suggests his profound, almost religious, commitment; Beatrice disastrously mistakes his enthusiasm for financial greed. The compact is sealed with her promise of a 'precious' reward; a reward he already anticipates as sexual – 'the thought ravishes' (2.2.128). Deflores' fantasies of sexual delight speak of reciprocal love, not rape. In his mind, he has been accepted in the role of courtly lover; he and Beatrice are now equals.

Now read Act 3, scene 3, 18–170. 📖

- *In a landmark essay on the play, Christopher Ricks analysed this scene through five key words:* service, blood, will, act, deed *all of which have two meanings, one always sexual. Look at the ways in which Deflores*

> *traps Beatrice through these double meanings, forcing her to accept his version of reality.*
> - *As the tension develops in the scene, Deflores moves between 'you' and 'thou' forms when addressing Beatrice. What significance can be found in his use of the more intimate 'thou'?*
> - *Thinking of the scene in terms of class dynamics, look at the ways in which Deflores systematically destroys Beatrice's assumptions of superiority.*

Deflores returns as the conquering lover, bringing as a trophy the severed finger and betrothal ring symbolizing his replacement of Piracquo and phallic ownership of Beatrice. She commences confidently, assuming that a generous monetary reward is all that is required, but Deflores is profoundly insulted by this – he has not murdered Piracquo and surrendered his soul to damnation for 'salary':

> Do you place me in the rank of verminous fellows
> To destroy things for wages? Offer gold?
> The life blood of man!
>   [. . .]
>   I could ha' hired
> A journeyman in murder at this rate,
> And mine own conscience might have slept at ease
>
>   3.3.64–70

But Beatrice has judged precisely in these terms – he is no more than the 'journeyman' to her. Her attempt to maintain hierarchical difference is undermined by her lack of morality, as Deflores reveals. Beatrice clearly regards class as the ultimate argument:

> Think but upon the distance that creation
> Set 'twixt thy blood and mine, and keep thee there.
>
>   3.3.130–1

Deflores redefines her theology of class absolutism: her parentage is irrelevant now that she is guilty of a mortal sin. He scorns her wealth and can only be appeased by the thought that 'thy virginity were perfect in thee'. In other words, he deserves the honour of the virgin bride. When Beatrice kneels to him, the gesture underlines the complete reversal of her expectations and class hierarchy. As Dollimore observes, the scene reveals '"blood" and "birth" to be myths in the service of historical and social forms of power' (Dollimore, 'Subversion', 178).

Beatrice articulates in conventional terms her horror at the violation of her honour. She does not, however, conform to the stereotype of the abused and broken woman who kills herself because she has been violated. Contemporary literature supplies numerous examples, all possibly deriving from the classical story of Lucrece in the first instance. In *The Revenger's Tragedy* (1607) Lord Antonio's wife has been raped by the Duchess's Younger Son. The latter is flippant and dismissive of the crime, but the wronged wife commits suicide rather than live with dishonour. Beatrice proceeds to marry Alsemero while evidently continuing her liaison with Deflores. Is this, perhaps, the most challenging aspect of the play for the audience of the time? Modern readers might suggest that the hysteria of Beatrice's initial loathing signifies her fear of being erotically attracted outside her own class – a love as transgressive as Desdemona's for Othello. The play certainly stresses that the forbidden love of servant and mistress continues beyond the 'deflowering': Jasperino informs his master that he and Diaphanta have heard the two together and Act 5 commences with troubling evidence that Alsemero must accept, 'the prospect from the garden'. The symbolism is intriguingly ambiguous: either Deflores is the serpent destroying Beatrice's Edenic world, or, conversely, the lovers meet in the traditional '*locus amoenus*' of courtly love. The complex substitutions of the wedding night also deserve consideration in terms of sex and class. Diaphanta is the changeling bride and Deflores the true lover who becomes the 'wondrous necessary man' (5.1.92). The role of the female servant has often been overlooked by critics; in fact this is equally subversive. Diaphanta's unhesitating enthusiasm for the scheme is itself interesting: she is eager to enjoy the 'first night's pleasure', perhaps she imagines that sex with a nobleman will be inherently more exciting. Secondly, the generous bribe will be sufficient dowry to enable her to improve her prospects:

> The bride's place,
> And with a thousand ducats! I'm for a justice now –
> I bring a portion with me, I scorn small fools.
>
> 4.1.125–7

It was certainly the case that young and ambitious servants aspired to better places and, ultimately, a household of their own. Unfortunately for Diaphanta's prospects, she enjoys her role too thoroughly. Yet, to the amorous 'husband', their passion has not betrayed any distinction of class. When the household responds to the danger of fire, Alsemero embraces Beatrice as his 'absolute treasure', displaying his bridegroom's possessiveness and her 'value' as virgin bride. Clearly, there is no difference here between gentlewoman and servant. As Liz Schafer observes, 'the bed trick points uncomfortably to the utter reification of women in the act of sex, as each woman becomes an anonymous body to be penetrated, not an individual with distinguishing marks' (Schafer, *Witch*, xxii). Meanwhile, Deflores has become the 'parfit gentil knight' in Beatrice's eyes; he rescues her situation from disaster – to ensure 'our pleasure and continuance' – by causing a fire within the castle. The seditious symbolism of fire within Vermandero's fortress is all too clear. But to Beatrice, Deflores has become 'a man worth loving' and the terms she uses typify the language of courtly love:

> How heartily he serves me! His face loathes one,
> But look upon his care, who would not love him?
> The east is not more beauteous than his service.
>
> 5.1.69–71

Her final gesture in the scene is bold and defiant: confronting the two figures of authority in her life, father and husband, she enquires with feigned innocence who first spied the fire and announces to the two men that Deflores should be rewarded for his pains. Even Deflores is astonished at her effrontery: 'Rewarded? Precious! Here's a trick beyond me!' (5.1.126). She has signalled her delight in him and their shared secret, as well as making it clear to him that both her husband and father can pay him tribute.

In the final scene Deflores again usurps the role of husband, defiantly lording it over his 'masters'. He has offered Piracquo's severed finger as a trophy to his beloved; he also presents the murdered Diaphanta as a sacrificial gift. The final gesture will be his appearance with Beatrice's dying body. Here, again, comparison with the source material is intriguing: in Reynolds's text it is Alsemero who – as tradition demands – discovers his wife's adultery and murders the lovers *in flagrante*. The play is more subversive as well as dramatic: the lovers are thrust together into a closet by Alsemero as his prisoners. Modern productions invariably suggest that Deflores stabs Beatrice at the climactic point of their final sexual act, her 'horrid sounds' being erotic as well as tortured. When Deflores then emerges carrying her in his arms, he is challenging both rival husband and father. His words defiantly proclaim his supremacy over his rival:

> her honour's prize
> Was my reward – I thank life for nothing
> But that pleasure; it was so sweet to me
> That I have drunk up all, left none behind
> For any man to pledge me.
>
> 5.3.167–71

He has made Alsemero the cuckold without right of redress and his suicide is a triumph over the assembled company, preventing either lawful punishment or revenge. His final words express no remorse but a command to his love: 'Make haste, Joanna,. . . / I would not go to leave thee far behind.' He has defeated Piracquo, his vengeful brother Tomazo, Alsemero and Vermandero. The comment by Alsemero that 'servant obedience' has been changed to 'master sin' is telling as is Vermandero's observation that 'An host of enemies entered my citadel / Could not amaze like this' (5.3.147–8). The ruling male class has been humiliated and dispossessed here; not by foreign invasion but by the enemy within.

'the madmen's morris'

The subplot to *The Changeling* was once judged as 'coarse and worthless' (Légouis cited in Levin, 3) whereas it now tends to be seen as an ironic parallel. In Alibius' madhouse, romantic love is folly or madness. This commercial and domestic world is dominated by Lollio, the servant, and Isabella, the mistress of the household. The wedding celebrations for Beatrice and Alsemero bring the two plots together as Alibius' inmates are to provide 'a frightful pleasure' by way of a carnivalesque interlude:

> A mixture of our madmen and our fools,
> To finish, as it were, and make the fag
> Of all the revels, the third night from the first
>
> 3.2.247–9

The audience has already seen Alibius' patients attired as birds or beasts; they play 'barley-brake' and attempt to 'catch the last couple in hell' – a reference echoed by Deflores in his dying words. Bringing the world of the madhouse into the castle, however, signifies the greater insanity of Beatrice's world; her substitutions and moral blindness being infinitely more dangerous. The play suggests comparisons and connections throughout by its structure; the juxtaposition of scenes and repetition of imagery creating a subtle patterning. In the opening scene of the play Deflores presents Beatrice with her discarded glove but she refuses to accept it from his hands:

> Now I know
> She had rather wear my pelt tanned in a pair
> Of dancing pumps than I should thrust my fingers
> Into her sockets here.
>
> 1.1.225–8

In the following scene, the elderly Alibius is confiding to his young servant Lollio that he fears his wife's fidelity when he is away from the household: 'I would wear my ring on my own finger'. Lollio agrees that rivalry is inevitable: 'You must keep it on still . . . one or other will be thrusting into't' (1.2.30–1). In Alibius, fear of cuckoldry is paramount and he appears too stupid to see what he is implying to the trusted servant, 'in my absence / Supply my place' – to which Lollio can only reply, 'I'll do my best, sir.' Both plots imply that female sexuality is untrustworthy; Lollio is simply a less intimidating version of Deflores. Indeed, he resembles the cheeky servant who can run rings around his master, typical of the city comedies of the time. The parallelism between the two plots is crucial to the central scenes of Act 3: the madhouse divides up the two key scenes between Beatrice and Deflores; one where he accepts her commission to murder Piracquo and the scene where he claims his reward. The playwrights achieve far more than comic distraction or a heightening of dramatic suspense here: Isabella's situation is uncannily close to Beatrice's. Three potential suitors address her; the two disguised courtiers Antonio and Franciscus, and Lollio himself. The courtiers attempt to woo her while remaining 'in character' as mad or foolish, Antonio seizing the opportunity to announce himself as the 'truest servant to your powerful beauties / Whose magic had the force thus to transform me' (3.2.117–18). Antonio has been observed by Lollio, however, just as Deflores sees Beatrice entertain Alsemero and Lollio, too, thinks he might take advantage of this situation:

> Come, sweet rogue: kiss me, my little Lacedemonian. Let me feel how thy pulses beat. Thou hast a thing about thee

would do a man pleasure, I'll lay my hand on't. [*Grabs indecently at her*]

3.2.225–7

Isabella, like Beatrice, can command and threatens Lollio that if he is not silent about the counterfeit, she will request Antonio to cut his throat 'For me enjoying'. Lollio, like Deflores, expects that a woman, once unfaithful will be promiscuously undiscriminating: 'My share, that's all!' (3.2.236). But Isabella succeeds in turning the tables against them all: her subsequent scene is again importantly placed between much darker events in the main plot: Beatrice's feigning of Alsemero's virginity test and the wedding night itself. Isabella schemes to reveal to Antonio how false his adoration is; Lollio is part of the plotting and again reminds her that if she should stray, he will 'fall upon [her]' (4.3.36). Disguise is a **motif** central to the play: Beatrice feigns the role of the fair and virginal heroine; Isabella disguises herself as one of her husband's patients. Dressed as a madwoman, she pays court to Antonio who scornfully rejects her. When she reveals herself, he cannot make amends: 'Dearest beauty!'

No, I have no beauty now,
Nor never had, but what was in my garments.
You a quick-sighted lover? Come not near me!

4.3.123–5

This subversive material establishes key points of contact with Beatrice: both castle and madhouse seek to imprison women, literally and metaphorically. Beatrice-Joanna overturns every moral code to defy the imprisoning rule of her father; Isabella allows herself the amusement of tricking her suitors and her husband, forcing them to realize that their judgements are false. In the main plot, the totemic figure of the bride is simply a veiled woman. In the madhouse, Isabella reveals to Antonio that he has fallen in love with her elaborate clothes. Both situations raise the question of whether class and status are merely performative, no more than costume and manner. Isabella is also crucial to the last scene, where, again, she challenges male authority. Antonio and Franciscus are brought back to the castle by Alibius as suspects; their absence coinciding with Piracquo's disappearance means that they are on trial. They are all, therefore, witness to the deaths of Beatrice and Deflores and the audience is visually presented with all the play's variations upon the theme of changeling substitutions. In the final exchanges, the authoritative voice is Isabella's, pointing to the need for male stereotyping to end:

ISABELLA
>   Your change is still behind [to come]
> But best deserve your transformation:
> You are a jealous coxcomb – keep schools of folly,
> And teach your scholars how to break your head.

ALIBIUS
> I see all apparent wife, and will change now
> Into a better husband

5.3.208–13

In Middleton's world, the feudal *régime* has had its day; modern commerce and an intelligent and resourceful woman show the way forward. Mark Thornton Burnett argues that Deflores' actions lay bare a 'pervasive blindness' and 'propel Alicante into a psychologically revitalized phase of its development' (Burnett, '*Changeling*', 307). This is perhaps truer of the commercial and domesticated sphere of the madhouse; Vermandero's castle is left with no heir, no child and no prospects for the future.

While *The Changeling* is certainly a text which connects with the drama and writing of its day, it also makes a covert reference to political events, in particular the story of Frances Howard, accused of murder, and gaining some public sympathy for her youthful, forced marriage. When Diaphanta refers to her virginity being searched 'like the forewoman of a female jury' (4.1.99–100) she clearly refers to the annulment of Howard's marriage to the Earl of Essex on the grounds of non-consummation. Howard subsequently married Robert Carr, then a favourite of James I, and was suspected of poisoning Thomas Overbury who opposed the marriage. It was believed at the time that when Howard was examined by a panel of noblewomen, she substituted a young cousin, veiled, to take her place. Howard and Carr were found guilty of the murder and imprisoned in the Tower; they were pardoned by the King and released in January 1622, just before the play was registered (see Lindley). To the historicist critic, Cristina Malcolmson, *The Changeling* 'is made up of a series of rebellions' rooted in the social and political world of the 1620s: 'At important moments in this play, women are morally and intellectually superior to men, servants to masters, and the members of the middle classes to the aristocracy. The play appears to be dismantling the principle of hierarchy' (Malcolmson, 322).

Compulsion (2009)

Middleton's play attracted two major turn-of-the-century film projects: Marcus Thompson's *Middleton's Changeling* (1998) is a consciously post-Tarantino work with extreme violence and disturbing sexuality, all conveyed in a stylized world mixing Imperial Golden Age Spain with modern fashion and music. A postmodern, ludic quality prevails throughout. Jay Stern's low-budget, independent film (*The Changeling*, 2006), offers a more restrained interpretation, with pared-down script, country house setting and vaguely historic costume suggesting a non-specific time past.

Compulsion, directed by Sarah Harding, was a TV drama for ITV, first broadcast on 4 May 2009; high viewing figures give it the rare distinction of being a Jacobean text watched by 4.7 million viewers, a 22 per cent share of the evening's (Bank Holiday) audience. Its popularity doubtless owed much to the two leads, Parminder Nagra and Ray Winstone, and the advance publicity which emphasized an 'addictive sexual relationship' leading to 'obsession, murder and tragedy' (*Compulsion*, Size 9 Productions). The drama needed to be finely judged around the commercial breaks to maintain suspense and Harding was highly aware of the juxtapositions created: 'the shrill retail counterpoint exposed the melodrama and extremity of the story' (Harding, 607). In common with the BBC filmed version of the play (Richard Curtis, 1993) there is no subplot. The sexual tension between Beatrice and Deflores is reinterpreted as class antagonism between Anjika and the family chauffeur Don Flowers. Anjika is beautiful and privileged, the indulged daughter of a wealthy Indian industrialist. Back home from Cambridge, wooed by eminently suitable boyfriend Alex, she expects to be able to enjoy life before deciding on her future. Like Beatrice, she is both spoiled and wilful. Cultural difference is a means of transferring Alicante's patriarchal world to a modern setting: Anjika discovers to her astonishment that her father expects her to marry Hardik, the son of fellow British-Asian businessman. Arranged marriage does not figure in her vision of her future life. The seventeenth-century obsession with virginity is paralleled in her father's anxious enquiry as to whether she has already 'disgraced' herself. The film, like the play, also highlights the hypocrisy of this conservative, patriarchal world: the strict father, whose own arranged marriage is celebrated in the opening anniversary party, pays discreet visits to his white glamorous prostitute. Equally, Anjika's brother, Jaiman, fully enjoys his Westernized freedom: he takes drugs, drinks profusely and dates and discards white girlfriends. Anjika, then, in the clashing world of Asian and Western mores, is the object of her father's ambitions and the obsessive lust of the family's middle-aged servant. Flowers is a menacing presence in the opening scenes of the film: he is large and ungainly (this presumably equates to Deflores' ugliness), old enough to be her father and unequivocally in a socially inferior position. One of the details of the play that is retained in the film is the erotic potential of the discarded glove: Anjika is elaborately dressed for a family evening party but clearly resents being on display. She removes the elbow length gloves, scorning Flowers when he attempts to return them to her. The camera fades on Flowers inhaling the scent of the gloves; later he drives past a line of prostitutes until he finds a suitable Asian girl whom he instructs to get in his car and put on the gloves as a prelude to sex.

In the play, it is Beatrice who first sees the potential of Deflores as potential hired assassin. The film makes subtle transactional changes: in the protected space of the family limousine, Flowers offers his services first, almost neutrally he claims that he can 'fix' anything she wants. Given that he also supplies cocaine to her brother, the offer might appear almost avuncular – indulging the wayward children of his employers. But Anjika makes her loathing of him abundantly clear, proclaiming that she hates him and that he is a disgusting pervert. The key scenes of negotiation, rejection and outmanoeuvring similarly take place within the enclosed space of the car – Flowers' world where he is, in every respect, the driver. Anjika is seen, silent and defeated through the driver's mirror – the viewer always seeing her reactions through Flowers' perspective. The claustrophobic nature of the space parallels the verbal intimidation of Beatrice in the play. Like Beatrice, Anjika makes every verbal effort to avoid her sexual fate; like Deflores, Flowers will not back down, reassuring her that their night together 'won't be that bad.' Anjika is seen making her dawn escape from her lover and almost frenziedly cleansing herself in her shower. The 'dark secret' of the film is the unexpected way in which Anjika then requests, later demands sexual satisfaction from Flowers. The play is perhaps simpler: because Alsemero is suspicious, Deflores risks everything to save Beatrice from disgrace and he is therefore 'a man worth loving'. In Anjika's case, the psychology is more complex: is she rebelling against family and upbringing in this transgressive act? She is perhaps no more than the high-spirited but spoiled child indulging a rebellious desire for mischief. The inoffensive boyfriend is sweet but tame; sex with the servant – especially in the family home – is the ultimate act of rebellion.

In a Jacobean tragedy murder is the norm and the corollary of revenge is inevitable. In *Compulsion*, murder is almost unexpected and, of course, there is no state death penalty to ensure the revenger's certain death. The unwanted suitor is not, at first, murdered but framed and disgraced. The engagement with a fellow Cambridge graduate is duly approved. But stray comments from Anjika's brother alert Hardik to the possibility of foul play and he confronts Anjika, surprising her when she is alone with Flowers. When he perceives the truth of her sexual bond with the servant, he threatens her with exposure and certain disgrace. Flowers strangles him and disposes of the body, reassuring her that he will take full responsibility if the crime is discovered. Later, Anjika reflects that she hardly feels guilty about the death as she seeks oblivion in the willing embraces of Flowers. Like Beatrice, Anjika is essentially a dislikeable personality. However, while her sexual confusion is disturbing, her decision to rid herself permanently of Flowers makes her a more troubled character than Beatrice. Once her trusted friend Claire has confided her suspicions about Anjika and Flowers to Alex, Anjika decides that this must be the opportune moment to act decisively. She informs Alex that Flowers is a perverted stalker who, she fears, might rape her. She then conceals a knife within her bed – which Flowers discovers as they make love. An emotionally highly charged and horrifying scene ensues. Flowers offers her love and an escape from her gilded cage; she scorns him as 'fat and ugly' and mocks his seaside retreat as 'trailer park' trash. Class instincts rule for Anjika. After a significant pause, Flowers appears to attack her sexually – in fact, he is giving her the excuse she desires. As he possesses her, he guides her hand to the knife and ensures that together they stab him, a modern equivalent to the 'Jacobean mix of sexual obsession and courtly service' (Harding, 609). In a key departure from the play, she herself is (physically) unharmed; she telephones the police to report a rape and possibly a death and weeps convincingly, if ambiguously.

The final frames reveal her participating in the formal Indian wedding ceremony and back in the totemic limousine, the new chauffeur deferentially in place. The viewer sees her choosing to wear the bracelet that was Flowers' gift to her. Sepia effects in the final shots create a dislocating effect as though Anjika proceeds through these events in a dream. She survives but she is damaged. The film attempts to identify the heart of the drama and make it authentic for a modern audience; to Harding, Flowers has a 'form of nobility' and Anjika discovers, only in the final scene with him, that she loves him (Harding, 610–11). Reviewers found the violence extreme and 'repulsive.'

Class, race and taboo

Richard Eyre's 1988 production of the play at the National Theatre also used the motif of racial otherness as a means of exploring class and cultural difference. In his attempt to find a modern correlative to the stratified class structure of Middleton's Alicante, he chose to set the play in a slave colony. The Grenadian British actor George Harris played Deflores as Vermandero's steward with Miranda Richardson as the blonde and indulged slave-owner's daughter. Taboo indeed. This inevitably emphasized the play's indebtedness to *Othello*: Beatrice clearly envisages herself as a guilty version of Desdemona when she says 'He cannot but in justice strangle me' (4.1.14). But a black Deflores had the effect of making him both Iago and Othello. Reviewers of the time commented that identifying Deflores as the racial outcast encouraged the audience to sympathize with both the character and the central relationship (Neill, *Changeling*, xliv). Ironically, then, an imaginative attempt to parallel the taboo of the original resulted in an effect at odds with the play's essential morality.

Further reading

Swapan Chakravorty, *Society and Politics in the Plays of Thomas Middleton* (Oxford, 1996)

T.S. Eliot, 'Thomas Middleton' in *Elizabethan Dramatists* (London, 1963)

Alison Findlay, *A Feminist Perspective on Renaissance Drama* (Oxford, 1998)

Christopher Ricks, 'The Moral and Poetic Structure of *The Changeling*,' *Essays in Criticism*, 10 (1960), 296–99

Anne Pasternak Slater, 'Hypallage, Barley-brake, and *The Changeling*,' *The Review of English Studies* 34 (1983), 429–40

5

Fatherhood, state and the dynamics of revenge:

The Spanish Tragedy and *Titus Andronicus*

One of the great hits of early commercial theatre was the revenge drama, a genre which managed to hold a place on the English stage from the late 1580s up until the closure of the playhouses in 1642. The driving force in the vast majority of these plays is a criminal act committed against an individual which, for a variety of reasons, rests unpunished. It is left to a solitary avenger (usually a relative or lover) to pursue the perpetrator of the crime and to seek the justice denied to them by what is, more often than not, a corrupt church and state. Playgoers, then, are offered a tantalizing glimpse of the private man (and very occasionally woman) standing up to the tyranny of institutional authority and asserting, however fleetingly, the right to take the law into their own hands. Unsurprisingly, given the increasing policing of the theatre, these clashes with the law – both theological and secular – did not take place on home turf: it was frequently the Catholic realms of Italy and Spain that saw the enactment of talionic codes. At the same time as enabling playwrights to circumvent the state censorship of stage performances, these settings also afforded some of them ample opportunity to indulge in a thoroughgoing vilification of the 'old faith'. If revenge plays had the potential to undermine state rule, they also held the potential to uphold its post-Reformation belief systems.

The late sixteenth century was an immensely exciting time for playgoers. Very much in its infancy, London's commercial theatres opened up a radical new form of entertainment for the city's inhabitants and the hectic pace and violent intrigue of the revenge drama must have contributed immeasurably to its rapid success. The better educated audience members may well have recognized the ancient amidst the modern. The structure, language and concerns of revenge dramas were heavily influenced by the Roman poet and philosopher Seneca, whose verse tragedies had been available in translation from the 1580s. There was, though, one essential departure from the classical model: Seneca's scenes of torture, mutilation and cannibalism, intended only to be read aloud, were repurposed to appeal to the political, social and ethical preoccupations of the later age. A relatively narrow range of early modern revenge plays has survived the passage of four centuries, with works by playwrights such as John Ford, Thomas Middleton and John Webster featuring more frequently in twenty-first century theatrical repertoires than at any time since the Restoration. How far the meaning and dramatic impact of these dramas have stood the test of time is a matter for keen debate. Those tasked with reviewing today's productions of revenge dramas frequently betray their own estrangement from the genre by selecting the default analogy of Quentin Tarantino movies to make sense of the violent spectacles in front of them. Based mainly on superficial likenesses, such a connection between the postmodern and the early modern can often obscure, rather than illuminate, one of the most influential dramatic impulses of the late sixteenth and early seventeenth centuries.

* * *

The professional criticism of the twentieth century was not always kind to the genre of revenge drama, at least not until the later decades. A scholarly tendency to expound a teleological account of the genre's development meant that works such as those featured in this chapter were dismissed as somewhat crude in their incipience. Shakespeare was often held to be above and beyond the tragedy of blood, with *Titus* being regarded as a young writer's folly and the later *Hamlet* as an 'anti-revenge tragedy' that marked the demise of a short-lived theatrical craze. Early modern scholars of the present century, however, are more likely to view *Hamlet* as an example of revenge drama at its most sophisticated and to argue that, while there is no doubt that plays such as *The Revenger's Tragedy* (1607) contain the kind of parodic elements associated with an artistic form passed its prime, there are a significant number of later plays – *'Tis Pity She's a Whore* being one notable example – which demonstrate that revenge continued to inspire radical, sophisticated theatre well into the Caroline era. One other scholarly habit which has sometimes diminished the status of the genre is the listing of what are perceived to be its chief characteristics in introductions to revenge playtexts; such a practice has served to compound the idea that it is formulaic, written to please an audience looking for cheap thrills.

The very notion of genre as an organizing principle is in itself highly problematic. Although necessary for imposing some kind of order on a vast array of artistic production, literary taxonomies are frequently found wanting. Like wayward children, certain poems, plays and prose fictions will always resist neat categorization; some will inhabit two or three genres at once, others will resist any at all. Moreover, organizing works into genres is a process some see as perpetuating a kind of hierarchical system wherein, for example, tragedy tops comedy or the novel tops the short story. Shifting social and cultural norms can also threaten the usefulness of generic orders. Take, for example, Shakespeare's *Cymbeline*, which was classified as a tragedy in the First **Folio** of 1623, a fable in Alexander Pope's 1725 edition of the complete works, and which is currently defined as a romance or a 'late play'. For all these complicating factors of genre attribution, revenge drama undeniably bears a number of distinguishing features.

📖 *The table opposite lists some of the features most commonly associated with revenge drama. Tick or cross to indicate which of these features are to be found in the two plays discussed in this chapter; if you're uncertain, indicate this with a question mark. What does the exercise reveal about the process of categorizing dramatic texts?*

What is immediately apparent from this exercise is that pinning down a generic characteristic is by no means straightforward and there is much to argue about in the selection and phrasing of the features represented. For instance, presenting the revenger and the revenge act in the singular assumes a primary focus, though a number of revenge plays have multiple revengers and revenge plots. Also striking is that neither play fulfils all of the 'typical' characteristics of revenge drama. Even *The Spanish Tragedy*, often thought to be a template for the genre, has some grey areas. Probably the most clear-cut judgements to make here are those concerning settings and the collateral damage of multiple deaths in so far as they are 'facts' of the dramatic texts. The appearance or otherwise of ghosts is also straightforward in these two instances (one of the cast of *The Spanish Tragedy* is actually listed as 'Ghost'), though this category might have received a question mark in the case of, say, *The Duchess of Malfi*, where some critics and directors have 'seen' the ghost of the Duchess appearing to Bosola at the end of 5.2 and again in the 'Echo scene' (5.3), and others have not. Perhaps one of the most difficult features to confirm is that concerning how far the revenge act exceeds the horrors of the catalyst crime. Comparing Tamora's consumption of her slaughtered sons' flesh and blood to the rape and

Features most commonly associated with revenge drama.

	Foreign setting	Corrupt state	Revenge act surpasses the violence of the original	Revenger's eventual descent into madness	Ghosts	Meta-theatrical elements	Revenge act carried out at a social event	Multiple deaths
The Spanish Tragedy								
Titus Andronicus								

dismemberment of Lavinia raises ethical questions about power, the body and societal taboos, questions which will be answered differently over time. Likewise, it is difficult to give a definitive answer to the question of how far the revenger is presented as 'mad indeed'. A survey of academic writing on the psychological state of both Hieronimo and Titus reveals considerable diversity of critical opinion; even more so in the case of *The Spanish Tragedy*, whose three hundred plus lines of 'Additions' in the 1602 **quarto** add several further layers of complexity to the presentation of the hero and his mental state.

* * *

The issue of revenge was widely and vigorously debated in early modern England as the state authorities sought to stamp out acts of private vengeance, often motivated by embedded codes of baronial honour. The public spectacle of hanged, disembowelled and dismembered bodies was not only a terrifying reminder of the consequences of wrongdoing, its ritualized violence also reinforced the idea that vengeance was the privilege of the state – not the individual. It was a view forcefully expounded by Francis Bacon (a prominent figure in the governments of both Elizabeth and James I) in his essay 'Of Revenge' (1625) and his treatise 'The Charge Touching Duells' (1614). A contribution to the debates of James I's anti-duelling campaign, the earlier document articulates the threat posed to the state by men taking the law into their own hands:

> [W]hen revenge is once extorted out of the magistrate's hand contrary to God's ordinance, 'Mihi vindicta, ego retribuam', and every man shall bear the sword not to defend but to assail, and private men begin once to presume to give law to themselves, and to right their own wrongs, no man can foresee the dangers and inconveniences that may arise and multiply thereupon ... so that the

state by this means shall be like to a distempered and unperfect body, continually subject to inflammations and convulsions.

BACON, 305

Bacon's treatise makes clear that the law's prohibition of private revenge upholds Pauline writ: 'Vengeance is mine, I will repay, says the Lord' ['Mihi vindicta, ego retribuam'] (Rom. 12.19–20) – to challenge earthly power is to challenge God himself.

* * *

Revenge dramas offered a playing out of what to all intents and purposes was a highly transgressive act, with revengers, often deeply compelling and sympathetic figures, committing acts bound to lead to their death and damnation. In the two tragedies treated in this chapter, both main figures are fathers seeking revenge for crimes committed against their children which the state refuses to pursue or punish. In placing their heroes in conflict with the ruling powers, Kyd and Shakespeare disrupt a well-established analogy: a father rules the family as a monarch rules a nation. It was an analogy that 'could be used to naturalize absolute monarchal authority' (Shuger, 227–8) and reinforce a sense of social and political stability. Prescriptive literature of the period repeatedly drives home the public–private parallel. *A Godly Form of Householde Governement*, insists that 'it is impossible for a man to understand to governe the common-wealth, that doth not knowe to rule his owne house' (Cleaver, 5); and in *A Treatise or Exposition Upon the Ten Commandements* (1603), the preacher-author, John Dod, insists on the father's duty to exact punishment on his children, just as the state exacts punishment on its citizens. Whereas this simple, but nonetheless powerful, analogy placed father and state on the same side, the dynamics of revenge theatre often positioned them as violently at odds.

> This chapter examines Kyd's *The Spanish Tragedy* and Shakespeare's *Titus Andronicus*, both of which are thought to have been composed sometime between the late 1580s and early 1590s. Violent, bloody and charged with immense rhetorical force, both plays engage their audiences with the plight of a father who opposes the authority of the state in order to avenge crimes committed against his family and who, it is sometimes argued, is driven to a state of insanity in the process.

The Spanish Tragedy

Thomas Kyd is commonly held to be the inventor of revenge drama. As Lukas Erne points out in one of the few extended studies of Kyd's work, *The Spanish Tragedy* can claim a number of theatrical firsts: '[t]he first modern revenge tragedy, the first Machiavellian villain, the first play which successfully mixes tragic and comic elements, the first play-within-a-play' (Erne, 96). There is convincing evidence that such novelty proved enormously appealing to the drama's original audiences. According to the diary of the theatrical agent and entrepreneur Philip Henslowe, the play was staged twenty-nine times between 1592 and 1597 and theatre records suggest that some of the leading actors of the time took on the role of Hieronimo. Moreover, the sheer number of references to the play in a variety of early seventeenth-century documents suggests that its profile was higher even than plays such as *Hamlet*. Yet for all its innovation and early popularity, the drama's post-Restoration performance history is slight to say the least. Nowadays, while it is much mentioned as a means of establishing the literary-historical context of other revenge tragedies, it rarely features in the repertories of national theatres or on pre-university literature syllabi. *The Spanish Tragedy*'s decline in fortune is often put down to changing theatrical tastes. Its sensational scenes of violence, murder and suicide are deemed evidence of an unrefined thrill-seeking public audience, while its powerfully rhetorical speeches are regarded as at odds with the psychological realism which developed over the first few decades of the seventeenth century. Arguably, such characterizations of the play's dramatic style have ossified into stereotype, obscuring the finer qualities of what Gurr suggests is '[p]erhaps the best revenge play in English' (Gurr, *Spanish*, vii).

To regard the *Spanish Tragedy*'s success as coming entirely from its spectacular violence is to overlook an important – and obvious – clue in its title. Although there is no definitive answer to whether or not the play was written before or after the Armada (1588), it was certainly composed during a period of considerable anti-Spanish feeling. It is more than probable, then, that elements such as Hieronimo's masque in Act 1, the Machiavellian deviousness of Lorenzo, and the annihilation of the Spanish dynasty at the play's close would have appealed to the Hispanophobics in the audience. However, it would be a mistake to label the play as crudely jingoistic. English audiences might have enjoyed seeing the utter defeat of the Spanish state, but they might also have been put in mind of their own monarch's unmarried status by Bel-imperia's steadfast refusal to enter into a politically expedient marriage. And while the Spanish may have been the enemy of the day, the grieving father figure at the centre of Kyd's tragedy serves to transcend national prejudices. Indeed, one of the remarkable features of the play is its insistence on breaking down fixed identities through its mixing of languages, belief systems and tonalities.

The individual versus the state

One of the commonalities of revenge drama is the revenger's rebellion against the state for refusing to right the wrongs inflicted on his (and occasionally her) family or lover. In some cases, the catalyst crime is committed by someone at the very centre of power: the Duke in *The Revenger's Tragedy* is responsible for the death of the revenger's betrothed; the newly anointed king in *Hamlet* is responsible for the murder of his predecessor. In such instances, the avenging heroes are obliged to operate within the corrupt world of the court. Vindice insinuates himself into the presence of power by taking on a physical disguise as the servant, Piato, and Hamlet, the prince in waiting, attempts to hide his vengeful self through the less literal disguise of an 'antic disposition' (1.5.170). In some revenge plays, the corrupt nature of the state is announced very early in the drama. In *The Revenger's Tragedy*, Middleton's employment of **aptronyms** leaves the audience in little doubt as to the health of the nation's leaders – a son and heir who goes by the name of 'Lussurioso' (lecherous) is unlikely to inspire confidence – and in both of his revenge tragedies, Webster demonstrates the corruption of church and state through the deeds reported in the plays' opening scenes. In *The Spanish Tragedy*, however, our initial impression of the state is altogether more positive. The Spanish King is first presented receiving the news of his country's victory over Portugal, a scene not unlike that which opens Shakespeare's comedy *Much Ado About Nothing*: the return of soldiers ready to celebrate their good fortune.

📖 *Read 1.2 (or better still, read it aloud).*

- *What impression do you gain of the Spanish court in this scene and how does Kyd's use of language contribute to this impression?*
- *Consider the significance of Kyd's initial presentation of Hieronimo.*

On the surface at least, this is a scene of measured formality and balance. In tune with the courtly audience, the turmoil of the past battle is compressed and steadied in the General's retrospective report, his tight command of Senecan rhetoric seeming to reflect his erstwhile command of the troops. The repetition of the **plosive** 'Both' at the start of lines 25–9 not only emphasizes that the warring sides were closely matched, thus heightening the eventual Spanish victory all the more, it also serves to convey the static tension of the pre-battle atmosphere. As the narrative moves to the fight proper, so verbs connoting mere gesture and display ('vaunting', 'raising') are replaced with those of battle action ('strove', 'Marched') and, as if conscious of the need to entertain as well as inform his aristocratic audience, the General shifts to the present historic tense which, along with the use of **deixis** at the start of lines ('While', 'When', 'Now'), brings home the immediacy of the military struggle at full pelt. And while the middle portion of the General's speech does not hold back from the gruesome realities of 'a body sundered from his head' and the 'legs and arms' lying scattered on the 'purple plain', its dramatic imagery, snippets of Latin, and climactic focus on the heroic deeds of named men all serve to present war as glorious and noble.

The fighting over, the King is eager to stress his gratitude to the troops who have fought so valiantly for their country through the ceremonial distribution of rewards. Such formalized munificence does more than just ensure the soldiers are kept 'on side'; it also reinforces the hierarchical order: a man's status in the army is signified by the number of ducats handed over to him as a sign of the monarch's 'largess'. At one point in this scene, however, the equation of status and reward is tipped off balance, as Lorenzo and Horatio enter the scene with the Portuguese Prince Balthazar held as prisoner between them. If the visual image on stage suggests that both men have an equal share in the capture of the enemy, it quickly becomes apparent that status will take precedence over valour. A run of 153 complete lines of **blank verse** is broken at the point at which Lorenzo and Horatio both claim to be Balthazar's captor. The two formally identical half-lines jar the ritual flow of the scene so far, with the brisk movement of the single-line exchanges which follow adding tension to this highly significant adversarial moment. As the social inferior of the two competitors, Horatio's countermanding of Lorenzo, underscored by the emphatic 'But' at the start of his lines, unsettles the decorum of the proceedings and it is left to the King to bring the court back in check.

The King's decision to offer the floor to the prisoner, while appearing to be the most reliable way of establishing the facts of the capture, is also a deft means of restoring social order. As Balthazar delivers his highly rhetorical reply (161–5), it is clear that class solidarity is asserting itself. While his lines might appear balanced (thanks to the precisely placed medial **caesuras**), their effect is to define Horatio as 'this other' and to associate his opponent with the courtly values of fairness, honour and loyalty. Likewise, though the measured repetition of the possessions seized in battle and then bestowed in reward (180–1) might create a sense of reasoned judgement, that the King chooses to address Lorenzo as 'Nephew' points to a resolution influenced more by close kinship and social status than valour. It comes as no surprise that the privilege of guarding the 'gracious' prisoner falls to Lorenzo, whose 'estate best fitteth such a guest'; thus, Horatio is excluded from the inner circle, rewarded with goods that can be transported back to his house – a house too small to accommodate the prisoner's entourage.

The march of the army through the court is a dazzling display of military strength, designed to promote national loyalty and pride. Yet the army that the King pronounces a 'gladsome sight!' is missing numerous members of its original company. Having earlier talked of 'some few . . . deceased' and 'little loss', the General's more precise estimate of 'three hundred or few more' is something of a shock. While the prisoner of high birth is treated as a 'friendly guest', the 300 or so casualties of war seem to be passed over with little concern. The court, then, is a place of rigid hierarchy, held in place by ceremonial procedure, the upholding of name over merit and the persuasive force of classical rhetoric. As Woodbridge points out, Kyd's final dramatic vision of 'leaving two royal families heirless' must have been 'satisfying to the frustrated and the powerless in the audience' (Woodbridge, *Revenge*, 240).

* * *

Hieronimo is presented as an obedient and well-respected servant of the court, whose pride in his son's achievements and hopes for his future are entirely bound up with the grace and favour of the sovereign. He prefaces his support for his son with a recognition of the immanence of the King's justice, at the same time recognizing his own bias as a natural father. Very much an observer for much of the scene, his relatively few lines suggest nothing other than that his deference to King and state is heartfelt. Unlike the opening of *The Revenger's Tragedy*, where a fully formed avenger, skull in hand, makes ready to exact a brutal and elaborately apt revenge for a crime committed nine years before the start of the action, *The Spanish Tragedy* presents a figure yet to feel the pain of loss and injustice. And where Middleton's audience is catapulted into a world of intrigue and revenge from the very first scene, Kyd's is led gradually from a state of equilibrium to one of utter chaos, the psychomachia of the hero making for highly compelling drama.

* * *

Once presented with the horrific sight of his murdered son, Hieronimo's absolute adherence to state authority becomes a thing of the past. His first response to the killing is to seek revenge, a desire that places him firmly outside the limits of the law:

> To know the author were some ease of grief,
> For in revenge my heart would find relief.
>
> 2.5.40–1

The rhyming of 'grief' and 'relief' here encapsulates the notion of revenge as a restorative, a view entirely at odds with Bacon's oft-quoted wisdom that 'a man that studieth revenge keeps his own wounds green' (Bacon, 348). Yet, when the authors of the crime are revealed to him in the form of Bel-imperia's letter, he is wary of rushing to action, looking instead to gather evidence in support of the revelation: an action tantamount to taking on the entire state apparatus. And even when Bel-imperia's letter is proven true, Horatio still retains faith in the integrity of the law, which he as Knight Marshal has assiduously upheld:

> I will go plain me to my lord the King,
> And cry aloud for justice through the court
>
> 3.7.69–70

It is only when Hieronimo's increasingly desperate pleas for justice fail to gain the attention of the King that he finally severs his royal allegiance and pronounces himself an enemy of the state:

> I'll make a pickaxe of my poniard,
> And here surrender up my marshalship,
> For I'll go marshal up the fiends in hell
> To be avenged on you all for this.
>
> 3.12.74–7

Ascribing Hieronimo's frenzied behaviour to his desire to have 'to himself/The ransom of the young Prince Balthazar' (3.12.85–6), Lorenzo effectively blocks the knowledge of Horatio's death from the court and insists that 'his office be resigned/And given to one of more discretion' (3.12.95–6). The King's response is entirely in keeping with that of a just leader: he insists that they 'see further in it' (3.12.98) before taking action against Hieronimo, regarding his outburst as that of a loving father too zealously guarding the fortunes of his son. Kyd seems to suggest, then, that events take their tragic turn not because the head of state is himself corrupt, but because the exigency of forging a 'sure inexecrable bond .../Betwixt the crowns of Spain and Portugal' (3.12.45–7) to keep the political system in place, leaves him vulnerable to the machinations of those just beneath him.

Grieving fathers and sweet sons

In terms of motivation and emotional engagement Hieronimo is one of the least complex avengers: his love for Horatio is all-consuming and the principal driver of his quest for retribution. If *The Spanish Tragedy* is an intriguing study in early modern statecraft, it is also one of the period's most intense and moving explorations of paternal grief. Placing such an affective work of art in its historical context is, however, fraught with difficulties because, as one recent study points out:

> the nature of that context is itself the subject of debate. In 1977 Lawrence Stone's weighty but stylishly provocative study, *The Family, Sex and Marriage in England 1500–1800*, initiated a major controversy about affective relations in the early modern family. Stone argues that from roughly 1580 to 1640 the norm in English families was a pernicious form of patriarchy in which the father became a 'legalized petty tyrant within the home.'
>
> TROMLY, 15

Since the early 1990s revisionist historians have drawn on an ever-widening range of sources to argue a correspondingly wide range of viewpoints concerning parental relationships. The poetry and drama of the early modern period offers evidence to support quite diverse conceptions of the father, from the 'petty tyrant' to one devoted to 'forgiveness, nurturing, and tenderness' (Shuger, 220). Certainly, no one who has read

Ben Jonson's poem 'On my First Sonne', or the scene in Shakespeare's *Macbeth* where Macduff struggles to comprehend the news that his wife and 'pretty ones' (4.3.216) have been slaughtered, could doubt that the early modern father–child relationship was often a very close and loving one.

The Spanish Tragedy presents a father whose grief at the loss of his son cannot be expressed through the usual rites of public mourning: it is channelled instead into his quest for justice and, when that fails, personal revenge. As the audience follow the trajectory of Hieronimo's revenge, they are given frequent insights into his psychological state through soliloquy. While Kyd is often credited with developing the dramatic potential of the device, his soliloquies are just as often dismissed as crude forerunners to the more introspective and nuanced pieces produced by playwrights such as Shakespeare.

📖 *Look closely at the first section of Hieronimo's soliloquy (3.2.1–23) and consider:*

- *how far Kyd's use of rhetorical devices can be seen as successful in conveying emotion*
- *the challenges that this speech might pose for a modern actor.*

What is immediately striking about this soliloquy is its wealth of rhetorical **tropes**. The first three lines alone offer examples of **apostrophe** (an exclamatory address to an absent person, object or abstract idea), **antithesis** (words or ideas set up in contrast with each other), **alliteration** and **anaphora** (the patterned repetition of a group of words or phrases, sometimes known as 'parallelism'). The opening of this soliloquy (lines 1–3) is both expansive and succinct, its repeated exclamations and patterned syntax commanding the listener's attention at the same time as summing up the nature and extent of Hieronimo's grief. The initial and medial caesuras, placed identically in each line, mark the tragic progress of the hero:

from having to not having. The nouns 'tears', 'death' and 'wrongs' are stressed by their end-of-line placing, serving to encapsulate Hieronimo's situation in three stark monosyllables.

For a modern audience, inclined to equate rhetorical style with manipulation and insincerity, these highly wrought opening lines might sound too contrived to carry any real sincerity of emotion; however, as the speech moves on, so the steadiness of its blank verse and its syntactical stateliness begin to show signs of breaking down, as if the speaker's initial control has deserted him. In a question which extends to seven lines (5–11), the triple repetition of the conditional phrase 'if this' and the delay of the main verb 'pass', convey Hieronimo's feelings of frustration and incredulity that his son's killers have not yet been brought to justice. The rhetorical question, directed to the divine powers, reaches its conclusion on a **heptameter** line, the additional syllables drawing attention to one of the key concerns of the drama: the nature of heavenly and earthly justice. Here, Kyd's Senecan rhetoric is given full rein as the Knight Marshal, once so secure in his relationship with the judicial system, attempts to make sense of its apparent contradictions. Hieronimo moves from the adjectival positive form 'just', to the negative adverbial 'unjustly' to the noun 'justice', an example of **polyptoton** (the repetition of a word with the same root in a different form). Kyd's use of the device here could be dismissed as cleverness for its own sake, though speaking the lines in question demonstrates how powerfully they portray Hieronimo's estrangement from the world and perhaps from language itself: however many times it is repeated or transformed into another part of speech, the root word 'just' no longer carries a stable meaning. Hieronimo's all-consuming sense of loss is emphasized through the negative prefixes woven into the speech ('unhallowed', 'unrevealed', 'unrevenged', 'unjustly', 'unfrequented'). It is, though, the line 'Of mine but now no more my son' that includes the most affective negation of all, raising as it does the agonizing question of whether the death of an only child is also the death of fatherhood.

* * *

It could be argued that the rhetoric of Hieronimo's speech is a linguistic means by which the hero's emotional turmoil is controlled, with any deviation from its patterns and balances suggesting inner struggle and potential mental breakdown. Yet while such an argument works well on paper, putting it into stage practice is rather more challenging – after all, the soliloquy bears more than a few linguistic affinities with Pyramus' lamentations over the dead body of Thisbe in *A Midsummer Night's Dream*. As Emma Smith points out '*The Spanish Tragedie* is a play writ large, which requires bold, gestic acting, a declamatory rhetorical style' (Smith, *Spanish Tragedie*, xix). Generally speaking, such theatricality is out of step with modern acting styles, which tend to favour making early modern blank verse as 'natural' to the modern ear as possible. Indeed, what is often perceived as the crudeness of Kyd's dramatic language could, in part, explain why *The Spanish Tragedy* is rarely performed on the professional stage and why, when it is, the director's impulse is to 'naturalize' it, often with dubious results. The *Daily Telegraph* reviewer of Bogdanov's 1982 production at the National Theatre observed that the 'dry, precise naturalness' of the actor playing Hieronimo (Michael Bryant) was 'so ill-suited to the vengeful father that he [had] to make a joke of his most terrifying speeches (Barber). And Peter Wight's performance of the role in The Royal Shakespeare Company's production at the Swan Theatre (1997) was seen as projecting 'the naturalness of a desk sergeant or chartered surveyor' (Macaulay) or, in the words of Benedict Nightingale, 'a bereft bumbler out of his depth: Polonius as hitman' (Nightingale). It remains to be seen whether today's theatre companies dedicated to original practices will manage to bring Kyd's groundbreaking tragedy to the attention of twenty-first-century playgoers – with all its declamatory energies still intact.

Adding to the tragedy: the 'enlarged' edition of 1602

The title page of the fourth quarto of *The Spanish Tragedy* promises its readers a 'Newly corrected, amended, and enlarged' version of the drama and delivers five new extracts, totalling 324 lines of prose and verse, which both add to and in some cases overwrite the text of Q1. While there remains no consensus regarding the authorship of what are generally termed 'Additions', there is currently strong support from scholars such as Warren Stevenson, Brian Vickers and Douglas Bruster for them coming from the pen of Shakespeare – a theory that will doubtless serve to attract further critical attention to these intriguing 'extras'. Having been consigned to the appendix sections of editions for most of the twentieth century, it is only in the past few decades that the Additions have been read with any real analytical rigour. Stage directors are nowadays obliged to consider which, if any, of the Additions to include in performance. Adding too many of the extra lines inevitably slows the pace of the revenge plot, and the numerous repetitions which occur from conflating the original text with that of 1602, while underlining the recursive nature of revenge itself, are unlikely to sit well with modern audiences.

Recent readings of the Additions have tended to focus on their presentation of Hieronimo's mental state. According to Neely, the Additions are 'significant textual revisions, that, by transforming Hieronimo's madness, make a new play' and chart the hero's movement 'from, in Freud's terms, melancholia to mourning' (Neely, 33, 36). Certainly, Hieronimo's 'madness', as portrayed in the Additions, seems more psychologically compelling than in the original text, where it is closer perhaps to Hamlet's 'antic disposition'. In the first Addition, the father seems incapable of identifying the corpse he has just cut down from the tree with his 'sweet Horatio', wondering 'how this fellow got his clothes' (15); it is a devastatingly poignant line, redolent, perhaps of Imogen embracing the headless body of

Cloten, dressed in her husband's clothes (*Cym*, 4.2.332). While Erne is surely right in seeing Horatio's behaviour here as 'mad flippancy' that 'powerfully jars with the tragedy of his son's death' (Erne, 125), it is worth acknowledging that this kind of denial of the death of a loved one is a well-established symptom of bereavement. In the third addition, Hieronimo's mood swings drastically as he moves from a disturbing misogyny, whereby a son can be figured merely as a 'lump bred up in darkness' to 'serve/To ballast these light creatures we call women' (6–7) to declaring Horatio 'my comfort and his mother's joy' (30).

If in the first and third Additions, Hieronimo could be seen as attempting, albeit unsuccessfully, to escape from the painful reality of his situation, in the fourth Addition, he seems to find some sense of integrity by means of 'identification and self-representation' (Neely, 37). Sometimes referred to as the 'Painter scene', the fourth Addition is by far the longest of the five and tends to be regarded as the most aesthetically successful. The scene brings the Knight Marshall into dialogue with the painter, Bazardo, who comes seeking justice for the murder of his only son, a situation broadly repeated in 3.13 with Hieronimo's encounter with the senex Bazulto (this replication is one of the reasons that this Addition is usually regarded as a replacement for 3.13.45–172, rather than an 'add-on'). In the fourth Addition, Hieronimo responds to Barzardo's declaration that 'no man did hold a son so dear' (90) without the least sign of empathy:

> That's a lie
> As massy as the earth. I had a son,
> Whose least unvalued hair did weigh
> A thousand of thy son's, and he was murdered.
>
> 91–4

Clearly, whoever the author of these lines may have been, he was not prone to sentimental notions of parenthood as a common and therefore unifying experience; rather, this particular moment brings to mind Freud's theory that parenthood revives and reproduces childhood narcissism, leading to a 'compulsion to ascribe to the child all conceivable perfections' (Freud, 19). Here, then, Hieronimo's conviction that his son is more precious than any other could be regarded as one of the prime psychological motivators of his revenge.

One of the reasons why the fourth Addition is often singled out for scholarly discussion (and perhaps why it is the most likely to make it to the stage) is that it engages with the complex issue of art and its ability to represent feeling. Hieronimo asks for the painter to convey his life in a sequence of pictorial forms, moving from the idealized vision of his complete family life to the horror of discovering his butchered child and, finally, to the stereotypical image of the revenger: 'Make me curse, make me rave, make me cry, make me mad' (154–5). Coming just before the '*Vindicta mihi*' soliloquy, wherein Hieronimo reasons between various courses of action, including suicide, before settling on 'I will revenge his death' (3.13.20), the Addition's engagement with the potential of art points the way to the play's climax: the author-avenger's play-within-a-play.

Things on stage

Since the mid-1990s certain areas of literary theory have concerned themselves with the investigation of the 'materiality' of things, once considered the preserve of disciplines such as museology, anthropology and archaeology. The research opportunities provided by theatres such as Shakespeare's Globe have generated some highly illuminating investigations into the materiality of early modern productions, ranging from the physical properties of stage make-up to the signification of body parts in performance. Other fields of material culture studies have been less concerned with the concrete realities of things and more interested in their theoretical potential. One particularly intriguing example is Bill Brown's development of 'Thing Theory', which explores ways in which things, far from being a kind of antonym to theory in their concreteness, might offer a focus for critical theory itself. Axiomatic to Brown's ideas is what he regards as the crucial difference between the terms 'object' and 'thing': 'You could imagine things ... as what is excessive in objects, as what exceeds their mere materialization as objects or their mere utilization as objects – their force as a sensuous presence or as a metaphysical presence, the magic by which objects become values, fetishes, idols, and totems' (Brown, 'Thing', 5). Applying Brown's distinction between 'object' and 'thing' to early modern drama, it might be argued that while every visible 'object' in stage performance is not necessarily a 'thing' (actors may well wear boots, drink from goblets, sit on chairs that have limited significance beyond their utility), when an object is named in the text itself, it is surely destined for 'thing' status. Put another way: 'it is only when an object is actively part of the performance that it gains a real theatrical value' (Karim-Cooper and Stern, 64).

The Spanish Tragedy has a higher than usual count of stage props that Brown would qualify as 'things', including the glove that Bel-imperia lets fall in 1.4; the empty box that promises, but ultimately fails, to deliver Pedringano's pardon in 3.6; the rope and dagger signifying Hieronimo's contemplation of suicide in 3.12; as well as the letters that lead the revenger to his victims. However, the stage object that could be said to contribute most powerfully to the play's exploration of the revenge dynamic is the handkerchief which travels from Bel-imperia to Andrea to Horatio and, finally, to Hieronimo. Like Desdemona's love token, this is a handkerchief whose signification is far in excess of its primary material purpose. As Janet Clare observes, it operates as 'a projection, a visible sign of grief and, as a stage prop, something to be held out and to be shown to an uncomprehending stage audience' (Clare, 34).

The handkerchief is first held out to the audience during Horatio's account of Andrea's death on the battlefield (1.4). Originating as a love token given by Bel-imperia to Andrea 'at his last depart' (47), Horatio recounts how he removed it from the fallen Andrea's 'lifeless arm' (42), retaining it to wear 'in remembrance' of his friend (43) and as a reminder of his duty to revenge his death. In requesting that Horatio wear it 'both for him and me' (48), Bel-imperia invests the cloth with dual signification: the enduring devotion of both a lover and a friend; yet as Andrew Sofer suggests, the transference of the cloth also makes it 'an unintentional **emblem** of Bel-imperia's faithlessness to Andrea' (Sofer, 141). As if carrying some kind of fatal charge, the fabric next appears 'besmeared with blood' (2.5.51) on the corpse of Horatio. From this point on a cathectic relationship forms between the grieving father and the handkerchief, now a bloody reminder of the revenge still outstanding, as well as a powerful visual marker for Kyd's original amphitheatre audiences, relatively new to the trajectory of revenge drama. The cloth's next appearance in 3.13 offers a telling exemplification of Brown's distinction between 'object' and 'thing'. Faced with the weeping father, Bazulto, Hieronimo tells him 'take my handkerchief and wipe thine eyes' (3.13.82). In this moment of spontaneous compassion, the cloth is merely an object of utility; however, as its owner draws it out of his pocket and identifies it as Horatio's (3.13.85), it becomes, once more, a 'thing'.

Making its next and final appearance in 4.4, the bloody memento is presented by the revenger as both sign of his completed mission and as a type of sacred object:

And here behold this bloody handkerchief,
    [*Draws out a bloody napkin*]
Which at Horatio's death I, weeping, dipped
Within the river of his bleeding wounds.
It, as propitious, see, I have reserved,
And never hath it left my bloody heart

4.4.121–5

Sofer links Kyd's focus on the handkerchief here back to the play's central symbol: the dead Horatio hanging from a tree planted by his own father, recalling the iconography of Christ crucified, a vicarious sacrifice for the sins of the world: 'Not content with displaying the body of the "Son", Hieronimo also elevates his blood. Brandishing the bloody handkerchief, Hieronimo travesties the ritual gesture of visual display common to the Mass and the religious drama of the *sudarium*' (Sofer, 145).

Hieronimo, so Sofer argues, is a transgressive figure, whose profane re-enactment of the Mass signifies the revenger's abandonment of any religious or ethical code. Certainly, the multiple killings carried out in his perverse choice of court entertainment (including the entirely gratuitous murder of Castile) suggests that the emotional softness of the devoted father has been replaced by the steely cruelty of what Bacon famously termed the 'wild justice' of revenge (Bacon, 347).

In the introduction to the Arden edition of *The Spanish Tragedy*, the editors note that, according to the promptbook of Michael Bogdanov's 1982 production for the National Theatre, 'Revenge took the bloody handkerchief from Hieronimo, stage-managing the action till the very end' (Calvo and Tronch, 80). It is a staging detail that insists on the importance of Kyd's use of Revenge as a framing device; it is also a detail that draws attention to how much can be lost in a reading of a playtext. The presence of Revenge on stage colours events, actions and speeches to an extent that is difficult to appreciate from the page alone. If the audience is encouraged to believe in Revenge's omniscience, then the struggles of the grieving father to right the wrongs visited on his beloved son can appear futile, even ridiculous. The character of Revenge is, then, the tuning fork of any production of *The Spanish Tragedy* and it is left in the hands of the director to decide just how far the grieving father can be '[a]uthor and actor in this tragedy' (4.4.146).

Further reading

John Kerrigan, *Revenge Tragedy: Aeschylus to Armageddon* (Oxford, 1996)

Chris McMahon, *Family and the State in Early Modern Revenge Drama: Economies of Vengeance* (New York, 2012)

Tanya Pollard, 'Tragedy and Revenge' in Emma Smith and Garrett A. Sullivan, Jr (eds), *The Cambridge Companion to English Renaissance Tragedy* (Cambridge, 2010)

James Shapiro, ', "Tragedies naturally performed": Kyd's Representation of Violence' in David Scott Kastan and Peter Stallybrass (eds), *Staging the Renaissance: Reinterpretations of Elizabethan and Jacobean Drama* (New York, 1991)

Brian Vickers, 'Identifying Shakespeare's Additions to *The Spanish Tragedy* (1602): A New(er) Approach', *Shakespeare*, 8 (2012), 13–43

Titus Andronicus

On 24 October 1955, the *Daily Mail* carried a short piece on Peter Brook's groundbreaking production of *Titus Andronicus* under the headline 'Old Titus makes them swoon at Stratford' ('Old Titus'). The review concerned itself primarily with the responses of the audience and tellingly captured the predominant mid-twentieth century view of the Roman tragedy as a drama of unrelenting violence, unfit to earn a place in the Shakespearean canon:

> Ten people were helped out by ambulance men during last week's performance at Stratford-on-Avon's Shakespeare Memorial Theatre. They had been overpowered by five acts of death and destruction. Said one of the ten last night: 'A woman behind us became hysterical. A man walked out looking sea-sick. Several dowagers drank whisky neat at the interval' ... Said one of last week's audience after

complaining to the theatre management: 'I cannot believe that Shakespeare ever wrote anything so horrible.'

Brook's production might have turned the stomachs of some of the Stratford faithful back in the 1950s, but it is now regarded as a seminal production, one whose stylization of bleeding and dismembered bodies brought a new aesthetic respectability to the play. Yet for all the success of this breakthrough production, it would take several more decades for the drama to become firmly embedded in the theatrical repertoire and to attract serious scholarly attention. Long dismissed for its ramshackle structure and cardboard characters, commentators laboured to find any moral purpose in what appeared to be its gratuitous violence and flagrant undermining of Roman virtues; moreover, its highly rhetorical language, replete with classical allusions and fragments of Latin, seemed to be disturbingly at odds with the brutality of its action. For many, such compositional infelicities were difficult to square with established thinking about Shakespeare and were often attributed to another author or explained away as a juvenile blunder.

The relatively recent turnaround in the play's academic fortunes can in part be attributed to the rise of post-structuralism in the second half of the twentieth century, which brought interesting new perspectives to bear on the play's language; at the same time, feminist theory offered fresh ways of interrogating its gender politics and, in particular, of interpreting Lavinia's 'martyred signs' (3.2.36). And while the play's reputation as a blood-and-guts spectacle still tends to go before it, over half a century or so of viewing television and cinema images of both real and fictional violence has done much to prepare audiences for the atrocities that so discountenanced those back in the 1950s. Far from being regarded as a work that indulges in violence for its own sake, it now tends to be read as a trenchantly ironic study of the vengeful human instinct and the self-defeating nature of revenge.

'Andronicus, surnamed Pius'

Titus was one of the earliest and most popular revenge tragedies of the early modern period. Set in the final days of the Roman Empire (though it mixes features of pre-Republican and Republican Rome), it charts a series of retributive acts that serve to problematize early modern notions of classical civilization. Titus' surname 'Pius' seems to mark him out as the embodiment of Roman values; however, it is a title that is put up for scrutiny with the hero's very first decision – to authorize the ritual sacrifice of Tamora's eldest son. Lucius' twice-stated desire to 'hew' (1.1.100, 132) the limbs of Alarbus calls to mind Shakespeare's Brutus articulating his vision of Caesar's assassination to his co-conspirator, Cassius:

> Let's kill him boldly, but not wrathfully:
> Let's carve him as a dish fit for the gods,
> Not hew him as a carcass fit for hounds.
>
> *JC*, 2.1.171–3

Considered in the light of Brutus' declaration, Lucius' intention to 'hew' the captive sounds more like base retributive violence than religious ritual: a truth driven home when Tamora accuses Titus of 'irreligious piety' (1.1.133), a memorable **oxymoron** that strikes a fissure between the hero and his 'surname'. And it is not only Titus' enemies that highlight the gap between his name and his actions. Before the first act is out, Titus' killing of Mutius will echo that of Alarbus, providing one of the play's numerous structural parallels – one reinforced by Marcus' proclaiming the deed one of 'impiety' (1.1.360).

Whereas the majority of revenge drama protagonists seek retribution only in response to what has been inflicted upon them or their loved ones, Titus could be regarded as the prime initiator of requital, his refusal to recognize any affinity between Tamora's parental grief and his own setting in motion a chain of horrific retaliatory crimes. From the outset, the dynamics of revenge are propelled by codes of honour whereby the political institution and the family are inextricably bound. On his return to Rome, Titus' defeat of the Goths is as much a victory for his family as it is for the state. Marcus announces that his brother 'with his sons' (1.1.29) has frightened away the enemy and Bassianus honours the successes of 'Titus and his sons' (1.1.53). Titus is, then, defined by his fatherhood and by the 'five-and-twenty valiant sons' (1.1.82) that have assisted him in public service. That twenty-one of this number lost their lives in the imperial cause is a testament not only to the family's loyal allegiance to Rome, but to Titus' authority as a father – an authority that is publicly challenged and shown to be tyrannical.

📖 *A number of scholars have suggested that the killing of Mutius is a late addition to the text, one that renders the play incoherent in several respects. Look closely at 1.1.294–319 and consider how far you would agree with this viewpoint.*

Titus' killing of his own child raises some puzzling issues, not least what the incident adds to the plotline. As the youngest son, the death of Mutius has no immediate hereditary consequences for the Andronici, nor is his death a direct factor in the play's politics of revenge. The incident itself sits rather awkwardly between Titus' request to follow him in pursuit of Lavinia (1.1.293) and Saturninus' reply some ten lines later, begging the question of how far the Emperor is aware of the barbaric act that has taken place in his absence. That he appears to give no response to an act as heinous as infanticide – an act he condemns as 'unnatural' (5.3.47) in relation to Titus' killing of his own daughter – is certainly perplexing. Also puzzling is Titus' inclusion of Mutius amongst his 'two-and-twenty sons' who 'died in honour's lofty bed' (3.1.10–11), when pleading for the lives of Quintus and Martius: a plain contradiction of his earlier denouncement of him as a 'villain boy'. Such textual oddities offer compelling, if ultimately unverifiable, evidence that Titus' killing of Mutius was a late insertion into an existing draft.

Whatever its textual history, the scene is undoubtedly crucial to the psychological development of the hero as avenger.

Mutius' public defiance of paternal authority is unconscionable for Titus, a humiliation so profound, it could be seen to influence his every subsequent action in the play. As Tom MacFaul observes: 'Titus' killing of Mutius seems to need no real justification ... The absolute quality of this paternal standard brooks no questioning. Titus has been "dishonoured by his sons in Rome" ... and in a sense he never really recovers from this' (MacFaul, 56). Titus enacts the Roman law of *patria potestas* in its most austere and ancient form whereby a father could kill a child of any age if he or she resisted his authority. That the killing is done in the time it takes to utter one **pentameter** line makes it appear a spontaneous response. Whether such spontaneity comes from a 'mistaken sense of honour and loyalty' (Bate, *Titus*, 7), built up over decades of inculcation into the patriarchal system or from the rash vindictiveness of an ageing patriarch, reacting against the public humiliation of not getting his own way, is open to question.

That Titus' killing of Mutius is immediately condemned by his remaining sons and brother underlines its aberrant nature, and that he desists from any further slaughter of rebellious family members, suggests that he too recognizes the error of his action. While Titus tells Lucius 'Nor thou, nor he, are any sons of mine', what appears to be a father's disinheritance never goes beyond a form of words. Doubtless, the hero's better judgement comes to the fore once the white-heat moment of Mutius blocking his path has passed, not to mention the sobering impact of the death of yet another son. Yet, as the extract clearly illustrates, Titus' decision to spare other unruly family members is also prompted by the gross ingratitude of Saturninus. Despite proving his unswerving allegiance to the principles of primogeniture over the will of the people in his support for Saturninus and his (unlawful) claim to Lavinia, Titus is nonetheless bracketed with his 'traitorous haughty sons'. For Titus, the Emperor's words are 'razors to [his] wounded heart', the violence of the **metaphor** conveying the sting of his disillusionment and anticipating the physical horrors to come. Though Titus puts up some initial resistance to burying Mutius with his 'brethren', he resigns himself to the family's will, a sign of forgiveness which he could be seen to extend posthumously to Mutius when he later counts him amongst the honoured twenty-two (3.1.10).

'The woefull'st man that ever lived in Rome'

For all its rhetorical excesses, *The Spanish Tragedy*, leaves an audience convinced that Hieronimo's grief at the death of his only child is intense and all-consuming. Titus, though, is likely to draw more ambivalent responses as a study of parental loss. As the father of twenty-six children, his killing of a son at the outset of the play and a daughter at its conclusion can be read as the actions of a man who accounts offspring expendable possessions, secondary to the Roman ideology he so staunchly embraces. One of Titus' first expressions of fatherly feeling concerns the burial rites of his sons who have fallen in battle:

> Titus, unkind and careless of thine own,
> Why suffer'st thou thy sons unburied yet
> To hover on the dreadful shore of Styx?
>
> 1.1.89–91

Here, Titus' use of **illeism** and his focus on public display strike a tonal note that seems – for a modern audience at least – out of tune with paternal grief; yet for this ultra-loyal Roman, observing due funeral rites is part of the 'natural' feelings of a father. And where Hieronimo speaks directly of his 'sweet son', Titus' terms of endearment are reserved for the family tomb, the symbol of his services to the state: 'O sacred receptacle of my joys,/Sweet cell of virtue and nobility' (1.1.95–6). Certainly, any examination of the revenge trajectory of *Titus* is complicated by the question of how far the Andronici's acts of retribution are driven and shaped by the unspeakable agony of a father, forced to witness the mutilation and suffering of his own children; or by an archetypal patriarch's desire to recover his own sense of honour.

The Andronici clan know full well the importance of the father's reputation in the eyes of the state. Lavinia pleads to be spared from rape 'for my father's sake' (2.2.158) and Marcus expresses her post-rape injuries as so horrific as to 'blind a father's eye' (2.3.53). In this honour culture, Titus is considered as much a victim of Chiron and Demetrius' attack as Lavinia and thus his pursuit of retributive justice is altogether more complex than the single-minded vengeance of Hieronimo.

While Titus' revenge is undoubtedly bound up with the public world of Rome, it also propels him into a private world of emotion that strips away the single-minded certainties of the warrior leader. His initial response to seeing his mutilated daughter has an austere power that anticipates late tragedies such as *King Lear*:

MARCUS
>This was thy daughter.

TITUS
>Why, Marcus, so she is.
>>3.1.63–4

Here, the bald half-lines suggest a moment where words falter; though, in outweighing his brother's utterance by one simple syllable, Titus' claim that Lavinia *'is'* rather than *'was'* proves the stronger. The sudden movement from full to half lines also marks a turning point in the play: Titus' humane assertion of his daughter's continuing existence reaches beyond any fear of losing face in Rome. Even so, alleviating the suffering of the child Titus declares is 'dearer than my soul' (3.1.103) is an undertaking for which he is ill-prepared. As he searches desperately for ways to ease Lavinia's suffering, he hits on an idea which is at once crazily grotesque and exquisitely tender:

> Or shall we cut away our hands like thine?
> Or shall we bite our tongues and in dumb shows
> Pass the remainder of our hateful days?
>> 3.1.131–3

Anticipating the severing of his own hand in a manner characteristic of the play's darkly comic irony, the bizarre suggestion demonstrates that this is a father more used to the brutality of the battlefield than the affective sphere of the family. At the same time, it insists that Lavinia should not be cast as Other – if she cannot be like fellow family members, then they must become like her.

Having entered the play world as a hero whose life has been shaped by the absolutes of state patriarchy and warfare, Titus, like Lear, encounters experiences that render him bemused, reduced to asking the desolate, helpless question: 'What shall we do?' (3.1.134). Aaron's deceitful offer of a reprieve for Quintus and Martius in return for Titus' severed hand gives him a momentary release from such confusion. Losing a limb holds no terrors for a man who has lived through years of military hardship and sacrificing his own hand to save his children is an action as automatic as his sacrificing of Mutius on the altar of patriarchy. It is only when this most Roman of sacrifices fails that Titus fully commits to the violent symmetries of revenge, to ensuring that 'all these mischiefs be returned again' (3.1.274). From this point forward, the family rallies to oppose the tyranny of the state: Lucius to lead a Gothic army, Marcus and Young Lucius to act as archer-messengers and the one-handed Titus, now fully retired from the warrior life, to cook up revenge in the kitchen.

The banquet scene completes the deconstruction of the binary opposition of barbarous Goths and civilized Romans established at the outset of the drama. Titus appears to have fallen into a state of abject depravity: feeding Tamora with the blood and flesh of her own children and killing his own daughter. Yet as any well-tutored schoolboy of Shakespeare's time would have known, both acts, however heinous, have roots in classical literature. The killing of Lavinia, underwritten by Livy's account of the killing of Virginia by her father to save her from the shame of rape, is carried out in the manner of an established ritual. The reverse structural patterning of Titus' farewell to Lavinia reinforces the Roman view that a daughter's disgrace duplicates through the father:

> Die, die, Lavinia, and thy shame with thee,
> And with thy shame thy father's sorrow die.
>
> 5.3.45–6

This, Titus' second act of infanticide, attracts a diversity of views. Is Lavinia complicit in the death or is it an imposition of patriarchal authority over an unwilling victim? Does Titus kill from fatherly compassion or as a means of asserting his ultimate control over his daughter's chastity? Or is it, at its core, an act of revenge for Lavinia's daring to choose her own marriage partner? It is only in performance that such troubling questions can be definitively answered – albeit temporarily.

'Old lad, I am thine own'

Described by one critic as a 'stunning metamorphosis' (Rutter, *Child's Play*, 95), Aaron's sudden transformation from out-and-out villain to loving father has intrigued audiences across the centuries. Edward Ravenscroft, whose adaptation of the play, *The Rape of Lavinia* (1687), played in Restoration theatres, clearly disapproved of such a sudden shift in sensibilities. In his version, the Moor's child is born prior to Titus' capture of Tamora and her sons, and nursed in secret, allowing time for the paternal bond to develop, thus making the eventual murder of the child at the hands of its own mother all the more distressing for the father to behold.

Today's critical readings tend to view Aaron's ardent paternity as a welcome sign of humanity in an unremittingly bleak drama. He is 'a better parent than either Titus or Tamora' (Jones, 59) whose 'feeling for the child ... has a quality of natural, unguarded affection' (Leggatt, 15). This may well be a valid reading though, as Emily Bartels observes, 'his tagging of his son as a "black slave," a "thick-lipped slave" ... has as much potential to convey antipathy as it does to convey affection' (Bartels, *Moor*, 91). Moreover, only a sentimentalist could ignore the possibility that Aaron's passion for his son is wrapped up in his own feelings of alterity. The only main character not to be 'incorporate in Rome' (1.1.467) at some point in the play, Aaron is offered the prospect of invading its territories through his son. His promise to bring him up to 'feed on berries and on roots' (4.2.179) in preparation for the warrior life provides an interesting parallel to *Antony and Cleopatra*, where Caesar relates how the heroic Antony would consume the 'roughest berry on the rudest hedge' (1.4.65) in order to survive the hardships of battle. In fact, Aaron's vision could be deemed a revenge fantasy, wherein 'his fruit of bastardy' (5.1.48) will grow to have the military fortitude of one of the great Romans – threateningly positioned within the enemy camp.

Whether Aaron's championing of his son is read as an extension of his own vengeful ambitions or as heartfelt fatherly love, what is certain is that any emergent humanity does not extend to empathy for others. Just as Hieronimo and Titus show little compassion for the paternal grief of others, so Aaron can love his own son at the same time as happily laughing at another father's loss:

> I pried me through the crevice of a wall
> When for his hand he had his two sons' heads,
> Beheld his tears and laughed so heartily
> That both mine eyes were rainy like to his

5.1.114–17

It falls to Lucius to determine the fate of Aaron and Tamora's offspring, though it still remains undecided at the play's close. Equally uncertain is whether the '[b]rave slip sprung from the great Andronicus' (5.1.9), whose initial insistence on a human sacrifice sparked a series of monstrous revenge acts, will manage to 'heal Rome's harms and wipe away her woe' (5.3.147).

Julie Taymor's *Titus* and the aesthetics of revenge

Julie Taymor's critically acclaimed adaptation of *Titus Andronicus* is classified as suitable viewing for adults only, a categorization that makes it a very rare thing indeed: an X-rated Shakespeare movie. The censor's rating was perhaps inevitable, given the film's extra-textual orgy scene and the director's refusal to stylize all of its spectacular atrocities – an approach that Brook's production helped to establish as a performance paradigm. Opting instead for a combination of stylization and realism, Taymor's directorial vision relied on keeping viewers alert to the play's horrors, desensitized neither by aesthetics nor by visceral actuality.

In what must count as one of the most memorable opening minutes of any Shakespeare film, a young boy in a makeshift paper-bag helmet sits at a typical 1950s American kitchen table, action figures and foodstuffs spread out in front of him. With the frenetic noise of television cartoons playing in the background, the boy's interaction with his toys grows ever more violent until the surface of the table – now splattered with blood-ketchup and layer-cake mud – resembles a battlefield in little. Visibly distressed, the child crouches underneath the table, a split-second before a blast shatters the kitchen window – and the frame of the twentieth-century world. Swept up into the arms of a burly man in motorbike helmet and goggles, the boy is carried through the door of his burning home and into a Roman coliseum, 'the archetypal theater of cruelty' (Blumenthal, 230). So the Rome of the play world is established, as the boy in the American kitchen becomes the Young Lucius of Shakespeare's tragedy and a major focalizer of the violent acts still to unfold. Indeed, the youngest character in the play carries much of the film's ideological weight. Though the child in the opening sequence appears to have the violent instincts of one of Gloucester's 'wanton boys' (*KL*, 4.1.38) and then, as Young Lucius, witnesses all manner of cruelty, the film's final slow-motion shot of him carrying Aaron's baby out of the coliseum and into a new dawn suggests a surprising victory for compassion.

The ending of *Titus* is regarded by some as a capitulation to Hollywood sentimentality, a turning away from the play's bleak, deterministic vision of retributive violence. Yet Taymor's ending, like Shakespeare's, is by no means unequivocal. Just as play audiences are left to wonder whether Lucius will manage to restore peace and stability, so film viewers have to wonder about Young Lucius' ability to protect the baby; this is, after all, the same baby that his father had earlier suggested should be hanged so that Aaron 'may see it sprawl' (5.1.51). Reflecting on the making of *Titus*, Taymor observed: 'Sitting safely in my New York apartment as war rages in Kosovo, Yugoslavia, brings home the horrible irony that we shot this film just a few months ago in Croatia. *Titus* will premiere as the millennium comes to an end. May the child finally exit the Colosseum as the new millennium rolls in' (Blumenthal, 243). It is a comment that underscores both an acute awareness of the perennial nature of violence and a reluctance to accept its absolute inevitability.

Representing Lavinia: The director's cut

The most frequently discussed sequence in *Titus* is the two minutes of screen time that capture Marcus' first encounter with the raped and mutilated Lavinia. This is a moment in the play guaranteed to exercise any modern film or theatre director, not least because today's sensibilities around the crime of rape differ so appreciably from those of Shakespeare's audiences. As Kim Solga points out: 'rape's dramatic representation among the early moderns reflects not what a modern audience might understand about the experience – the victim's heinous bodily and psychic suffering – but rather what rape means to those to whom it is reported . . . who also bear the heavy responsibility to absolve the victim of any potential complicity and to mobilize the force of the law'

(Solga, 31). While it is wise to be alert to overestimating just how much more enlightened modern attitudes are to rape, Jonathan Bate is surely right in asserting that, for today's female directors, 'rape matters ... more than it could possibly have done to Shakespeare writing for Marcus' (Bate, *Titus*, 63).

Read Marcus' speech (2.3.13–57) and evaluate the challenges it presents for modern stage or film performance.

Marcus' speech has attracted diverse readings. It has been viewed as 'partly transforming the immediate horror of the spectacle into something more iconic and emblematic' (Dillon, 31), as underlining 'the *failure* of Lavinia's body to fit even those classical tableaux of horrific rape' (Little, 54) and as a verbal means of repeating the 'atrocity in a different key' (Leggatt, 18). Yet whatever the intellectual challenges the speech might offer to critical readers, it is the practical implications of the speech that prove testing to directors. However much audiences nowadays might accept that early modern drama was not a realist art form, it is nonetheless difficult for them to fathom the sight of an uncle delivering an **ekphrastic** monologue, while his niece stands bleeding before him. As several critics have quipped, this seems more a time for first aid than fancy words.

In such circumstances, Marcus' speech is prone to coming across as crass and insensitive, its focus on Lavinia's physical appearance offering disturbing parallels with the **blazon**. Yet Shakespeare is by no means alone in defamiliarizing and subverting this courtly love convention: Ford subjects it to a savage vivisection in *'Tis Pity She's a Whore* in which the eloquence of Giovanni's itemizing of Annabella's body in poetic terms becomes a bloody anatomical reality; and Middleton exposes its dark underside through Vindice's apostrophizing to Gloriana's skull, whose 'unsightly rings' had once been 'two heaven-pointed diamonds' (*Revenger's Tragedy*, 1.1.19–20).

*Watch Taymor's treatment of Marcus' encounter with the 👁
mutilated Lavinia and think about the following:*

- *How is the aftermath of the attack on Lavinia represented?*
- *How is Marcus' response to the sight of his niece conveyed to the viewer?*

One of the most striking aspects of this brief sequence is its desolate environment. Redolent of one of Paul Nash's haunting First World War landscape paintings, the swamp, with its pools of muddy water and bare, gnarled tree stumps functions as 'a metaphor for the ravishment of Lavinia' (Blumenthal, 236). The abrupt shift from the relative realism of the pre-rape forest setting to this strange marshland seems to enact Lavinia's abrupt shift of consciousness from confident newly-wed to traumatized rape victim. Moreover, though Marcus' allusions to the story of Philomel are cut from the script, the gauzy white undergarment immediately signifies her violation, prompting the viewer to recall the moments when Chiron savagely cuts the buttons off Lavinia's heavy black riding habit to reveal glimpses of that same underwear.

As a prelude to the rape, Tamora's sons forcibly remove Lavinia's black leather gloves to reveal the white fingers inside, fingers which they lick in a manner that anticipates both her rape and dismemberment. However, nothing prepares the viewer for what is surely the most striking image of Taymor's sequence: the sight of the raped Lavinia, twigs appearing to grow, Daphne-like, from out of her stumps. Just as Brook translated the imagery of the 'crimson river' and 'bubbling fountain' of Lavinia's blood into bright red ribbons hanging from Vivien Leigh's mouth and wrists, so Taymor takes the arboreal image of hands being 'lopped and hewed' as her inspiration, 'a poetic metamorphosis in the manner of Ovid' (Blumenthal, 184). While modern cinematic techniques can picture bodily wounds with verisimilar precision, Taymor uses such techniques to achieve rather less literal effects: 'Using blue-screen gloves we were able to digitally remove the actress's hands and through computer-generated imagery create a splay of twigs in their place. The result is surreal and poetic, in keeping with my vision of the work and not falling into the trap of utter realism' (Blumenthal, 236). Exhibited on a tree-stump pedestal, Lavinia is figured as the cruel reality behind the courtly love language in which Chiron and Demetrius express their 'passions for Lavinia's love' (1.1.535).

* * *

Marcus' poetic monologue in response to Lavinia's horrific injuries has often been cut completely in stage productions. However, where the theatre director has little or no option but to keep Lavinia in full view of the audience while Marcus delivers his speech, the film director has complete control of how long and how intensely they gaze at her at this point in the narrative. That is not to say that a performance of this scene always benefits from the freedoms offered by the camera. Jane Howell's BBC television production (1985) retains all but a line and a half of Marcus' speech: an editing decision that does not sit easily with the camera's starkly realistic capture of a bruised and bloody Lavinia, staring in terror and bewilderment at her stumps. As if heeding the lessons of Howell's version, Taymor keeps only the first seven and the last six lines of Marcus' speech and presents Lavinia with a much greater degree of abstraction.

A **tracking shot** presents Marcus walking through forest trees to the **diegetic** sound of loud birdsong, emerging abruptly on the edge of desolate swampland: a transition that seems to mirror that of the rape victim. An **establishing wide shot** of the bleak new terrain fixes Marcus' viewpoint prior to his identifying the figure of his niece in the distance. Alternating shots of Lavinia, stranded on a tree stump, and of the rapidly approaching Marcus, capture his perspective from first recognition to the moment of horrified realization – marked by the highly realistic blood that gushes from Lavinia's swollen lips, a seemingly furious answer to the question 'Why dost not speak to me?' Marcus' response to this shocking instant is captured in a twenty-second **close-up reaction shot** that seems to freeze the action and create the dream-like quality suggested in the opening line of the monologue: 'If I do dream, would all my wealth would wake me'. As if shaking off a moment of paralysis, Marcus takes three steps forward, the scene's first **two-shot** capturing the moment when, compassion overriding horror, he sweeps her up into protective arms.

* * *

Some performance critics have evinced discomfort at the way in which some of *Titus'* most violent scenes are made ravishing to the spectator's eye. Yet, as Taymor herself points out to her cast in a pre-production meeting (*The Making of Titus*, YouTube), there are many beautiful art works that depict the brutal and the grotesque. And, like all such art works, the degree of aesthetic pleasure to be found in Taymor's *Titus* will ultimately rest with the viewer.

Further reading

Pascale Aebischer, *Shakespeare's Violated Bodies: Stage and Screen Performance* (Cambridge, 2004)

Warren Chernaik, *The Myth of Rome in Shakespeare and his Contemporaries* (Cambridge, 2011)

Cary DiPietro and Hugh Grady, 'Presentism, Anachronism, and *Titus Andronicus*' in Cary DiPietro and Hugh Grady (eds), *Shakespeare and the Urgency of Now* (Basingstoke, 2013)

Erika T. Lin, *Shakespeare and the Materiality of Performance* (New York, 2012)

G. Harold Metz, *Shakespeare's Earliest Tragedy: Studies in* Titus Andronicus (Madison, 1996)

6

Transgressive desire:

Measure for Measure and *'Tis Pity She's a Whore*

In a thought-provoking Afterword to a recent study of early modern sexuality, Valerie Traub recommends that teachers of *Romeo and Juliet* ask their students what they think Romeo and Juliet get up to on their wedding night (Bromley and Stockton, 303). While there is clearly no definitive answer to such a provocative question, just attempting to find one highlights some of the challenges that inhere in exploring sixteenth-century sexualities in the twenty-first century. One such comes from contemplating a thirteen-year-old girl having sex which, according to Western law today, is in itself a transgressive act, one that is potentially abusive and damaging for the 'natural' development of the young person. In order to suspend their sensibilities surrounding age-appropriateness, modern audiences are inclined to regard the sexually-active Juliet as a product of her time, readily accepting the drama as a romantic love story and, in so doing, acknowledging that attitudes to sexual behaviour change over time. However, estimating precisely how and to what extent notions of normative sexuality shift from century to century is highly problematic, especially when dealing with a dramatic text.

Plays tend to gather their energy from extreme behaviour and scenarios and *Romeo and Juliet* is no exception. Shakespeare's sexualizing of an early-teenage girl, while not carrying the associations it does today, was nonetheless provocative. By choosing to set the play in a Catholic country where young brides were more usual than in England (where the average age of marriage was closer to the mid-twenties than the mid-teens), Shakespeare presents a situation that was, even by Elizabethan standards, 'foreign'. Considering early modern drama's treatment of sexuality, then, requires a diachronic perspective that is at once alert to historical, social and cultural difference, as well as to the nature of theatrical representation itself.

After taking account of the age-of-consent issue, the next stage in answering Traub's question involves imagining exactly *how* the lovers have sex. Perhaps the most obvious response is to assume that sex is transhistorical and to picture them doing much the same as lovers might today. But this seemingly common-sense view fails to take into account that nowadays there is no common agreement about what actually constitutes 'sex'; opinions vary appreciably as to whether, say, phone sex, mutual masturbation or toe-sucking count as 'having sex'. However, Bromley and Stockton are surely right in their assertion that penile–vaginal intercourse remains the most commonly understood definition (Bromley and Stockton, 3). Such a definition has been significantly shaped and perpetuated by psychoanalytic theory, with its firm conviction that sex is an unchanging instinctual drive whose 'normal' aim is penetrative heterosexual intercourse. Inevitably, this demarcation of the normative brought with it correlative definitions of the 'perverse' and the 'deviant', as the emerging turn-of-the-century science of sexology began to embed terms such as 'heterosexuality' and 'homosexuality' into mainstream discourse. Such conceptions of sexuality were comprehensively interrogated around the mid-twentieth century when works such as Michel Foucault's three-volume *History of Sexuality* mounted an intellectually brilliant 'constructionist' challenge to the prevailing 'essentialist' paradigm. According to Foucault:

> Sexuality must not be described as a stubborn drive, by nature alien and of necessity disobedient to a power which exhausts itself trying to subdue it and often fails to control it entirely. It appears rather as an especially dense transfer point for relations of power: between men and women, young people and old people, parents and offspring, teachers and students, priests and laity, an administration and a population.
>
> FOUCAULT, *Will*, 103

Sexual feelings and practices are not 'natural' but predetermined by political, social and cultural forces and their associated discourses. Foucault held up for scrutiny the late nineteenth-century medicalization of sexual behaviour and the persecution of 'perverse' sexual behaviours, averring that while the 'sodomite had been a temporary aberration; the homosexual was now a species' (*Will*, 43). Seen from a Foucauldian perspective, those sexual activities considered transgressive in the early modern period would not have marked out those who engaged in them as belonging to any particular 'species': sex acts were what humans *did* not who they *were*.

Any serious scholarly endeavour to understand the sexual feelings, behaviours and attitudes of the early moderns requires the study of a range of contemporary writings such as legal documents, medical writings and conduct books. Taken together, such printed materials offer diverse, often conflicting, perspectives and 'facts' about areas such as reproductive anatomy, sexual arousal and gender difference. A common thread running through such works is the citing of biblical text to illustrate the difference between licit and transgressive sexual conduct. As biblical literalists, the early moderns looked to the Pentateuch for their model of human sexuality. In the well-known treatise *The Secret Miracles of Nature* by Dutch physician Levinus Lemnius (first published in Latin in 1564),

Genesis is interpreted in a way that presents the companionate marriage as fundamental to God's design, a means of controlling the carnal desire that prompted humans to be 'fruitful and multiply' (Gen. 2.28):

[H]e gave a woman for an helper and companion, and he put into them both force to love, and a greedy desire of procreating their like ... For unlesse this were natural to all kind of Creatures, that they should care for posterity, and propagate their like; mankind would quickly be lost ... Since this Passion is so forcible and so unruly that it can hardly be subdued (and but a few can bridle their passions) God granted unto man the use of the matrimonial bed, that he might be bounded thereby

LEMNIUS, 1: 8–9

While Lemnius' exegesis confirms the libido as entirely natural, it also insists on its predisposition towards the transgressive, a tendency vividly exemplified in Genesis's stories of adultery, masturbation and incest. Bible readers who ventured a little further into the Old Testament would find plenty more tales of sexual 'abominations'; Leviticus 18, for instance, includes cautions against sex during menstruation, intercourse with a neighbour's wife, sodomy and bestiality. And it was not only the fire-and-brimstone pages of the scriptures that were quoted to mark out certain sexual practices as aberrant. Equally fitted to the purpose were Pauline teachings on sexual morality and marriage, which included the dire warning that 'neither the immoral ... nor adulterers, nor sexual perverts' (1 Cor. 6.9–10) should inherit the kingdom of God.

If the Bible alerted sexual sinners to the punishment they should expect to endure in the afterlife, tracts by polemicists such as Philip Stubbes drew their attention to more earthly torments. Those who indulged in 'whoredom' (a catch-all term for sexual promiscuity) would bear the consequences in their flesh: '[I]t dimmeth the sight, it impayreth the hearing, it infirmeth the sinewes, it weakneth the joynts, it exhausteth the marow, consumeth the moysture and supplement of the bodie, it riveleth the face ... it weakeneth the whole body, it bringeth consumption, it causeth ulceration, scabbe, scurffe, blaine, botch, packes and byles, it maketh hoare haires, balde pates' (Stubbes, 54).

Those convinced by Stubbes's invective might well have considered abstinence the safest route to physical well-being but this, too, carried a health warning. In post-Reformation England, celibacy was associated with Catholicism and the tyranny of the papacy. Monasticism was viewed as unnatural, liable to lead to the type of sexual transgressions outlined in Robert Burton's encyclopaedic study of human learning, *The Anatomy of Melancholy*: 'Nature, youth, and this furious passion forcibly inclines, and rageth on the one side: but their order and vow checkes them on the other ... from such rash vowes, and inhumane manner of life proceed many inconveniences, many diseases, many vices, mastupration, Satyriasis, Priapismus, melancholy, madnesse, fornication, adultery, buggery, Sodomy ... and all manner of mischiefes' (Burton, 586). Too little or too much control over desire could, then, lead to damnable sexual practices. Getting the balance right was crucial to an individual's social standing; burdened as they were by original sin, no human was free from sexual urges and only those who practised appropriate restraint would deserve their community's respect.

Given the harmful social consequences of sexual transgression, such as venereal disease, illegitimate children and family breakdown, the responsibility for curbing desire was not left to the individual. As the early modern historian, Laura Gowing, explains:

> Seventeenth-century sex was intensively regulated. Sex outside marriage was subject to the discipline of the church courts, the local courts, the quarter sessions, and – in cases of rape – the assizes ... Illicit sex was the business both of secular magistrates, who were charged with punishing fornicators and establishing the paternity of illegitimate

children, and of the church courts, whose responsibility was
the moral crimes of adultery and fornication.

GOWING, 85

The 'facts' on which such external governance of sexuality were based were deeply flawed and often plain wrong. Though the physiological sciences developed rapidly in the early modern period, they were still at a rudimentary stage (with England some way behind the Continent), knowledge about sexual reproduction being informed more by a mix of classical writings and biblical commandment than by the empirical method. A baby born with physical abnormalities (a 'monstrous birth') was taken as evidence of maternal sexual deviancy and was for some a reassuring sign of God's providence. And women were often the victims of erroneous medical knowledge if they fell pregnant as a consequence of rape. The common belief that conception only occurred with the female orgasm meant that the pregnant victim was often not believed in court: if she had experienced a sexual climax, then she had clearly consented. While this conception myth was beginning to be challenged by medical scholars such as Helkiah Crooke who, although conceding that the best chances of conception come from mutual orgasm, argued that 'women do sometimes conceive without pleasure ... against their wils' (Crooke, 283), it was firmly rooted in the thinking of the period and, surprisingly, would carry some influence well into the twentieth century.

Where the church and state sought to control the population's sex lives, the theatre was a place where they could be represented and opened out for debate. For those with no great interest in exploring the complexities of human sexuality, the stage provided ample titillation in the form of the bodily presence of the actors and the sexual puns, innuendoes and rhythms of their speech. Unsurprisingly, the representation of sexual desire on an open platform in broad daylight proved anathema to opponents of the theatre, who made much of the close proximity of the playhouse and the brothel. Henry Crosse, thought to be a Puritan minister, held the theatre to account for inciting the whole gamut of transgressive conduct in his 1603 work, *Vertues Common-wealth or the High-way to Honour*:

> For is not vice set to sale on open Theaters? is there not a *Sodome* of filthinesse painted out? and tales of carnall love, adulterie, ribaldrie, leacherie, murther, rape, interlarded with a thousand uncleane speeches, even common schooles of bawdrie? is not this the way to make men ripe in all kinde of villanie, and corrupt the manners of the whole world?
>
> CROSSE, 112

How far Crosse's contention that the dramatic representation of vice would be imitated by theatregoers had any basis in fact is impossible to establish, though he was certainly correct in his assertion that plays of the time dealt with some highly transgressive subject matter. Fornication, adultery, homoerotic desire, incest, prostitution, rape and libertinism were all staples of the early modern theatrical repertoire and were treated with an explicitness that would prove offensive to post-Shakespearean audiences well into the twentieth century.

This chapter examines two plays that deal with abidingly controversial sexual issues. How far these issues continue to be thought of as 'transgressive', however, varies from play to play. *Measure for Measure* is a particularly interesting example of how historical distance can skew what might have been a drama's original emphasis. While today's audiences are probably more inclined to consider Angelo a rapist than their Jacobean counterparts, they are far less inclined to view premarital sex as a transgressive act. *'Tis Pity She's a Whore*, on the other hand, focuses on sexual behaviour that sat – and still sits – outside the majority view of the 'acceptable': brother-sister incest.

Measure for Measure

The Victorian writer and critic, Walter Pater, found in *Measure for Measure* the 'true seal of experience, like a fragment of life itself, rough and disjointed' (Pater, 170). Certainly the play world is closer to the lived experience of its original audiences than some of Shakespeare's earlier comedies – it is hard to imagine a red-light district in *Twelfth Night*'s Illyria or one of the Athenian gentlemen of *A Midsummer Night's Dream* discussing the local bawd's sciatica. Much of the play's realism comes from its concentration on issues such as prostitution, sexually transmitted diseases and illegitimacy. This engagement with social 'problems' often regarded as perennial makes it more than usually open to presentist approaches, which take the here-and-now as the point of departure for any critical reading. Since the 1960s, the play has been repurposed in response to new ways of thinking about gender equality, sexuality and marriage, as well as to sexual health challenges such as the emergence of HIV and AIDS. And in the past few decades there have been plenty of headline news stories offering fresh frames of reference for this early modern text: Britain's Director of Public Prosecutions cautioned for kerb-crawling in the early 1990s; Bill Clinton's denial that he had had sexual relations with a White House intern during his term of office; and historic sexual abuse cases involving high-profile figures from both the US and Europe, too numerous to name.

What is accounted sexually transgressive is to a large extent dictated by a particular culture at a particular time, though even in the same time and place universal agreement over sexual morality is rare (look, for instance, at the current variation in the age of consent across European jurisdictions and, until 2015, in the same-sex marriage legislation across American states). For some earlier generations, *Measure for Measure*'s focus on sexual transgression proved rebarbative. The early nineteenth-century editors of the hugely popular *Family Shakespeare* found the comedy resistant to their usual textual deep-cleansing on account of 'the indecent expressions with which many of the scenes abound' (Bowdler, 86). And although by the late nineteenth century, progressives such as George Bernard Shaw were hailing *Measure for Measure* as ready and waiting for the dawn of the twentieth century, it would take until the second half of that century for the play to enter the mainstream Shakespearean repertoire. Peter Brook's Stratford production of 1950 is often identified as the turning point in the play's theatrical fortunes, a shift buoyed up by increasingly liberal social attitudes towards sex. Twenty years later, the relaxation of theatre censorship would bring even greater freedom for directors of the play, paving the way for sexually explicit stagings of Vienna's sex-addiction (joyless *fellatio*, masturbating to pornography, and sex workers strutting around in fetish gear have all become staple background activities for today's productions).

If theatrical interpretations of *Measure for Measure* incline towards filling the historical gap between Shakespeare's age and the present, any academic study of the play needs to take account of the historical specificity of its setting. The laws and attitudes that governed sexual behaviour in the early sixteenth century are far removed from those that regulate sexuality in the Western world today. Unmarried mothers are no longer imprisoned or brought before the bawdy courts; nor are they regarded as having committed a 'sin of heavier kind' (2.3.28) than the father's. And while the stigma of illegitimacy is now more or less a thing of the (quite recent) past, in the early modern period, children born outside of marriage were commonly viewed as both a drain on the economy and a threat to social cohesion. As Alison Findlay explains: 'The absence of the father in the little commonwealth of the family was an implicit challenge to Renaissance authority ... The existing hierarchy was suddenly not as natural as those who promoted it suggested' (Findlay, 3–4).

One other essential difference between the milieu of *Measure for Measure* and that of the present lies in the conflicts between old and new faiths that underwrite much of the play's treatment of sexuality. Indeed, how far original audiences would have responded to the play as an endorsement of Isabella's elective chastity or as an indictment of conventual life is a compelling, if ultimately unanswerable, question.

'All sects, all ages, smack of this vice'

When Angelo urges Isabella to sleep with him, he defines the sensation of sex as 'sweet uncleanness' (2.4.54), an **oxymoron** that might stand for *Measure for Measure*'s view of human sexuality. That sex is 'sweet' is evidenced by the sheer number of characters from all classes in Viennese society who have given into its temptations; that it is 'unclean' is reinforced by the text's insistence on its consequences: venereal disease, bastardy and prison. As countless academic studies have pointed out, the play bears more than a trace of Shakespeare's Sonnet 129, which defines sex as 'A bliss in proof, and proved, a very woe'. Claudio laments his sexual transgression in similar terms:

> Our natures do pursue,
> Like rats that ravin down their proper bane,
> A thirsty evil; and when we drink, we die.
>
> 1.2.128–30

Though Claudio and Juliet's relationship is sometimes held up as the play's sole example of healthy, natural sexuality (with Lucio's agricultural imagery at 1.4.41–4 often cited in support), Claudio's comparison of erotic desire to vermin glutting on their own poison is at odds with such a romantic reading. Likewise, the brief detail that the finalizing of the marriage had been postponed '[o]nly for propagation of a dower' (1.2.147) tinges the pair with the city realities of pecuniary exchange. What *does* set Claudio and Juliet's sexual relationship apart from the rest of the play, however, is its mutuality. In one of the principal literary sources for *Measure for Measure*, Cinthio's *Hecatommithi* (1565), Vico, the Claudio figure, is arrested because he 'had done violence to a virgin' (Lever, 156); Shakespeare's insistence on the couple's sin being 'mutually committed' (2.3.27) radically changes this element of the story, rendering it much less transgressive for original playgoers, most of whom would have inclined to the view that fornication between an established couple should incur no more harsh punishment than an appearance at the 'bawdy court'.

In the play's final scene, the Duke, still disguised as a friar, reports that he has 'seen corruption boil and bubble/Till it o'errun the stew' (5.1.316–17). Audiences at the Globe would doubtless have recognized in this vision of Vienna the image of their own city. As Leah Marcus points out in an important new-historicist reading of *Measure for Measure* 'reform was very much in the air in London, 1604. The city was taking on a reputation for exceptional vigor against vice' (Marcus, *Puzzling*, 175). Playgoers travelling past – or even visiting – the 'stews' of Bankside on their way to the theatre would have encountered the vices in question writ large. A survey of playtexts circulating in the early years of James I's reign reveals a preoccupation with the world of the brothel. Prostitutes appear as the eponymous heroines of Thomas Dekker's provocatively titled two-part city comedy *The Honest Whore* (1604) and John Marston's *The Dutch Courtesan* (1605), performed in 1613 to honour the marriage of James I's daughter, the Princess Elizabeth. And in *Pericles* (1607–8), Shakespeare would revisit the brothel-world of *Measure for Measure*, though with rather more focus on the life of the prostitute. Marina, a young princess, is stolen by pirates and sold to a pimp. As the brothel keepers vainly attempt to initiate her into the ways of the world and '[c]rack the glass of her virginity' (4.5.146–7), the drama underlines the extent to which women's bodies were treated as commodities to be appraised, priced and sold. Yet while the low-life scenes of *Pericles* are in some respects more sexually explicit than *Measure for Measure*'s, Marina's conversion of a potential client to the path of righteousness, and her eventual release thereby, takes the play away from the often dark world of the problem comedies and into the more benign world of the romance.

In the Restoration period, public taste turned away from brothel scenes on stage and adaptations of *Measure for Measure*, such as William Davenant's *The Law Against Lovers* (1662) and Charles Gildon's *Measure for Measure; or, Beauty the Best Advocate* (1700), erased them entirely. It would take well into the twentieth century for what Peter Brook called the 'roughness and dirt' of the brothel to be reinstated (Brook, 88).

📖 *Read the first brothel scene in* Measure for Measure *(1.2.44–115) and then consider the text in light of the critical extract below, taken from Tony Tanner's* Prefaces to Shakespeare.

> Dr Johnson found them [the brothel scenes] 'very natural and pleasing' . . . Walter Pater is even more enthusiastic. 'It brings before us a group of persons, attractive, full of desire, vessels of the genial, seed-bearing powers of nature, a gaudy existence flowering out over the old court and city of Vienna, a spectacle of the fullness and pride of life which to some may seem to touch the verge of wantonness.' *Touch the verge!* One applauds the tolerance, but perhaps has to deprecate the idealizing – some of the figures are amiable enough, and they certainly provide the only *comedy* in the play; but they are meant, surely, to be seen as emissaries from a pretty foul and degraded world.
>
> TANNER, 277–8

This extract engages with an enduring critical question concerning the play's low-life scenes: are they life-affirming in their bawdy vitality or expressive of a sordid world, where human beings are bought and sold? Justification for both perspectives can be found in Shakespeare's brothel scene. As the master of licentiousness, Lucio's banter with the unnamed gentlemen brings a lively urbanity to the scene, and the easy, quick-paced prose that passes between two contrasting social groups – the gentlemen and the bawd – promotes a certain democratic spirit. After the gentlemen exit, Pompey's insistent punning and refusal to be cowed in the face of the proclamation that the suburban whorehouses are to be 'plucked down', seem to confirm what Pater calls the 'fullness and pride of life'. Yet, there is surely more in the language of the extract to support Tanner's contention that the audience is presented with 'emissaries from a pretty foul and degraded world'. The quick-fire puns of the libertines who haunt Mistress Overdone's establishment revolve around syphilis and its physical consequences: baldness, bone disease and sciatica. Early audiences of the scene would doubtless have been acutely aware of these debilitating effects on the body. As Bruce Boehrer explains in *Environmental Degradation in Jacobean Drama*, the gruesome physical symptoms of syphilis (including ulcers, rashes and granulomas), not to mention the incapacitating neurological conditions that took hold in the tertiary stage, meant that the disease 'came to be identified with the ostensible moral decay of early modern urban life' and '[w]ith the spectacle of syphilitic suffering and degradation constantly before their eyes, the writers, actors, and playgoers of Jacobean London had good reason to obsess about the disease' (Boehrer, 25). The brothel-banter of 1.2 could, then, be read as the brittle verbal surface covering a city-deep malaise.

Pompey's vulgar innuendo ('Groping for trouts') and punning on the verb 'to do' might also function as a comic means of masking the darker reality to be found in Overdone's lines, all of which are grounded in the plain fact of her indigent condition. As she makes plain, the brothel is a place stamped with sweat, war and the gallows, a version which is hard to square with Pater's. Faced with the very real threat of losing her trade, her situation and that of the gentlemen she serves seem miles apart: the brothel might bring all sectors of the community together, but, syphilis notwithstanding, it is the poor who will suffer most from its destruction. As the soon-to-be reformed libertine Freevill argues to his soon-to-be-corrupted puritanical friend, Malheureux, in *The Dutch*

Courtesan, the sex trade was often the only means of survival for those down on their luck:

> A poor decayed mechanical man's wife, her husband is laid up; may not she lawfully be laid down, when her husband's only rising is by his wife's falling?
>
> 1.1.102–5

The perils of celibacy

One of *Measure for Measure*'s most unsettling features is its refusal to offer any satisfactory corrective to the 'wanton stings and motions of the sense' (1.4.59) or any means of escaping its damaging consequences. The novitiate Isabella's entry into the celibate life of the convent is interrupted when she is compelled to plead for her brother's life, a task which requires her to defend the very vice she claims to 'abhor' (2.2.29) and which exposes her to the sexual aggression of a man who proves more 'virgin-violator' (5.1.43) than upright official of 'stricture and firm abstinence' (1.3.12). So the central transgressive act of the play, Claudio's 'untrussing' (3.2.172), becomes imbricated in the sexual desires and resistances of both his prosecutor and defender. Angelo and Isabella are commonly noted as a well-matched pair: both absolutists and confirmed celibates. Following the logic of this neat structural parallel, they are frequently diagnosed with the same psychosexual disorder brought on when 'virginity has itself become a mode of excess' (Garber, *Age*, 130); or, alternatively, as the two halves of a sadomasochistic union. In the play's analogues, the sexual relationship between the man in authority and the erring brother's sister is more a matter of fact than speculation. Cinthio's tale sees Epitia agree to Iuriste's sexual demands and concludes with the two marrying and living together 'in great happiness' (Lever, 165). Similarly in Whetstone's *The Historie of Promos and Cassandra*, the heroine sleeps with the blackmailer and ends up married and 'tyed in the greatest bondes of affection' to him (Lever, 167). In contrast, Isabella and Angelo are never brought together in any physical or marital union, their sexual 'compatibility' emerging instead from psychoanalytic readings of the text's rich linguistic ambiguities.

There is certainly plenty of textual evidence to construct a persuasive case for erotic affinities between Angelo and Isabella, although there are some striking differences to be found in the degree to which their sexual feelings are rendered explicit. Angelo's desire provides the main focus for his soliloquies, its strength calculable from the way in which it drives much of the play's action. How far Isabella is subject to sexual yearnings, if at all, is made much less explicit. Her one and only soliloquy at the end of 2.4 speaks her determination to continue a celibate existence, concluding with one of the most frequently discussed lines of the text: 'More than our brother is our chastity' (2.4.184). Isabella's decision to put her chastity above all else has often been attributed to her 'sex inhibitions' (Knight, 102) and while feminist scholars have taken such views to task, offering alternative, female-centred readings, there remains a critical reluctance to accept her stance as one of reasoned principle. Certain of Isabella's speeches have attracted a store of close readings, with critics detecting richly erotic undercurrents, unconscious innuendoes and even conscious sexual provocation in and between the lines. Informed by psychoanalytic theory, her behaviour has been interpreted as demonstrating classic signs of repressed sexuality, masochistic tendencies and even a predilection for sadism. A good deal of this critical attention has rested on just four lines:

> were I under the terms of death,
> Th' impression of keen whips I'd wear as rubies,
> And strip myself to death as to a bed
> That longing have been sick for, ere I'd yield
> My body up to shame.
>
> 2.4.100–4

This passionate vision of self-harm is frequently read as one of the most sexually transgressive moments of the play. David McCandless speculates that: 'Isabella may be sufficiently aware of her provocation of Angelo, sufficiently appreciative of the power she thereby commands, and sufficiently distressed by a sting of reciprocal attraction to feel that her own stimulated, errant flesh stands in need of corrective flaying' (McCandless, 106). Reluctant to contemplate a sexless Isabella, McCandless suggests that not only might she be aware of the sexual power she wields over Angelo – an awareness that does not necessarily require her to have any desire of her own – she might also be physically excited by him.

If the absence of any direct expression of Isabella's sexuality in the playtext generates multiple readings, so too does its rather more explicit presentation of Angelo's carnality. Readings of the Deputy's sexual transgressiveness have, inevitably, changed substantially over time. Writing back in the 1950s, F.R. Leavis's conviction that '[i]f we don't see ourselves in Angelo, we have taken the play very imperfectly' (Leavis, 172) situates Angelo as a kind of everyman figure; whereas Alan Sinfield finds in Angelo 'the misogyny of the rapist, who desires to spoil the pure, to violate, to hurt and degrade' (Sinfield, *Authority*, 182), a twenty-first-century viewpoint in step with modern feminist thinking. While the majority of today's critics agree on the abusive nature of Angelo's behaviour towards Isabella, theories accounting for why his dormant libido awakens so abruptly yield considerable variety: it is stirred 'by prohibition' (Maus, *Norton*, 2024), by the 'pleasure of rhetorical debate' (Knapp, 277) or because Isabella 'addresses him as a human being rather than as a man' (Dusinberre, 224) – to cite but a few examples. Yet while it is feasible, indeed desirable, for academic study to encourage and accommodate such a multiplicity of perspectives, a director faced with bringing the playtext alive on stage must arrive at some kind of definitive reading.

Read 2.2 in its entirety, looking especially closely at lines 162–87.

- *Analyse how Shakespeare presents Angelo's sexual awakening here.*
- *How far does the soliloquy encourage a sympathetic audience response to Angelo?*

As one influential scholar of Shakespeare in performance observes, '[t]he presentation of sexual passion has very special difficulties for a dramatist, especially at a time when plays were performed on open stages almost surrounded by a potentially unruly audience' (Brown, 'Sexuality', 169), and this first meeting between Angelo and Isabella must have offered plenty to excite an amphitheatre crowd. Placing the incorrigible libertine Lucio on stage adds an undertow of licentiousness to the scene, as he commentates in asides on how well his theory that 'when maidens sue,/Men give like gods' (1.4.80–1) works in practice. Urged on by Lucio, Isabella, the 'woeful suitor', delivers over twice the number of lines as the powerful Deputy. Angelo's near silence offers ample opportunity for an actor's face and body to register his response to Isabella's rousing rhetoric as well as to her 'prone and speechless dialect' (1.2.180) as she engages him with the subject of fornication. At the same time, Isabella's loquacity in the face of male authority carries suggestions of sexual availability, of transgressive openness, prevented in the order of Saint Clare by rules that dictate that 'you must not show your face;/Or if you show your face, you must not speak' (1.4.12–13). The erotic impact of Isabella's embodied speech is announced in the first of Angelo's two asides, his revelation that his 'sense breeds' suggesting both the tumescence of erection and its potential consequences for the female body: pregnancy.

Placed after a lengthy stretch of stage time (2.2.107–62), during which Angelo speaks a mere handful of lines, his first soliloquy of the play bursts forth with an energy borne out of restraint, conveying intense physical excitement and mental confusion. The pace of the speech is accelerated by its frequent repetitions. Uttered three times in the first line, the demonstrative preposition 'this' is often taken as a cue for the actor playing Angelo to look down at, or even clutch, his penis to illustrate the unnamed referent. How such a stage gesture would have been received in the raucous atmosphere of the early modern amphitheatre can only be imagined – though it might well have been taken as confirming the commonly held theory that an erection is 'not always at our commaundement either to move or to appease as we may doe our armes, legges and eyes' (Crooke, 248). Angelo's discovery of his sex drive destabilizes his sense of self and prepares the way for the deed that later 'unshapes' him (4.4.21). The Deputy's soliloquy contains no fewer than eleven questions which serve to both accelerate the pace of the speech and to underscore his estrangement from his former ascetic self. As the soliloquy progresses, its frequent shifts of address suggest a man desperately trying to rationalize his feelings. Initially questioning himself in the first-person singular and finding only an image of himself as alike to 'carrion', he then attempts to move away from his self-loathing and outward to the refuge of misogynistic generalities. Adopting the first-person plural, he scrutinizes one of the precepts he has relied upon to shape his worldview: 'woman's lightness'. Finding the experiential evidence pointing in quite another direction seems to place him entirely outside himself, indicated in the text when he suddenly addresses himself in the second-person: 'What dost thou, or what art thou, Angelo?' – a question whose existential anguish would not look out of place in a tragedy. Though in the lines that follow Angelo moves once more between first-person singular specifics and first-person plural generalities, it settles finally in the singular: Angelo's dilemma is his alone.

* * *

The speech's numerous **caesuras**, irregular line lengths, and exclamatory phrases convey Angelo's mental and somatic perturbation. The energy and urgency generated by its lexical oppositions, its saints and sinners, virtues and evils, dramatize a mind torn between extremes. The speaker's declared awareness of his own culpability and hypocrisy, notwithstanding that it is sometimes expressed in hypothetical rather than personal terms, encourages a sympathetic audience response, though perhaps one mixed with gratification at seeing a man of 'severe restraint' fall by the wayside. Yet if this early soliloquy leaves an actor plenty of room to elicit audience sympathy, it also forms a kind of preface to the turpitude he goes on to display in later scenes. Angelo's ability to identify and articulate the sexual transgression that beckons him means that, when he actually falls to it, he does so in a state that meets all three conditions of a mortal sin laid down in the Catholic Catechism: gravity, full knowledge and deliberate consent. And while the confusion Angelo exhibits in the speech seems to validate Isabella's claim that 'A due sincerity govern'd his deeds/Till he did look on me' (5.1.443–4), it cannot excuse the cruelty and violence that is unleashed once he gives his 'sensual race the rein' (2.4.159). This is also a speech which concludes that all women, be they saint or harlot, are to be reviled. As Pascale Aebischer notes: 'The doubleness of the whore here becomes the doubleness, the deceptiveness, of the virtuous maid ... It is this speech which prepares the audience to hear "double" in Isabella's words when she next encounters Angelo and to detect, in the famous "ruby" speech with which Isabella most passionately *rejects* sexuality (2.4.98–104), undertones of sexual domination and masochistic subjection' (Aebischer, 13).

O curse of marriage?

It could be argued that one of the most transgressive aspects of *Measure for Measure* lies not in its treatment of illicit desire but in its presentation of the licit state of matrimony: the institution held up by the church of Shakespeare's day as the God-given means of controlling and sanctifying human sexuality. As critics frequently point out, the marriages in *Measure for Measure* seem to be imposed on the play world so as to fit the generic model of early modern comedy and, in the case of Lucio and Angelo, come more as a form of punishment than reward. Of all the play's marital unions – or potential unions – that between Mariana and Angelo is perhaps the most disturbing for modern audiences. Brought together by the bed-trick, their marriage begins with a deception – one recommended, ironically, by the chief authority figure of the play. Mariana's claim that Angelo 'knew [her] as a wife' (5.1.229) might be true in the biblical sense of the word, but not in any sense more general. Academic readings of the bed-trick range from somewhat literal-minded explorations of its physical realities – one critic, for example, wonders how Angelo, not being able to see hymeneal blood on the sheets in the dark, knows he has penetrated a virgin 'beyond the feel of a tight vagina' (Jankowski, 100) – to those who insist that it is best 'accepted as a *donnée*' (Corbin, 41).

A common narrative feature of folklore tales and other traditional literature, the bed-trick would have been quite familiar to Shakespeare's audiences. The contrivance appears with some frequency in early modern dramas, including Shakespeare's *All's Well That Ends Well*, a dark comedy that explores the nature of sexual desire, and which is thought to have been composed around the same time as *Measure for Measure*. However, what might once have been accepted as nothing more than a plot device is often found disturbing and transgressive by modern audiences. As critics frequently point out, the sexual tryst at the moated grange is inextricably bound up with violation, whether it be a bizarre form of male rape, or the rape of Isabella in conscience, if not in body. It is difficult, then, to receive the Duke's command 'love her, Angelo' (5.1.522) as striking anything other than one of several jarring notes in a finale where comic harmony seems more a matter of form than spirit.

Casting Isabella

In literary-critical studies, treating dramatic characters as 'real people' possessed of a backstory, inner feelings and a future that extends beyond the end of the playtext tends to be regarded as perpetuating a liberal humanist fallacy. In the ostensive world of theatre, however, the moving, speaking corporeity of the actor creates a verisimilitude that works directly against the notion of character as merely an effect of the text. As one leading semiotician of the theatre notes: 'the sign created by the actor tends, because of its overwhelming reality, to monopolize the attention of the audience at the expense of the immaterial meanings conveyed by the linguistic sign; it tends to divert attention from the text to the voice performance, from speeches to physical actions and ... to the physical appearance of the stage figure' (Veltruský, 115).

Nowadays, audiences of early modern drama tend to anticipate that stage figures will 'look the part', despite that 'look' being largely unspecified in the script. In particular, characters who are positioned as the play's object of desire are often expected to conform to normative conceptions of physical attractiveness. To go against such expectations can radically change the impact of the piece.

Measure for Measure is a work that engages emphatically with the complex nature of sexual arousal, with Angelo's desire for Isabella providing its most psychologically intriguing case. In this regard, casting the role of Isabella presents a real challenge: to choose a conventionally beautiful actress could be seen as 'normalizing' Angelo's sexuality; to choose one that goes against the grain of cultural-aesthetic expectations deepens the play's transgressive tone. One production whose casting of Isabella proved particularly controversial was that directed by Roxanna Silbert at the RSC's Swan Theatre in 2011–12. Male reviewers, perhaps taking Lucio's address to 'pretty Isabella' (4.3.151) as a plain statement of fact, were more than a little put out by what they perceived to be the physical unattractiveness of the actress playing the role.

Charles Spencer considered 'Jodie McNee's plain, plodding Isabella ... highly unlikely to have inflamed ... passion in the first place' (Spencer), while Paul Taylor found the 'sharp-featured' (Taylor, 'MM') actress brought little sexual electricity to her encounters with Angelo. Quentin Letts, a theatre critic notorious for needling the 'politically correct', deemed McNee 'not so much chaste as plain ... no sexier than carbolic soap', and far from Shakespeare's conception of her as 'pretty enough to yank the lusts of two powerful men' (Letts, 'Isabella'). It is interesting to note that none of the critics quoted above refers at any point to the physical appearance of the actor playing Angelo, though it goes without saying that this, too, must have an impact on the drama's sexual dynamics and meaning. In effect, all three reviewers inhabit the **gaze** of Angelo, only to find the object of that gaze inadequately ravishing. It seems that actresses playing Isabella – or any other female Shakespearean heroine for that matter – are much more likely to have their appearance put under critical scrutiny than male cast-members.

It seems clear from the descriptions of the actors' appearances given in the introductory notes that accompany Silbert's production that Isabella's 'look' was intended to contrast significantly with that of the other two upper-class women of the play. Where Juliet and Mariana could have been taken straight off the cover of a romantic novel (the former has 'a heart-shaped face' and 'tousled, shoulder length chestnut curls'; the latter is 'tall and slender, with long, strawberry blonde curls'), Isabella is described plainly as having 'brown hair ... severely braided around her head' (Notes to Roxanna Silbert's *Measure for Measure*, 3, 5, 4; RSC website). Some male theatre critics, unable to see past the disquieting experience of seeing a 'plain' woman staged as the unwilling partner in Angelo's initiation into the ways of the flesh, were therefore unable to fully appreciate the play's suggestion that sexual desire is not easy to categorize – and frequently surprises. Perhaps, a conventionally attractive Isabella would have allowed them the more comfortable option of figuring Angelo's desire as 'normal', because directed towards a 'typical' victim of sexual predation, making his crime more fathomable and thus more easily forgivable.

Costume adds another important layer of signification to the figure of the actor, the colour, shape, movement and even the sound of clothing, jewellery and footwear contributing to the impression a character makes in performance. That audiences are alert to the semiotics of costume was tellingly demonstrated back in 2012, when the actor playing the Cardinal in the Old Vic's production of *The Duchess of Malfi* wore a black sling on his left arm. Assumed to be an item of costuming, it set the audience wondering about its significance. Did the broken limb symbolize a broken soul? Was the contrast of black against the ecclesiastical scarlet a hint at the devilish? It was, in fact, a matter of necessity: the actor had fallen off his bike and injured his arm. The decisions made in selecting Isabella's costume will have a direct influence on how the character is read by the audience. If, as is sometimes the case, a director decides to dress Isabella in secular garments, she inevitably appears more part of the everyday world of Vienna; in addition, the idea that Angelo is excited by the sight of an animated woman in a nun's habit, a sartorial maker of chastity, is inevitably diminished. Opting for religious garb can also bring its problems. The nun's habit is an outfit freighted with erotic signification; the image of the 'naughty nun', breasts bared against a background of black serge is, after all, something of a pornographic cliché, one that can be traced back several centuries. To clothe Isabella in a habit that is even remotely becoming is, then, to risk evoking the 'double vigour, art and nature' (2.2.184) of the 'strumpet' Angelo claims never to have found arousing. Stills from a range of productions mounted over the past decade or so reveal a tendency to plump for the safely drab, with Anna Maxwell Martin's long black velvet gown and simple silver cross worn in the Almeida Theatre's 2010 production proving a notable exception. More the robes of a priest than a novitiate, the costume conferred a distinctive authority on the figure of Isabella, a welcome change from the more usual schoolgirl staples of thick black stockings and ill-fitting habits.

The past decade or so has witnessed the rise of the 'big name' in the casting of high-profile Shakespeare productions, with the likes of Benedict Cumberbatch, Sienna Miller and David Tennant guaranteeing sell-out runs. It is a practice that adds yet another – some might say artistically undesirable – signification to the stage figure. Whether or not the role of Isabella will ever be played by a major celebrity remains to be seen, though if responses to Jodie McNee are anything to go by, casting directors would do well to look for someone 'pretty'.

Further reading

James M. Bromley, *Intimacy and Sexuality in the Age of Shakespeare* (Cambridge, 2012)

Katherine Crawford, *European Sexualities, 1400–1800* (Cambridge, 2007)

Christine Dymkowski, '*Measure for Measure*: Shakespeare's twentieth-century play', in Christine Dymkowski and Christie Carson (eds), *Shakespeare in Stages: New Theatre Histories* (Cambridge, 2010)

Keir Elam, *The Semiotics of Theatre and Drama* (London, 2002)

Ivo Kamps and Karen Raber (eds), *Measure for Measure: Texts and Contexts* (Boston, 2004)

'*Tis Pity She's a Whore*

In the autumn of 2014, London playgoers settled down in the candle-lit intimacy of the Wanamaker Playhouse to watch *'Tis Pity She's a Whore*. Primed by the play's title to expect a provocative theatrical experience, few were disappointed as scenes of incest, adultery, murder and mutilation were played out in what was often alarmingly close proximity to the audience. Believed to be the first play to place a consummated incestuous relationship at its centre, Ford's drama must also have had a powerful impact back in the late 1620s when it was first performed at the Phoenix Theatre (also known as the Cockpit) in Drury Lane. Nowadays, in keeping with the generally accepted dating of this first performance, *'Tis Pity* is classified as Caroline, though it was labelled Jacobean, or even Elizabethan, by previous generations of scholars. While such anachronistic labelling can be put down to changing academic conventions, it is also symptomatic of the critical tendency to regard Caroline playtexts as somewhat jaded products of late-Renaissance theatre. As Julie Sanders observes: 'It is too often a fact that theatre histories of the seventeenth century gloss over the Caroline period, either ignoring it completely or presenting it as a period of aberration, of a falling-off from the high aesthetic achievements of the Elizabethan and Jacobean eras' (Sanders, 4).

Engaging with the specificity of the Caroline context of *'Tis Pity* makes for a fuller appreciation of a play too often dismissed as decadent and thrill-seeking. As the 2014 Globe performance demonstrated, the design of the seventeenth-century indoor theatres where Ford's independently authored plays would have been performed created a significantly different spatial dynamic from the amphitheatres. The nearness of actor and spectator allowed for a more nuanced tonality of line delivery as, in such a tight space, performers could range from a roar to a whisper; Ford may well have borne these **paralinguistic** aspects of performance in mind when composing the intimate exchanges between Annabella and Giovanni.

The shift to the indoor playhouses, with their significantly higher admission charges, inevitably brought about changes in the audience demographic. Being seen in the indoor playhouse was a means of establishing social status at a time when plays were increasingly acknowledged as 'respectable literature' and it is broadly accepted that the playgoers at the hall venues would have included both gentry and those with 'new money'.

In an auditorium where the leisured dandy might sit shoulder to shoulder with the middle-class trader, the jilted Hippolita's sneering reference to Annabella as '[y]our goodly Madam Merchant' (2.2.48) would not have gone unnoticed.

Ford entered this theatrical world in his mid-thirties, having up till then only tried his hand at poetry. The early 1620s saw him collaborate with various dramatists, most especially Thomas Dekker, before producing a run of single-author works approximately dated from 1627 to 1638. While the 400th anniversary of Ford's birth prompted a critical reappraisal of his work, there is still a tendency for his plays to be examined through the lens of dramas that hold a more central place in the literary canon. With the play frequently seen as derivative of tragedies such as *Romeo and Juliet* and *Othello*, critics such as Raymond Powell have argued that *'Tis Pity* 'became both a record and an extension of what Ford had learned from Shakespeare' (Powell, 583). Others, though, have resisted viewing Ford's reworking of well-known Elizabethan playtexts as simply the practice of a literary magpie; rather, they have identified a more sophisticated spirit of intertextuality at work. Emily Bartels, for example, argues that, in modelling the story of Giovanni and Annabella on Shakespeare's *Romeo and Juliet*, Ford 'familiarises the desire that we might otherwise reject as immoral, unnatural or unthinkable, prompting us to take seriously the love story beneath the taboo' (Bartels, *''Tis Pity'*, 252). Readings such as these have helped to rescue Ford's play from earlier critical stances that dismissed it as lacking in innovation, a typical product of Caroline 'decadence'.

'Cursed be he who lies with his sister' (Deut. 27.22)

That Ford was not afraid to provoke is apparent from his choice of title. Omitting *'Tis Pity* entirely from his 1831 edition of Ford's dramatic works, William Harness cannot even bear to name the play, referring to it in his Introduction as 'Annabella and Giovanni', and explaining in a footnote that this title stands in lieu of 'a much coarser one' (Harness, 1: xviii). Yet for all the shock value of the title, it lends no precise clue to the transgressive elements within. If Ford's play was not the first to include 'whore' in its title (Dekker's *The Honest Whore* is as early as 1604), it was the first to pin the main dramatic focus on a fully consensual sexual relationship between consanguine family members. Romeo and Juliet may violate the laws of patriarchy, but Giovanni and Annabella commit two heinous sins in addition: incest and adultery.

Though there were an estimated sixty or so plays published during this period that engaged in some way with the issue of incest, in the vast majority of them incestuous sexual acts are committed without full knowledge, consent or erotic desire. In Peele's biblical drama *David and Bethsabe*, Thamar is raped by her half-brother Ammon; in Middleton's *Women Beware Women* Isabella only consummates her love affair with her uncle after being tricked into believing that he is not a blood relative; and in *The Revenger's Tragedy*, also by Middleton, an incestuous affair (in this case between relations by marriage) is instigated more from a mutual desire for vengeance than from sexual longing. In *Pericles*, Shakespeare engages with the seldom touched-upon theme of father–child incest through the mutually affectionate relationship of Antiochus and his daughter, and in *Hamlet*, with the incestuous marriage of Gertrude and Claudius. However, unlike *'Tis Pity* neither of these plays makes incest its core concern.

In seventeenth-century England, incest was considered the most ungodly and injurious to society of all sexually transgressive behaviours. As the Bishop of Bath and Wells pointed out to his congregation in a sermon of 1628:

> *Fornication* violateth the good order that should be betweene single persons, through unruly Lusts; *Adulterie* addeth thereunto a confusion of Families, and taketh away the distinction of Heires, and Inheritance; but *Incest* moreover abolisheth the reverence which is ingraved by

nature, to forbid that persons whom nature hath made
so neere should one uncover the others shame, as speaketh
the Law

LAKE, Fourth Alphabet, 12

The 'law' to which Lake refers is derived from various texts found in the Pentateuch. Genesis urged exogamy whereby 'a man leaves his father and his mother and cleaves to his wife' (2.24) and Leviticus 18 and Deuteronomy 27 laid down prohibited relationships between close kindred, forming the basis of the table of 'Kindred and Affinity' which underwrote English church law. It is evident from this table that no clear distinction was made between relationships of 'consanguinity' and those of 'affinity', an organizing principle which, as Lake explained, is underpinned by biblical authority: 'Whatsoever you have heard of Consanguinitie, is true also of Affinitie: because by wedlocke man and wife become *one flesh* and so their parents, their children, their brethren, their sisters, are as neere to the one as to the other: Affinitie maketh them as neere as if they were of one blood' (Lake, Fourth Alphabet, 22).

Of course, a literalist reading of the scriptures raises the awkward question of how humankind was propagated from the marriage of Adam and Eve without sexual congress between blood relations. Again, Lake's sermons provide a useful explanation: '[W]hen there were none but Adams children, brothers and sisters must needs match, and then did God dispence with the first collaterall degree of consanguinitie' (Lake, Fourth Alphabet, 22). A necessary dispensation to kick start the human race, God's approval of sibling coupling was nothing other than temporary; Giovanni and Annabella could not look to the story of Cain and his sister-wife to justify their relationship.

In Western societies today, objections to sexual relations between family members tend to be grounded in biological and psychological science; in Ford's day, however, God's word reigned supreme. The Friar's vain attempts to persuade

Giovanni from his sister's bed rest more on the commandment of holy writ, than on any understanding of incest as 'unnatural'. The Friar insists to Giovanni that 'nature is in heaven's positions blind' (2.5.34): to be sexually aroused by family members is wrong because the Bible tells us so and not because of any 'natural' aversion. In the same way, the 'monstrous births' that were thought to come from incestuous intercourse were regarded as divine punishment and not as the biological consequences of inbreeding, hence the prescience of Hippolita's dying wish that Annabella's womb should 'bring forth/ Monsters' (4.1.101–2).

Giovanni: 'angel like' or 'black devil?'

How far *'Tis Pity* casts a sympathetic light on the subject of incest is a long-debated question. Broadly speaking, today's critical opinion inclines towards ambivalence, as captured in Richard McCabe's view that Ford's play 'neither wholly exonerates nor wholly condemns its protagonists' (McCabe, 228); it also tends to interrogate the modern habit of romanticizing the love between the protagonists. Sonia Massai, editor of the Arden edition of *'Tis Pity*, argues that the critical habit of considering Ford's work in parallel with *Romeo and Juliet* is an approach that 'glamorizes incest by reading Giovanni and Annabella *only* as sympathetic victims' (Massai, 3). Certainly, the poster advertising the 2014 Globe production went all out to 'glamorize' the siblings. Featuring a mid-range shot of brother and sister embracing, both blonde, bronzed and naked from the waist up, it was an image that proved too daring for Transport for London, who banned it from their billboards.

The diversity of views surrounding *'Tis Pity*'s treatment of incest has, perhaps inevitably, arisen mainly from responses to the erring siblings. Giovanni has been seen as sophistic and obdurate, an affected exponent of the 'rhetoric of the courtly Platonic vogue endemic to the late 1620s and 1630s' (Clerico, 420), whose university education has given him the wherewithal to dress up sexual appetite in florid words. In an important essay on early modern drama, T.S. Eliot declared Giovanni 'almost a monster of egotism' (Eliot, 198) and, indeed, the brother's frequent iteration of the first-person possessive pronoun could be seen to invite such condemnation. Determined to pursue his own desire, even if it entails lying to his sister about the 'counsel of the holy Church' (1.2.249), some critics have read Giovanni's behaviour as disturbingly coercive, a perspective that invites connections to Ford's *The Broken Heart*, whose tragedy is largely brought about by Ithocles' insistence on controlling the life of his sister, Penthea. Other responses to Giovanni are, to some degree, more sympathetic. For some he is an isolated figure whose father seems to have written him off; for others he is a youth trapped in a state of 'spiritual stagnation' (Woods, 124). And for Mario DiGangi he is the sole male in the play to express any real human tenderness, admirable for his 'idealized yearning for the emotional and spiritual harmony of love' (DiGangi, 575).

📖 *Read 1.2.216–59.*

Keeping in mind the critical viewpoints touched upon in this section so far, consider your responses to the following:

- *Some critics consider that Giovanni is presented as the more manipulative of the pair. How far does a close reading of the extract persuade you to such a view?*
- *Consider the stage business with the dagger both in terms of its dramatic impact and its significance for the play in its entirety.*

Giovanni's offering of the dagger, his high-voltage courtly rhetoric and exclamatory tone can either be taken as indicators of a young man who is both inspired and transformed by passionate love or as mere gesture to cover over the urgent promptings of the flesh. It is true to say that modern readers and audiences tend to respond to *amour courtois* with a degree of cynicism; this was also to some extent true of the early moderns, who frequently satirized the idealized **hyperboles** found in forms such as the sonnet and the **blazon**. That Giovanni is well-schooled in courtly cliché is underscored by his sister's calling him a 'trim youth!'. Like Juliet's charge that Romeo kisses 'by th' book' (*RJ*, 1.5.109), Annabella's **epithet** brings a certain linguistic self-consciousness to the scene, closing down any possibility that she is naively taken in by her brother's rhetorical embroidery. Giovanni's description of his amatory sufferings conforms closely to that of the courtly lover: the 'tortured soul', the 'sighs and groans', the 'untuned ... harmony' of the self. As if to counter any sense that Giovanni's language is mere surface, Giuseppe Patroni Griffi, director of *Addio, fratello crudele* (1971), the only cinematic adaptation of the play, adds scenes that actualize the physical and mental torments only reported by the hero in the play. The viewer watches as Giovanni casts himself into a disused well, where, like Jesus in the wilderness, he endures hunger and thirst as a means of conquering the temptations of the flesh. Unlike Jesus, however, Giovanni succumbs to the promptings of desire, rising from the muddy pit of despair to pursue his own damnation.

Yet for all the familiar conventionality of this extract, there is something in the rhythms of its rhetoric that strike the ear as authentic. Take, for example, when Giovanni articulates having '**Reason**ed against the **reason**s' of his ardour or when he insists on the '**nearer near**ness' of his fraternal bond with Annabella. In these instances, the **trope** of **polyptoton**, draws attention to word roots, adding to the impression of a brother who cannot move away from his own family origins, the rhetorical repetition (especially in the second example) helping to convey a sense of a life stalling. Numerous critics have drawn attention to the lie that Giovanni tells to convince Annabella to sleep with him: that the relationship has been sanctioned by the 'holy Church'. That Annabella does not respond to such an outrageous statement could be read as unquestioning faith in the word of male authority, placing her as the passive victim of her brother. This is, though, a difficult view to reconcile with a duologue in which lines are frequently shared and where the 'captive' of the pair competes eagerly for the prize of most long-suffering lover. Indeed, any assumption that Giovanni's lie is premeditated is complicated by the lines that follow on from it ('and 'tis just/That since I may, I should, and will, yes, will!') which have about them an air of improvisatory excitement.

* * *

Giovanni's dagger is of major significance to the design of the drama, serving as structuring agent, **polysemic** symbol and sensational stage object. Here, it is at once a sign of his willingness to die should she refuse him and a phallic representation of his desire. Ford's scenario of the courtly lover, physically exposing the region of his heart to the violence of the beloved, would once have had a conventional signification; as Michael Neill explains, the body in Renaissance culture 'was both a biological entity and an assembly of emblematically arranged parts each with its own allegoric meanings, among which the heart as the supposed seat of the affections had a peculiar prominence' (Neill, 'Riddle', 156–7). This duality of flesh and spirit is deconstructed by Ford in the course of the play, culminating in one of the most memorable stage directions of the period: '*Enter GIOVANNI with a heart upon his dagger*' (5.6.8). If Giovanni hands Annabella control of the dagger in this early scene, by the play's close she is indisputably its victim. Its phallic symbolism is carried through to a fatal climax in Giovanni's announcement that '[t]his dagger's point ploughed up/Her fruitful womb' (5.6.30–1), a **metaphor** gruesomely realized in the 2014 Globe production when Giovanni appears to stab Annabella through the vagina. And if Ford settled for preserving the metaphorical import of the title of his tragedy, *The Broken Heart*, in having only 'silent griefs . . . cut the heart-strings' (5.3.75) of the bereaved Calantha, he exercised no such restraint in *'Tis Pity*. Giovanni's deranged entrance is perhaps the apogee of early modern drama's fascination with the love–death nexus, a dramatic *tour de force* that Neill acutely notes as 'eloquent' (Neill, 'Riddle', 155). A condensed visual expression of the play's preoccupations with sex, religion and familial bonds, it also lays bare the courtly art of the blazon when Giovanni's verbal anatomizing of his sister's beauty (2.5.49–58) takes on a physical reality. As the cultural historian, Jonathan Sawday, observes: 'The human body may, in the Renaissance, have been "emblazoned" or embellished through art and poetry. But to "blazon" a body is also to hack it into pieces, in order to flourish fragments of men and women as trophies' (Sawday, ix).

'A wretched, woeful woman's tragedy'

'Tis Pity is often remarked upon as a play obsessed with blood, one critic estimating that the word itself appears in the script thirty-four times (Gibson, 64). Annabella's blood is a particular focus of dramatic interest and her progress through the play can be tracked through its ebbing and flowing: the hymeneal blood lost to her own brother, the cessation of menstrual blood as a consequence of the resulting pregnancy – the symptoms of which are ironically misdiagnosed as 'a fullness of her blood' (3.4.8) – and the final terrible blood-letting of her murder, prefaced by Giovanni's chilling scrutiny of her 'well-coloured veins' (5.5.75). Annabella's trajectory in blood is directed by her choice of a consanguine sexual relationship: a choice that runs contrary to Parmesan society's demand for exogamy. As Verna Foster observes: 'The inhabitants of ... Parma are members of closely knit households of kin and dependants. Family aggrandizement through marriage arrangements and the preservation of honour ... are important constituents of the [play's] action and atmosphere' (Foster, 182).

In Cheek By Jowl's 2014 production of the play at London's Barbican, the audience was never allowed to forget the all-pervasive pressures of this aspirant mercantile society, as even in the first intimate love scene between the protagonists, members of the cast lined the perimeter of the stage, looking on and echoing the lovers' vows as if reciting church liturgy.

In the course of the play, the citizens of Parma are revealed as self-centred, conniving and corrupt, and the audience cannot help but sympathize with Giovanni and Annabella's attempts to isolate themselves from such venality. And although this isolation is inextricably wrapped up in transgressive sexual behaviour, outright condemnation is rendered far from straightforward by the couple's exhibiting a tenderness of emotion that is singularly absent in the wider play. As Kathleen McLuskie notes, Annabella's choice of an incestuous relationship is mitigated to some extent by Ford's dramatic construction: '[T]he structure of lovers rejected and a lover chosen leads the audience to accept Annabella's choice in spite of the startling danger of incest ... [Giovanni] occupies the position of contrast to the unsuitable lovers dismissed in the dialogue between Annabella and Putana' (McLuskie, 130).

There is no 'man of wax' waiting in line for Annabella as there is for Juliet; she has the pick of the foolish Bergetto, the brutal Grimaldi, or the arrogant adulterer, Soranzo. Though Giovanni provides a blissful sanctuary from this motley collection, it comes at a cost. From the moment she conceives, she loses control over her own destiny; the child in her womb is incontrovertible evidence of her disobedience to church, family and state, leaving her no option other than to enter the marriage she had sought to avoid. While Giovanni is able to take refuge in being 'devoted to his book' (1.3.5), that privilege is not extended to his sister. As an important market resource, her body must be put on display to attract the most prestigious buyer and she must be kept sexually 'intact' to guarantee that the transaction goes through. If, as some scholars insist, genealogies evidenced a predisposition towards endogamy among the aristocratic classes, merchant-fathers like Florio, were obliged to look outward to marriage partners who would enhance the family's social standing. As Lisa Hopkins points out: 'This invisible but impenetrable border between the classes to which incest is permitted and those to which it is not ineluctably scars both the civic and the psychic landscapes of *'Tis Pity She's a Whore*' (Hopkins, 'Incest', 105).

Read 3.6.1–42 📖

- *How does this scene contribute to the play's discussion of incest?*
- *How might an audience respond to Annabella here?*
- *How far does Annabella's behaviour in this scene cohere with that in the remainder of the play?*

Friar Bonaventura pulls out all the fire-and-brimstone stops in his attempt to turn Annabella away from sin, leaving the audience in no doubt as to the church's condemnation of her relationship with Giovanni. The Friar's choice of imagery when accusing Annabella of having 'unripped' her soul, unwittingly recalls Giovanni's exhortation: 'Rip up my bosom' (1.2.218), an echo that suggests the omniscient wisdom of the church. The repetition of words such as 'weep', 'wretched' and 'burning' and the extended run of **enjambement** across lines 12 to 19 lend an urgency to the speech, underscoring the inexorability of damnation. As one gruesome punishment follows swiftly on the heels of another, so this paradoxical world of 'never-dying deaths' and 'lightless sulphur' begins to take on an alarmingly physical reality. And lest Annabella should think of hell as a place for other people, the Friar personalizes it through adding direct speech from her lover: '"Oh, would my wicked sister / Had first been damned, when she did yield to lust."' By putting such words into the brother's mouth, he pulls down the full force of anti-feminist tradition on the sister's head. Annabella is the 'wicked' sister who, in yielding to her fleshly desires, repeats the sins of Eve; she is the originator of incest and cause of her beloved's damnation.

One of the sources for the Friar's lecture is Ford's own *Christ's Bloody Sweat* (1613), a devotional poem based on Christ's prayerful agony in the Garden of Gethsemane where, according to Gospel tradition, he sweated drops of blood. Included in its 2,000 or so lines are Jesus' words to the damned, which, though similar in tone and content to the Friar's lecture, differ in one important respect: they make no direct reference to incest. Named for the first time in the play at 3.6.26, the sin stands bare, no longer occluded by Giovanni's courtly love language or cod-philosophy, its climactic position as the last offence specified in the lecture, driving home its gravity. The **sibilance** of the Friar's denouncement of the couple's 'lawless sheets/And secret incests' seems to evoke the hissing of Eden's serpent; while the **transferred epithet** ('lawless sheets'), suggests the shifting of blame from human beings to bed sheets, perhaps indicating the lovers' obstinate refusal to acknowledge their own sinfulness.

* * *

Post-Reformation England had moved away from the Catholic practice of individual confession to communal confession spoken by the congregation, though the cultural memory of the old faith was no doubt fresh enough for a Caroline audience to appreciate the theological tensions of this scene. One such tension is whether or not Annabella, in confessing her sins to the Friar, does so with what the Catholic church defines as a 'firm purpose of amendment'. On the surface, at least, she demonstrates quiet obedience to ecclesiastical authority. Despite speaking just five lines out of forty-three (only one of them metrically complete), her few words express a spiritual journey from self-castigation, to pleading for mercy, to resignation. Yet the very sparseness of Annabella's responses might also leave an audience wondering about the nature and extent of her contrition. Might the Friar's coercive lecture have brought about what amounts to a forced confession? Is Annabella merely paying lip service to religious dogma, espoused by a churchman whose pragmatic approach to the sacrament of marriage could hardly be accounted holy? Is her contrition no more genuine than Juliet's when she assures her father that she has 'learnt ... to repent the sin/Of disobedient opposition' (*RJ*, 4.2.17–18)?

* * *

As the Friar rests his case and the penitent agrees to resist the 'baits of sin', so the forces of patriarchal Parma close in on Annabella, subjecting her to the will of her father, her husband-to-be and, less publicly, to that of her brother. Yet for all the weight of male authority pressing down on her, she demonstrates a devil-may-care defiance when confronted with Soranzo's violent rage at discovering her past 'belly-sports' (4.3.12). Laughing, singing and praising the father of her unborn child in adulatory terms that some critics have read as suggestive of the Annunciation, Annabella's behaviour seems to fly in the face of her earlier repentance. Yet, as Virginia Woolf suggests in *Notes on an Elizabethan Play*, '[a] dramatist . . . is forced to contract. Even so, he can illumine; he can reveal enough for us to guess the rest' (Woolf, 77). So the reader or spectator must 'guess' how deeply Annabella's contrition is rooted, aided by the moments Ford chooses to 'illumine'. One such moment is when Annabella, in her one and only soliloquy, shapes her own chronicle as '[a] wretched, woeful woman's tragedy' (5.1.8), as if anticipating and countering the Cardinal's final condemnation of her as a 'whore'. Contemplative and resigned, she holds the stage here with a dignity reminiscent of the Duchess of Malfi at the lowest point in her fortunes. At the same time, her choice of epithet reiterates the '[w]retched creature' of 3.6, confirming, perhaps, that the sacrament of reconciliation has indeed done its work.

The Cook, the Thief, his Wife and her Lover: Peter Greenaway's theatre of blood

Peter Greenaway is one of the most innovative and influential film-makers of contemporary cinema. Tirelessly resistant to the narrative clichés of Hollywood, his work is characterized by its intellectual challenge, its arresting visual language and its exploration of the two subjects Greenaway considers central to European cinema: sex and death. *The Cook, the Thief, his Wife and her Lover* (1989) was one of a number of his films to be influenced by early modern theatre as Greenaway himself explains:

> the model is classic Revenge Tragedy out of the 'theatre of blood' with its obsession for human corporeality ... More particularly the model is satirical English Jacobean theatre which was invariably erotic and certainly violent. Most particularly it could be modelled on the example of a drama like John Ford's *Tis Pity She's a Whore* [sic] that looks seriously, compassionately and without flinching, at a taboo subject on the far reaches of experience.
>
> GREENAWAY, Introduction, n.p.

Greenaway's treatment of his seventeenth-century model is a complex one. While the film concerns itself primarily with signifying the rampant consumerism of late-Thatcherite Britain, it also makes frequent allusions to the art and culture of seventeenth-century Europe. The tonalities of Dutch still-life painting are captured in numerous food shots; Franz Hals' 1616 painting, *Banquet of the Officers of St George Civic Guard*, forms the backdrop to the long table where Albert Spica (the Thief) and his cronies dine; and Cavalier fashion meets 1980s designer-label fetishism in the extravagant lace collars and cuffs worn by the male gang members (costumes created by Jean Paul Gaultier).

Yet for all the film's visual signification of its early modern template, anyone expecting precise parallels between *Cook* and *'Tis Pity* would be disappointed. Greenaway departs from Ford in choosing, instead of incest, the taboo of cannibalism to 'suggest that when you've finally devoured everything there is to be eaten, you end up eating one another' (Greenaway in Gras and Gras, 85). Another major departure is in Albert Spica, 'an anti-Semite, fascist, sexist, racist pig' (Greenaway in Gras and Gras, 72), a figure so vile that his nearest seventeenth-century cousin would be more Middleton's Duke in *The*

Revenger's Tragedy than any single character in *'Tis Pity*. There are, though, some significant general connections to be found between *Cook* and its model. Both play and film depict a society influenced by a rapidly expanding middle class; both exploit the relationship between the figurative and the literal, especially regarding bodily functions; both present a heroine whose body is treated as a male possession; and, perhaps most noticeably, both deal with multiple revenge plots and their consequences.

Greenaway's interest in the revenge genre is evident from the film's opening four minutes. In the car park that forms the sordid backstage area to the sumptuous interior of Le Hollandais restaurant, Spica's gang wreaks vengeance on their hapless victim, Roy, stripping him naked, smearing his face and body with dog faeces, and urinating over him. Captured in **long-shot**, Roy's befouled body, lying prostrate on the dank floor, prefigures the film's final revenge tableau: the cooked body of the Lover, laid out on a bier-cum-salver. And there are plenty of retaliatory acts that occur in between these first and last scenes – more than enough to match the multiple revenge strands of *'Tis Pity*. In keeping with Greenaway's key **motifs**, vengeance is frequently linked to the alimentary. The diner guilty of being in the wrong place at the wrong time has soup poured over him; the woman who announces the Wife's adultery is stabbed in the face with a fork; and the Thief, the final revenge victim, is made to eat the cooked body of the bookseller-Lover, himself the victim of what Spica terms a 'dignified revenge killing' (Greenaway, 78) – being stuffed to death with his own books. Greenaway brings the cannibalistic overtones of Giovanni's presenting Annabella's heart on the dagger like a piece of 'dainty fare' (5.6.22) to a shocking realization when the cooked flesh of the Lover is offered to the cuckolded Albert as a gourmet anniversary treat. Just as the speared organ proves a frightful incarnation of Giovanni's **Petrarchan** tropes and of Soranzo's threat to 'rip up' (4.3.53) Annabella's heart, so Michael's oven-baked body brings to full material reality Albert's earlier threat, 'I'll kill him and I'll bloody eat him!' (Greenaway, 66). In true revenge tragedy style, the poetic irony of the moment is underlined by Georgina's steely command, '[Y]ou vowed you would eat him. Now eat him', and by her arch suggestion, 'Try the cock Albert. It's a delicacy. And you know where it's been' (Greenaway, 92).

While Greenaway's climactic revenge act corresponds with Ford's in its focus on the ritualistic and the anatomical, it differs from it in allowing the abused female character to inhabit the role of killer rather than victim. Dressed for much of the film in clothing that evokes a sense of entrapment and restriction, Georgina's final outfit is a visual sign of her transition from trophy wife to powerful avenger. The black feathers emanating from the yoke of her dress make her appear spider-like, an image enhanced by a long black net train, carried by one of the waitresses – now under her employ rather than Spica's. Yet where Giovanni disrupts an entertainment planned by the enemy (Soranzo's birthday party), Georgina's revenge recalls that of Titus Andronicus, as she takes sole charge of the catering for the final 'private function'. And where Giovanni stands isolated in his moment of berserk retaliation, the Wife is supported by a host of characters who have been subjected to Spica's brutality, foremost among them Pup and the Cook, who are afforded the privilege of handing her the gun that will fire the fatal bullet. By means of a rare point-of-view **close-up shot**, the spectator is taken into the regard of Spica's victims to stare at their isolated and terrified abuser as he vomits and then, hands trembling, takes a morsel of the cooked flesh into his mouth. And it is at this moment that viewers, having spent two hours in Spica's boorish company, are apt to cheer on the abused Wife as she shoots her monstrous husband, proclaiming him a '[c]annibal': an utterance that places him firmly and finally as Other.

However, the manipulation of the viewer in the film's final minutes is more subtle than a straightforward recounting of events suggests. Douglas Keesey is surely right in asserting that the distancing long-shots that dominate the final scene, 'are deliberately calculated to take us out of the vengeful frame of mind and to get us to look at these plotters from the outside, as if they were schemers on the stage of a Jacobean revenge tragedy' (Keesey, 96).

The audience might be cheering Georgina on, but they are ultimately brought to realize that the revenge-crew, assembled as if for a formal photograph, are themselves tainted by the 'wild justice' of revenge (just as those who smear excrement on Roy cannot avoid smearing it on themselves in the process). Indeed, the Cook's mistaken assumption in an earlier scene that Georgina wants her lover cooked so that they 'can always be together' (Greenaway, 88) points up that the bitter promptings of retribution have won out against the former tenderness of the love affair. The 'ice cool' (Greenaway, 92) tones of the Wife-avenger that cut through *Cook*'s concluding moments indicate that she, like Giovanni, has 'grown insolent in [her] butcheries' (5.6.75).

Further reading

Angela Carter, 'John Ford's *'Tis Pity She's a Whore*'; Carter's short-story adaptation of the play, published in *American Ghosts and Old World Wonders* (London, 1993)

Ira Clark, *Professional Playwrights: Massinger, Ford, Shirley, & Brome* (Lexington, 1992)

Lisa Hopkins, *John Ford's Political Theatre* (Manchester, 1994)

Amy Lawrence, *The Films of Peter Greenaway* (Cambridge, 1997)

Susan J. Wiseman, '*'Tis Pity She's a Whore*: Representing the Incestuous Body', in Lucy Gent and Nigel Llewellyn (eds), *Renaissance Bodies: The Human Figure in English Culture, c.1540–1660* (London, 1990)

7

Damnation:

Dr Faustus and *Hamlet*

The nature of religious belief and the almost universal acceptance of the chief tenets of Christianity marks one of the greatest differences between present-time and early modern society. Leaving aside, at first, the religious differences between Catholic and Protestant that dominate and scar the period, all lives are lived *sub specie aeternitatis*, encompassed by belief in God as Creator and Judge. Equally the vast majority of Shakespeare's contemporaries would have held an absolute belief in the perpetually tormenting presence of the Devil, a malign being forever seeking the damnation of every individual soul. The biblical narratives that commence with creation and progress through Jewish history to the life, death and resurrection of Christ were perceived as a teleological scheme that would culminate in the Parousia (the Second Coming of Christ) at which point earthly time would end. For some, this Last Judgement was not a remote event: prophetic writings of the time expressed an urgent conviction that the Last Days might be at hand. Meanwhile, existence itself was characterized by its brevity and uncertainty; death and the fear of damnation permeates the poetry of the late Middle Ages and remains a constant presence throughout the seventeenth century. The uncompromising nature of belief is ubiquitous at this time: a reflective decision to reject certain tenets of faith, or an intellectual position of total indifference is almost inconceivable in a context where dissent could mean state-sanctioned torture and the most hideous forms of public execution.

Death itself – its physical realities and spiritual rituals – also marks profound differences between early modern society and current attitudes. Nowadays, it is quite common not to hold a 'funeral service' but a 'thanksgiving'; not infrequently, this follows cremation so that the deceased is no longer present. In Western culture, visible reminders of death are deemed to be unacceptable. The Elizabethan funeral ceremony, on the other hand, refers unflinchingly to 'the corpse' and stresses the impermanence and trials of existence. In Cranmer's Reformation Prayer Book, the newly established vernacular rite for the Burial of the Dead takes as its first premise the biblical exhortation, 'Man that is borne of a womanne hath but a shorte time to lyve, and is full of misery: he cometh up and is cut downe lyke a floure: he fleeth as it were a shadowe.' Cranmer's text discards the 'Popish' invocation of Saints and prayers for the dead and concludes with a Collect (prayer) that thanks God for delivering the deceased from the perils of the world, with the accompanying rubric that 'the corps is made ready to be layde into the earth.' The visual artistry of medieval funeral monuments is also a world away from modern tastes. In England 'cadaver tombs' appeared as *memento mori* from the later fifteenth century as graphic representations of decay, a dignified and idealized stone form lay in state above the stone figure of a decayed corpse. Scenes of the Last Judgement and the torments of the damned were accessible to all as stained-glass windows or highly coloured wall-paintings in churches until removed or whitewashed during the Reformation. Nowhere is the eschatological drama expressed more vividly than in the poetry and prose of John Donne (1572–1631). His Holy Sonnets or 'Divine Meditations' encapsulate the visceral fear of the moment of death:

> This is my play's last scene, here heavens appoint
> My pilgrimage's last mile

> [...]
> And glutt'nous death will instantly unjoint
> My body and soul, and I shall sleep a space,
> But my ever-waking part shall see that face
> Whose fear already shakes my every joint
>
> 'Divine Meditations'
> 6, 1–2, 5–8

'Gluttonous death' is a monstrous figure that anticipates the grotesque **personification** of Milton's Death in *Paradise Lost* (Book 2). Equally, the 'unjointing' of soul and body suggests the torturous pains of the rack. Death itself is fearsome but, as Claudio observes in *Measure for Measure*, the fear of what lies beyond is infinitely more terrifying:

> The weariest and most loathed worldly life
> That age, ache, penury and imprisonment
> Can lay on nature, is a paradise
> To what we fear of death.
>
> *MM*, 3.1.128–31

The immortal soul is destined for Heaven or Hell: again, a world away from sentimental twentieth-century notions of the departed 'only slipped away into the next room' (Scott Holland). Fear of judgement created Donne's terror of sudden and unexpected death – like Hamlet's father 'disappointed' of the preparation necessary to encounter the next world: 'In my night of ignorance he may come, and he may come in my night of wantonness; in my night of inordinate and sinful melancholy and suspicion of his mercy, he may come; and he may come in the night of so stupid or so raging a sickness' (Sermon, 19 November 1627 in Donne, 552, n. 1). Donne's eschatological anxiety was not an individual paranoia: biblical authority teaches the prudent believer to 'Watch, therefore: for ye know neither the day nor the hour wherein the Son of Man doth come' (Mt. 25.13, KJV).

At an unknown point in the future, worldly time itself will end and 'all the tribes of the earth' shall see 'the Son of Man coming in the clouds with great power and glory' (Mk 14.26, KJV). To the medieval Catholic, this is the 'Dies Irae' (Day of Wrath) when the suppliant and miserable soul fearful of the 'flammis acribus' (flames of bitterness) awaits judgement. Redeemed souls will inhabit their celestial body for an eternity of bliss; those unregenerate souls who cannot be redeemed are destined for endless torment. The powerfully prophetic but impenetrably symbolic book of Revelation which concludes the Christian New Testament, introduces the further troubling notion of numbered souls: 'the hundred and forty and four thousand, which were redeemed' (Rev. 14.3). Calvin and his followers preached their doctrine of predestination and election from these verses; a theology which became increasingly deterministic. Church historian Diarmaid MacCulloch explains 'double predestination' whereby 'before Adam and Eve had committed sin by disobeying God in the garden of Eden, God had drawn up his complete scheme of the damned and the saved in the human race' (MacCulloch, 374). At the extreme end of the Calvinist argument, Christ had died only for the elect few.

In England this cosmic drama was a familiar theatrical as well as theological event: the cycles of Corpus Christi plays dramatized the entirety of human and cosmic time, beginning with the Creation and concluding with the Last Judgement. As Helen Cooper establishes, the 'dominant living theatrical experience [of] a large number of the playgoers of the 1590s was religious drama carried forward from the Middle Ages.' Popular cycle plays had survived long enough to be 'part of the cultural memory of Shakespeare and his audiences' (Cooper, 55).

Shakespeare's personal religious views have been earnestly debated, and it is clear that this is an area of speculation which is unlikely to be satisfactorily resolved. Catholic writers such as Peter Milward pursue 'enlightened conjecture' in an attempt to connect Shakespeare's schoolmasters in Stratford to a network of Lancastrian Catholic families with Jesuit connections; Arthur Marotti argues that Shakespeare 'may have outwardly conformed to the official state religion [but] could not, and apparently did not wish to, sever his or his culture's ties to a Catholic past and its residual cultural presence' (Marotti, 232). Arguments in favour of a Catholic Shakespeare speculate upon the 'lost years' of Shakespeare's youth: was he a schoolmaster known as 'Shakeshafte' in a recusant household in Lancashire? Did his father retain Catholic sympathies? The possible discovery of a Catholic 'Spiritual Testament' in the rafters of the Henley Street house has been dismissed by biographer Katherine Duncan-Jones who claims that it 'disappeared almost as soon as it was seen' (Duncan-Jones, xii). Even more speculatively, do the plays and sonnets conceal buried references to the faith of the past? Famously, the nostalgic evocation of 'bare ruined choirs/Where late the sweet birds sang' (sonnet 73) has been recruited to suggest sympathy for the music of the past. Yet the drunken Porter of *Macbeth* appears to be consigning the Jesuitical 'equivocator' to 'the everlasting bonfire' (*Mac*, 2.3.8–10) and monasticism is not venerated in *Measure for Measure*. Shakespeare was born thirty years after Henry VIII's break from Rome, some six years after the accession of Elizabeth. By the time he was writing *Hamlet*, 1599, England had conformed to Reformation Protestantism for over sixty years. Greenblatt argues 'a fifty-year effect' whereby survivors of revolutionary change 'look back with longing at the world they have lost' (Greenblatt, *Hamlet*, 248). This is speculative, however, and fascinating as the scrutiny of Shakespeare's putative religious affiliations might be, such feelings remain 'hidden from the eyes both of contemporary audiences and of modern scholars' (Milward, 68). Of course, for some readers of the twentieth century, Shakespeare had simply adopted the agnosticism of their own age; George Santayana was one of the first to argue religious nihilism in Shakespeare: '[For] Shakespeare, in the matter of religion, the choice lay between Christianity and nothing. He chose nothing; he chose to leave his heroes and himself in the presence of life and of death with no other philosophy than that which the profane world can suggest and understand' (Santayana, 94).

Twentieth-century readers would like to discover in Shakespeare the pluralism and relativism that corresponds with present-day sympathies but attempts to locate any systematic agnosticism or atheism in the period have failed to identify any common corpus of thought. On a personal level, any proclamation of atheism would simply have been too dangerously subversive. Dissent throughout the struggles of the seventeenth century tended to mean dissent from the orthodox Anglican position, generally towards a more radical Puritanism. Bacon gives some consideration to Stoic philosophy that excludes Christian notions of God but even here argues that 'depth in philosophy bringeth man's minds about to religion' (Bacon, 371). When Bacon thinks about the 'contemplative atheist' he is referring to classical thinkers, not his own contemporaries. In language that resembles Hamlet's he also proposes that man's own nature is defined by likeness to God: 'They that deny a God, destroy man's nobility, for certainly man is of kin to the beasts by his body; and, if he be not of kin to God by his spirit, he is a base and ignoble creature' (Bacon, 372).

But does the drama of the time offer possibilities of radically questioning religion? Tourneur's *The Atheist's Tragedy* (published 1611) would seem to offer a tantalizing protagonist in D'Amville. He certainly begins the play with a declaration of attachment to natural philosophy, comparable to Edmund's philosophy of Nature in *King Lear*. His companion Borachio observes that 'there's nothing in a man above/His nature' (1.1.13–14), a denial of the transcendent which elicits from the protagonist a commitment to his own hedonistic pleasures: 'Let me have all my senses feasted in/Th'abundant fullness of delight at once' (1.1.18–19). But D'Amville is created in the theatrical mould of the Machiavellian villain and as such he represents not philosophical scepticism but rather the ruthless desire to gain wealth and power through any means. His 'atheism' is no more than confirmation of his depravity. As Robert Watson shows, in Jacobean usage, 'atheism' was 'a term of anathema applied to anyone who deviated from the writer's preferred form of Christianity rather than a specific term for those denying the existence of God' (Watson, *Silence*, 25). The thrust of Tourneur's play is to force D'Amville to reconsider his brutal pursuit of self-interest. At the opening of Act 5 he is discovered worshipping his gold in a manner resembling Volpone, when the Ghost of one of his victims appears announcing that he is a 'wretched miserable fool' about to witness the 'confusion of [his] projects' (5.1.29–31). At this point servants bring in the body of his younger son just as D'Amville hears the dying groans of his elder son. Deprived of both, he announces, 'Now to myself I am ridiculous' (5.1.115) and repudiates his belief in Nature. In the sensational final scene, he seizes the executioner's axe and strikes his own head rather than witnessing the execution of his (innocent) victims. He dies, conceding the futility of his failure to believe in a 'power above'. For the playwrights of the period, death and damnation offer unlimited theatrical possibilities: what could be more compelling than the Cardinal in *The Duchess of Malfi* bleakly contemplating his end and 'puzzl'd in a question about hell' (5.5.1)? Michael Neill argues the centrality of tragic drama to early modern thinking about the realities of death itself: 'the extraordinary burgeoning of tragic drama ... was among the principal instruments by which the culture of early modern England reinvented death' (Neill, *Death*, 3).

Recent critical theory has begun to re-engage with religious perspectives; where critical theorists pursuing materialist or historicist arguments tended to avoid discussions of spiritual perspectives, post-1990 and presentist studies explore religion as crucial to the understanding of early modern culture, 'a complex reality of the early modern period and an important dimension of its historical alterity in relation to our own times' (Fernie, 24, n. 1).

> This chapter examines the dramatization of damnation and the individual in *Hamlet* and *Doctor Faustus*, looking at early modern ideas of the Ghost, Satan and Hell. The political implications of *Hamlet* are also explored through Grigori Kozintsev's film interpretation.

Doctor Faustus

Reviewing a production of Gounod's nineteenth-century opera *Faust*, the novelist Philip Hensher examines the enduring popularity of the *Faust* myth, from ancient sources to the present day. It is certainly the case that the essence of the story – the insatiable desire for knowledge or power; a diabolic pact; the pursuit of extremes of indulgence; and, finally, a terrible reckoning – has been reprised across centuries in literature, music, art and, now, computer games. Hensher concludes that while theatrical effects differ significantly across centuries, audiences remain profoundly engaged with the fundamental Faustian: 'What would you do to attain the thing you dream of?' The transgressive nature of Faust's ambition has led writers to connect Marlowe's protagonist with the author himself and the highly coloured accounts of Marlowe's rebellious pugilism and blasphemy. For George Buckley, as an early twentieth century critic, Marlowe typifies Renaissance man: 'All the currents of thought that made for religious unbelief ... combined in him to produce one of the best examples of Renaissance paganism' (Buckley, 129).

Buckley traces a connection between Marlowe's Cambridge education and the writings of Machiavelli, then circulating in intellectual circles. Recent scholarship has tended to query inferences about Marlowe's beliefs and seditious affiliations, however. Thomas Healy argues that Marlowe was historically unlikely to be the personality that his subsequent reputation has established; where his literary works are bold and adventurous, the life might be altogether less glamorous. On the one hand, accusations against him for blasphemy were extracted under torture from fellow spies, Thomas Kyd and Richard Baines and secondly, once Marlowe had been killed, 'his reputation could be forged to suit a variety of ends' (Healy, 343). Denunciations against Marlowe were quite possibly fabricated for the political exigencies of the troubled 1590s. Whatever the truth of Marlowe's private views, his heroes have been regarded through the prism of Renaissance ambition and individualism: '[The] epitome of Renaissance aspiration ... all the divine discontent, the unwearied and unsatisfied striving after knowledge that marked the age in which Marlowe wrote' (Roma Gill, cited in Dollimore, *Radical*, 122).

Marlowe's source was the German *Faustbuch*, published in 1587 in the Lutheran city of Frankfurt by the prominent Protestant publisher Johann Spies and rapidly translated into English as *The Historie of the Damnable Life and Deserved Death of Doctor John Faustus*. The text is a didactic work, exploiting the contemporary interest in tales of sorcery and witchcraft while demonizing Faustus for dealing with the devil. The author, as well as emphasizing the grisly horror of Faustus' end, seizes every opportunity to moralize on the tale and warn against the temptations of ambition: 'Therefore I wish all Christians to take an example by this wicked Faustus and to be comforted in Christ, contenting themselves with that vocation whereunto it hath pleased God to call them, and not to esteem the vain delights of this life, as did this unhappy Faustus' (*Faustbuch*, 98). The historical Faustus, a vagrant scholar and magician (existing probably *c*.1480–1540) was not unique in Protestant Germany: there was a widespread interest in the occult, magic, witchcraft and necromancy which religious authority attempted constantly to repress. Indeed, the very beginnings of Christianity record the attempts of Simon Magus to buy supernatural power from Christ's disciples (Acts 8.9–20). The English magus John Dee (1527–1608) was a Renaissance polymath, notable astrologer, scientist and mystic who founded England's Rosicrucian Order. He claimed to receive information directly from angels, and asserted that by occult means he had prevented the Spanish Armada from reaching England. The esoteric writings of Hermeticism and the influence of Paracelsus created what MacCulloch describes as a 'febrile excitement' (MacCulloch, 682) across Protestant Europe. The combination of new ideas in theology together with belief in 'natural science' created possibilities for unlimited speculation.

Disputing with the devil

At the opening of the play Faustus is engaged in the scholarly exercise of disputation – with himself, however, rather than with his peers or his students. His pleasure in the world of academic debate has already been signalled in the Chorus's Prologue to the action: 'whose sweet delight disputes/In heavenly matters of theology' (Chorus, 18–19). The scholarly world he inhabits is itself fraught with contradiction; a discipline based on classical learning within a framework of 'divinity'. Healy draws attention to Marlowe's own academic life in Canterbury and Cambridge: 'Marlowe was raised in an academic environment that was formally highly orthodox in upholding ... the religious status quo, but that then gave him access to materials that challenged these positions' (Healy, 339). When Marlowe emphasizes the intellectual world Faustus inhabits, he is making a specific point: for Faustus, as for Hamlet, Protestant Wittenberg represents 'new wisdom'; to Jan Kott, Wittenberg is a 'vision of man as master of the universe – and of his being!' (Kott, 'Kozintsev', 386). Faustus' opening soliloquy establishes at the outset the fascinating complexity that will unfold. The tragic hero in soliloquy might seem to be the hallmark of the Renaissance protagonist: the dramatic realization of a wholly new individuality and interiority. In Faustus though, 'the Renaissance soliloquy [renders] precarious precisely the unified subjectivity which it is its project to represent' (Belsey, 44). So the audience see the unified subject that is the speaker but the 'subject of the utterance ... is fragmented, discontinuous' (Belsey, 46). In fact Marlowe presents Faustus through a complex divided perspective: the audience hear his innermost thoughts yet are invited to see the errors of his thinking. Indeed, the Chorus has set him up as 'swollen with cunning of a self-conceit' (Chorus, 20). His hubris is displayed at the outset as he considers the various branches of learning in which he excels only to dismiss them for not sufficiently satisfying him. Analytical logic? 'read no more, thou hast attained the end' (1.10); medicine? 'hast thou not attained that end?' (1.18). Faustus evidently knows everything; like Alexander he has nothing left to conquer. And in common with a later Faustian figure, Mary Shelley's Frankenstein, only the possibility of defeating death itself inspires him. Legal studies offer only 'external trash' (1.35) and so he is left with divinity and his Latin bible. The syllogism he produces when consulting the scriptures reveals the deficiencies of his logical reasoning: 'we must sin,/And so consequently die/... an everlasting death' (1.44–6). But he misquotes his biblical sources: 'For the wages of sin is death; but the gift of God is eternal life through Jesus Christ our Lord' (Rom. 6.23, KJV). Faustus quotes only the opening clause 'Stipendium peccati mors est' as he does with his following biblical verse, 'If we say we have no sin we deceive ourselves ... If we confess our sins he is faithful and just to forgive us our sins' (1 Jn 1.8–9). Does Faustus wilfully deceive himself in order to reach his desired conclusion – that necromancy is the only world of 'profit and delight,/Of power, of honour, of omnipotence' (1. 53–4)? Or is Marlowe suggesting that Faustus lacks both honesty and insight? He later dismisses divinity as base: 'unpleasant, harsh, contemptible and vile' (1.109) – is this because it fails to offer him the uniqueness and supremacy he yearns for? Divinity teaches him that God's mercy is available to all but Faustus, like Tamburlaine, does not desire a common humanity:

> [Nature] doth teach us all to have aspiring minds
> Our souls, whose faculties can comprehend

> The wondrous architecture of the world
> And measure after knowledge infinite
> And always moving as the restless spheres
> Will us to ... never rest.
>
> *I Tamburlaine*, 2.7.20–5

Faustus' Promethean ambition typifies the Marlovian 'overreacher' but when he declares 'A sound magician is a mighty god' (1.62) is he a hero or a charlatan? Once he turns away from divinity he is 'glutted' with the prospect of magic. Faustus' crucial first three scenes with Mephastophilis circle around ideas of hell, damnation, knowledge and free will. The first revelation made by Mephastophilis (1.44–50) should perhaps dampen Faustus' enthusiasm – it is not magic that has summoned Hell's messenger, rather he comes 'in hope to get his glorious soul' because he hears Faustus renouncing God. The second, which instantly moves the drama beyond medieval iconography and preaching is Mephastophilis' existential definition of Hell:

> Why this is hell, nor am I out of it.
> Think'st thou that I, who saw the face of God,
> And tasted the eternal joys of heaven,
> Am not tormented with ten thousand hells
> In being deprived of everlasting bliss?
>
> 3.75–9

His evocation of a terrible loss resembles Milton's Satan who acknowledges, also, '[which] way I fly is hell; myself am hell' (*Paradise Lost*, 4.75). Both have known former glory and, in despair, can only find relief in revenge.

📖 *Now read scene 5.*

- *Consider to what extent Marlowe characterizes Faustus as an individual making a free choice?*
- *Analyse the dramatic effects of blood, fire and devils.*

The structure of the opening scenes, moving between Faustus (both in soliloquy and in debate with Mephastophilis) and the parodic scenes where first Wagner and then Robin attempt magic tricks, has a profoundly reductive effect. Faustus aspires beyond human limitation; Wagner also promises metamorphosis but the Clown's highest ambition is to be 'a little pretty frisking flea' so that he can 'tickle the pretty wenches' plackets' (4.61–2). Robin, in scene 6, similarly wants only to conjure naked maidens to 'see more than ere I felt, or saw yet' (6.4–5). While there is, of course, a degree of comic contrast here, the parallelism and parody also has the effect of associating Faustus with their delusional and carnivalesque attempts to conjure. On stage, the comic pairings of Clown and Wagner, Robin and Rafe where first the Clown and then Rafe are the butt of mockery further imply that Faustus is no more than an object of derision to Mephastophilis. Faustus' scenes leading up to his pact all commence with Faustus alone, as he will be at the end of the drama. At the beginning of scene 5 he doubts and questions: 'thou must needs be damned', both resisting and urging himself on. His theology is entirely contradictory: 'what boots it then to think of God or heaven?' (5.4). The Good Angel reassures him that 'contrition, prayer, repentance' can 'bring [him] unto heaven'. Hope is always accessible. Faustus undoubtedly exercises free will here: Mephastophilis does not threaten but tempt. A cruder version can be seen in Dekker's *The Witch of Edmonton* (1621) where Satan in the form of Dog offers Mother Sawyer the satisfaction of revenge against her enemies if she 'make a deed of gift/Of soul and body' (2.1.132–3) which, similarly, must be sealed with her blood. As she wavers, Dog threatens that he can 'tear thy body in a thousand pieces' (2.1.136). Marlowe clearly wants to emphasize Faustus' willing cooperation at this stage; later, in fact, when Mephastophilis hears Faustus yearning to repent, he produces the identical ominous warning: 'Revolt, or I'll in piecemeal tear thy flesh' (12.67). At this early stage of the bargaining, Mephastophilis promises to 'be thy slave and wait on thee' and Faustus immediately capitulates, 'I give it thee' (5.48).

Clearly the signing in blood is the play's ultimately transgressive moment, concluded with appositely blasphemous words, 'Consummatum est', the final words of Christ on the cross (Jn 19.30). To Stephen Greenblatt the words represent 'the uncanny expression of a perverse despairing faith, an appropriation to himself of the most solemn and momentous words available in his culture' (Greenblatt, *Self-fashioning*, 214). The congealing of the blood functions dramatically and symbolically as if some inner core of selfhood attempts to protect him from himself. On a literal level, the deed of gift cannot be executed without a signature; he has an opportunity to reconsider. Symbolically, it is as if Nature itself recoils from his act: to wound himself physically with the intention of destroying his soul everlastingly. And it is fire itself – clearly signifying the flames of Hell – which enables the contract to be concluded. Dramatically horrifying, the suspended moment realizes the force of Faustus' internal conflict; his identification with Christ's words could not be more ironic: '[In] the Gospel . . . the words are a true end; they are spoken at the moment of fulfilment and death. In *Doctor Faustus* they are rather a beginning, spoken at the moment Faustus is embarking on his bargain' (Greenblatt, *Self-fashioning*, 214).

Marlowe's staging is remarkable for the way in which he undercuts the tension: Faustus' cry of '*Homo fuge!*' is the despairing acknowledgement that his soul is irretrievably lost; yet a dance of devils who present him with 'crowns and rich apparel' suffices to restore him: 'there's enough for a thousand souls' (5.88). In *The Tempest*, it is Stephano and Trinculo who are distracted by 'frippery'; even Caliban knows that it is 'but trash' (*Tem*, 4.1.225). The carnivalesque nature of Mephastophilis' choice of entertainment has the effect of trivializing the macrodrama of Faustus' soul and undermines his intellectual aspirations.

Faustus' questions return always to the nature of Hell yet he discounts the replies he receives from Mephastophilis and professes not to believe in its existence. Marlowe's definitions of Hell are radical: Hirschfield argues that this is a 'watershed moment in the canonical literature of hell, emphatically defining it as a place of spiritual torment, a state of mind, rather than a geographical locale' (Hirschfield, 59):

> Hell hath no limits, nor is circumscribed
> In one self place; for where we are is hell,
> And where hell is must we ever be.
>
> 5.120–2

Marlowe's influence on *Paradise Lost* is evident: when Milton's Satan arrives on earth, he brings Hell within him, 'nor from hell/One step no more than from himself can fly' (*Paradise Lost*, 4, 21–2). The intensity of the tragedy derives precisely from this obsessive concern on Faustus' part with the nature of Hell and the fate of his immortal soul yet his determination to grasp the diabolic. Mephastophilis deceives Faustus: he gives the great scholar a single book which purports to contain 'all spells and incantations ... all characters and planets of the heavens ... all plants, herbs and trees' (5. 163, 66–7, 71). When Faustus questions him on astrology, the replies are scarcely beyond the capacity of his student, Wagner. Yet Mephastophilis does not deceive Faustus on the subject of Hell; in their first meeting he requires Faustus to 'leave these frivolous demands,/Which strike a terror to my fainting soul' (3.80–1).

Scene 7 concludes the alternating pattern of the play whereby the debates between Faustus and Mephastophilis are juxtaposed against the foolery of the parodic scenes. Again, Faustus dwells on his own damnation but speaks of his regret and desire for repentance. He begins with an unconscious biblical quotation, 'When I behold the heavens, then I repent' (7.1). The biblical psalm hovering behind Faustus' expression of regret is ironical in two respects: it celebrates the majesty of both God and man and anticipates Faustus' later demand: 'Tell me who made the world' (7.64). In the language of the Geneva bible (1560) the similarity is striking: 'When I behold thine heavens, even the works of thy fingers, the moon and the stars, which thou hast ordained' (Ps. 8.3). Faustus dwells on his own damnation but speaks of his regret and desire for repentance. As a scholar of divinity Faustus knows well that the advice of his Good Angel is correct – that genuine repentance will elicit God's mercy. Yet Faustus is doubly defeated: first by the determinism of his inner Bad Angel – 'but Faustus never shall repent' (7.17) – and secondly by his worldly desires, '[hath] not sweet pleasure conquered deep desire' (7.25). The bathos of the latter is central to Faustus' tragedy: he is as easily distracted by the superficial as Rafe is wooed by promises of Nan Spit. When he calls upon Christ to save his soul it is with the confidence that Mephastophilis is fearful of articulating the name of God. This moment could be a turning point for Faustus but the appearance of Lucifer with a show of the Seven Deadly Sins seems to offer compensatory distraction: 'That sight will be as pleasing to me, as Paradise was to Adam, the first day of his creation' (7.98–9). This final scene of the several that make up the event of Faustus' damnation is arguably the most Calvinist in intention. Marlowe portrays a tragic hero who exemplifies the anguish of the soul predestined to damnation. The Evil Angel's 'Faustus never shall repent' neatly sums up the entire dilemma: is Faustus predestined to be damned, incapable of ever avoiding the immutable scheme ordained by God before creation itself? Or, does Faustus wilfully bring damnation upon himself because of his refusal to repent and inability to believe in the possibility of salvation? If free will is an illusion, then the tragic hero can do no more than rail against his destiny. Chief among the English adherents of Calvinist theology was William Perkins (1558–1602), an exact contemporary of Marlowe's at Cambridge. Perkins was a prolific writer on the subject of predestination and had, indeed, published diagrams of the path to salvation. His theological work, *A Golden Chain, or the Description of Theology* (published 1590 in Latin and 1592 in English) was his account of 'the decree of God by which he hath ordained all men to a certain and everlasting estate: that is, either to salvation or condemnation for his own glory' (cited in Kastan, 250–1).

When Mephastophilis hands Faustus one small volume to satisfy the scholar's vast intellectual yearnings, this could be a warning that there is an epic dichotomy between Faustus' undefined desires and the reality granted by Mephastophilis. Faustus' twenty-four years of glory amount to very little, particularly in the A-text where the scenes between Faustus and Mephastophilis dominate the drama. This makes a significant moral and spiritual point: not simply that Mephastophilis lies and deceives but also that Faustus' aspirations are essentially undefined. Unlike Tamburlaine, for whom military conquest is the goal, Faustus' desire for knowledge and power remains ambiguous and elusive. The scenes of triumph amount to some mischief in the Vatican, conjuring in the court of the Emperor, half drowning a horse-courser and commanding a bunch of unseasonal grapes for a pregnant Duchess. Where critics once found these scenes embarrassing for detracting from the central tragedy, it is now more usual to find a compelling irony in the discrepancy between Faustus' ambition and its apparent realization. Structurally, these scenes are punctuated by Faustus' reflections upon time and his destiny, as well as by the ironic juxtaposition of Robin and Rafe. Scene 10 opens with the Emperor praising Faustus' reputation 'for the rare effects of magic' and concludes with the promise of a 'bounteous reward' (10.85–6). Yet this scene of courtly triumph is followed by Faustus wearily requesting of Mephastophilis that they should return home:

Now Mephastophilis, the restless course
That time doth run with calm and silent foot,
Shortening my days and thread of vital life,
Therefore sweet Mephastophilis, let us make haste to
    Wittenberg.

10, 87–91

Equally, the ducking of the horse-courser in the pond is interrupted by Faustus contemplating the inescapable reality that time draws to an end:

> What art thou, Faustus, but a man condemned to die?
> Thy fatal time doth draw to final end.
> Despair doth drive distrust unto my thoughts;
> Confound these passions with a quiet sleep,
> Tush, Christ did call the thief upon the cross
> Then rest thee, Faustus, quiet in conceit.
>
> 10, 117–22

There is a carefully structured dualism here, exemplifying Faustus' conflict. Marlowe implies that Faustus never escapes the reality of his situation. Helen's two appearances in Scene 12 further illustrate this effect. The fact that it is the scholars who request a sight of Helen's beauty is itself significant, as if Faustus has returned simply for the final reckoning. The scene opens with Wagner confiding that 'I think my master means to die shortly' – where 'means' seems to suggest a degree of volition rather than acquiescence. When Helen first passes across the stage, there is no response from Faustus – it is the scholars who admire her beauty. They depart with bleakly ironic words, 'Happy and blest be Faustus evermore' (12.32) as the Old Man returns to spur Faustus to revoke his earlier contract: 'Break heart, drop blood, and mingle it with tears' (12.38). Contrition and grace can effect salvation, as Faustus knows – 'Hell strives for grace with conquest in my breast' (12.63). Like John Donne, Faustus is caught in the Protestant dilemma:

> Yet grace, if thou repent, thou canst not lack;
> But who shall give thee that grace to begin?
>
> DONNE, 'Divine Meditations' 4, 9–10

Mercy can be shed upon those who seek for grace but – the Protestant Catch-22 – grace is the prerequisite for initiating that movement towards repentance. However, Mephastophilis concedes that '[his] faith is great, I cannot touch his soul' (12.77) which raises the intriguing question of whether Marlowe did originally intend that Faustus should cheat Satan. Certainly it would have been a significant departure from the *Faustbuch* and, presumably, far too radical for the theatre of the time. William Empson argued that censorship had meant cuts in Marlowe's original text: any suggestion that Faustus could escape Hell would have been profoundly heretical, particularly to the more Calvinist Protestants of the audience (Empson, 64). Mephastophilis' unexpected statement seems to suggest that Faustus is not yet beyond redemption. Meanwhile Faustus' spiritual torment is assuaged by Helen, 'make me immortal with a kiss' (12.91) – yet even if 'heaven be in these lips' (12.94), Faustus' moment of judgement cannot be stalled. It could be predicted that Faustus' story would be entirely different for the Romantics. Hazlitt defines him as 'a personification of the pride of will and eagerness of curiosity, sublimed beyond the reach of fear and remorse' (Hazlitt, *Lectures*, 57). Goethe's creative life was entirely dominated by the Faust legend and his *Part Two* was completed shortly before his death in 1832. His verse drama concludes with the defeat of Mephastophilis and the redemption of Faust whose soul is carried to heaven by Angels singing, 'For he whose strivings never cease/Is ours for his redeeming' (Goethe, 282). It seems wholly improbable that Marlowe might ever have considered a conclusion of this kind. Textually, the play begins by **emblematizing** Faustus as Icarus – he is doomed to fall – and, historically, it is inconceivable that any play set in a recognizably Christian context, would vindicate diabolism.

In the A-text, Faustus' final soliloquy is only preceded by the love and reassurance of his followers; they remind him that God's mercy is infinite, pray for him even, in one case, offer to stay with him. The later text adds tormenting comment from Mephastophilis who freely confesses his role in Faustus' damnation:

> 'Twas I, that when thou wer't i'the way to heaven,
> Dam'd up thy passage; when thou took'st the book
> To view the Scripture, then I turned the leaves
> And led thine eye.
> What weep'st thou? 'Tis too late; despair; farewell.
>
> GILL, B-text, 13.87–91

At this point, interestingly, the Good Angel leaves too. To the writer of the later text, there is now no hope for Faustus and the Bad Angel appears, gloating over particularly nasty punishments.

📖 *Now read Faustus' final soliloquy, 13.55–111.*

- *Look back at Faustus' opening soliloquy: what does Marlowe achieve in these introspective speeches?*
- *Pay close attention to Marlowe's fusing of dramatic time with the unfolding imagery of time in Faustus' speech.*

Faustus begins, as he does at the beginning of the play, by addressing himself, 'Now hast thou but one bare hour', but here he has come full circle; his opening soliloquy constantly draws to an end his various studies, the word 'end' being repeated several times. In the final scene, he confronts the end of physical time but, terrifyingly, eternity will commence. Faustus will be seized out of time to the unending world of Hell. Throughout, he moves between personal pronouns and direct address to God, 'I'll leap up to my God! ... ah my Christ'/'O God, if thou wilt not have mercy on my soul ...' and an externalized objectifying of himself, 'Faustus may repent ... Let Faustus live in hell a thousand years') as if he is both subject and object of the scene. At the same time, his pleas move between the macrocosmic – that the planets will cease their orbit, that time itself will stand still or create perpetual day – and the vividly immediate and personal, 'I'll burn my books'. He is apocalyptic: in calling for mountains to fall upon him he cites the book of Revelation, 'Fall on us and hide us from the face of him that sitteth on the throne, and from the wrath of the Lamb; for the great day of his Wrath is come; and who shall be able to stand?' (Rev. 6.16–17). Heather Hirschfield draws attention to the 'compulsive calculation and measurement' throughout – 'one bare hour . . . A year, a month, a week, a natural day' (Hirschfield, 63). Against which pleading for increments of time, Faustus' plea is that he should live in hell 'a thousand years/A hundred thousand, and at last be saved'. As well as the time that he can no longer inhabit, he is tormented by the notion that there is no place of safety for him: the earth will not harbour him; he desires transformation, to become 'like a foggy mist' or a 'brutish beast'. In contrast with the blood and fire of his contract with Satan, he wishes now to evaporate into 'little water drops' or air itself. His vision of Christ's blood streaming in the firmament is the frightening corollary to the congealing of his own blood in signing away his soul. Here, 'one drop would save my soul, half a drop' yet fear and torment dispel the vision and the brief moment of hope. The scene is brilliantly paced: the bell tolls the half hour nearer the end of the monologue, as if time speeds up for Faustus. The uniqueness of this scene has been widely discussed, the soliloquy is 'the advent of modern tragedy, the portrayal of a despairing protagonist . . . the compelling exploration of interiority' (Cox, 127). To the writer of the *Faustbuch* this is a moral tale with an inevitable and minatory outcome:

> And thus ended the whole history of Doctor Faustus his conjuration and other acts that he did in his life; out of which example every Christian may learn, but chiefly the stiff-necked and high-minded may thereby learn to fear God and to be careful of their vocation and to be at defiance with all devilish works . . . to the end we may remain with Christ in all endless joy: Amen, amen.
>
> *Faustbuch*, 181

Present-day readers, less inclined to be fearful of such warnings, might rather agree with Alan Sinfield that, although the play sustains a Reformation reading, it is 'entirely ambiguous – altogether open to the more usual, modern free-will reading. The theological implications of *Faustus* are radically and provocatively indeterminate' (Sinfield, *Faultlines*, 234).

Performing *Doctor Faustus*: Stage on Screen (2010)

Stage on Screen have made a significant contribution to the academic and theatrical commitment to move away from 'myopic bardolatry' (Karim-Cooper, 56), producing filmed versions of key early modern texts: *Doctor Faustus*, *Volpone*, *The Duchess of Malfi* and the Restoration comedy, *School for Scandal*. *Doctor Faustus*, directed by Elizabeth Freestone, is a two-hour production based on the earlier and shorter A-text of 1604. As a live performance from the Greenwich Theatre it conveys something of the intensity and immediacy of the theatrical experience, including audible audience response. A filmed performance can obviously draw on the additional resources of the genre, camera angles concentrating on individual detail such as the facial expressions of Mephastophilis while the fixed wide angle shot also ensures that the viewer is aware of movement and interaction across the entire stage. As a staged event, however, it maintains the continuity of a single performance and the special effects must be those available to the theatre director rather than the unlimited resources of modern **CGI**. One of the factors typical of staged rather than commercially filmed productions is the far smaller size of the acting company. Stage on Screen double or triple parts in order to dramatize, uncut, the unexpurgated text. For Lois Potter it is a practice that 'has tended to enforce a pessimistic reading' (Potter, 'Marlowe', 265). Challenging connections can be implied: the Evil Angel who tempts Faustus at the beginning of the play is also Helen of Troy, to be greeted rapturously by him at the end.

The fact that she appears in the same costume might suggest that all Faustus' inner voices and external manifestations are illusions. Alternatively, the doubling might suggest that the seductive voice of wickedness is, for Faustus, sexual temptation. Parallelism is achieved as the Good Angel and the benign figure of the Old Man are also doubled. In John Barton's RSC production (1974), the entire action was set, claustrophobically, in Faustus' study as a psychodrama within the mind of the protagonist. As David Bevington explains, Faustus was presented as a troubled schizophrenic 'stunned by his own indecisiveness as he listened to the Good and Evil voices who were, in this performance, held and operated by McKellen himself as he spoke their lines' (Bevington, 54).

Michael Kirwan, reviewing the production for his website *Bardolatry*, suggests that the overall aesthetic connects the text with the world of Shelley and *Frankenstein* – the costumes of Faustus and his fellows being loosely based on Regency styles. The choice of moving away from Marlowe's Elizabethan world has the effect of implying an Enlightenment ethos with the concomitant desire to question authority, making the final reality of Hell more terrifying for Faustus who, after all, has commenced the play informing Mephastophilis that he does not believe in the existence of an infernal dimension. Faustus' semicircular wall of books establishes his intellectual world from the outset and connects him with Shakespeare's later mage, Prospero. The galleried space above Faustus' study is used to strong effect, often enabling striking and unexpected appearances of Mephastophilis and Lucifer. The first dramatic climax is, inevitably, the conjuring of Mephastophilis. The stage is darkened, Faustus' spells appear initially futile and then suddenly with lightning and a piercing scream from Faustus (echoed from the audience) Mephastophilis appears above Faustus as a terrifying horned creature. The characterizing of Mephastophilis is distinctly unusual. It is particularly intriguing to compare him with the non-professional actor, Andreas Teuber, in the eccentric Burton/Taylor film (1967) directed by Oxford's Merton Professor of Poetry, Nevill Coghill. In the opening scenes Teuber is a compelling but quiet presence; his words seem to come from depths of alienation and despair. Tim Treloar for Stage on Screen is an angry and often bullying presence, shouting about his prior knowledge of heaven. Often performed as a Machiavellian villain full of subtlety and intrigue, Treloar plays him as a grim and violent manifestation, lacking any humanity. Textually speaking, this is an original but consistent interpretation of the role – he is doomed to serve Lucifer and to suffer Hell, and is full of rage and hatred. He appears particularly terrifying at the very end of the play when Faustus is dragged off to damnation. Mephastophilis stares, wide-eyed, after him – a mysterious facial expression whether of terror or satisfaction is impossible to say. The performativity of Hell and its inhabitants on stage is itself a challenging question – there are traditions and imagination but no possibility of mimetic realism. In the RSC production of *The Witch of Edmonton* (2014) Dog was played as a disturbing hybrid, neither man nor beast, in a costume that suggested nakedness, and black body paint. Dog's presence on stage in all the scenes of violence had the effect of blurring boundaries between the human world and supernatural evil. The Burton/Coghill film of Faustus, contrastingly, drew on surreal and hallucinogenic effects to convey the numinous in ways that did not necessarily appeal to the film's original audience. Renata Adler described the film as 'of an awfulness that bends the mind' (Adler). Marlowe's original audience brought to the theatre their real fears of the diabolic: the Puritan Prynne drew on an old tale of 'the visible apparition of the Devil on the stage at the Belsavage Play-house ... (to the great amazement both of the actors and spectators) while they were there profanely playing the History of Faustus' (cited in Hattaway, 166). And when the play was performed later, in Exeter, there was a general conviction that 'there was one devil too many' on stage; the audience rushed the doors. While it is easy to assume the credulity of the early modern audience, it might also be worth recalling that in plays such as Jonson's *The Devil is an Ass* (acted, 1616), the notion of one of Satan's servants appearing on earth to recruit souls for Hell, is a subject only of comic satire. The play is characteristic of Jonson's city comedies – but framed by scenes in Hell. The joke of course recoils on Pug, Satan's useless sidekick, when he discovers that London is such a den of iniquity that he is shocked by it and longs to return to Hell, protesting that 'Hell is/A grammar school to this!' (4.4.70–1).

Stage on Screen's Faustus (Gareth Kennerley) is played with youthful febrile energy. When he has signed the fatal deed – an exceptionally blood-soaked bond – he writhes and groans as if possessed. His final soliloquy commences with a melancholy tolling bell and then silence – there are no special effects as he pleads for more time. His spiritual torment is clearly envisaged as the solitary soul confronting a terrifying inevitability. Then – lightning, demons and the watchful presence of Lucifer take over. The pared-down A text is played to good effect here: Stage on Screen offer a bleak reading and there is no room for sentimentality or pity. Again, the sombre and reflective disillusionment of Richard Burton strikes a very different note: he lingers over words such as 'Hell' and pauses as he contemplates the enormity of his decision.

The increasing appeal of the play through the twentieth century to the present day raises interesting questions. The London stage has seen Jude Law playing at the Young Vic (2002) as well as a recent production at the Globe theatre (2011). Theatre critic Michael Billington, discussing the enduring popularity of a religious play in a secular age, suggests that *Faustus* offers much more than 'a Hieronymus Bosch floor show book-ended by great poetic passages of desire and damnation' (Billington, *Faustus*). Just as Jan Kott sees *Hamlet* as a sponge that can soak up different meanings for different generations, Billington argues that *Faustus* 'is set in an eternal present in which material wealth, scientific knowledge and sexual fantasy become the objects for which we trade our own integrity'.

Further reading

Emily C. Bartels and Emma Smith (eds), *Christopher Marlowe in Context* (Cambridge, 2013)

Patrick Cheney (ed.), *The Cambridge Companion to Christopher Marlowe* (Cambridge, 2004)

Lisa Hopkins, *Christopher Marlowe, Renaissance Dramatist* (Edinburgh, 2008)

David Scott Kastan (ed.), *Doctor Faustus*, Norton Critical Edition (New York, 2005)

William Tydeman, *Doctor Faustus Text and Performance* (Basingstoke, 1984)

https://blogs.nottingham.ac.uk/bardathon/ (accessed 28.05.2015)

Hamlet

Hamlet and Purgatory: 'thoughts beyond the reaches of our souls'

Hamlet, like *Macbeth*, opens with the numinous – the disturbing possibility that no more than a gossamer veil divides the mortal, empirical universe from the mysterious and otherworldly. And at the end of *Macbeth*, the malevolence of the 'weird sisters' presumably coexists alongside human events. Where *Macbeth* opens with a certainty – the three speakers will next meet 'upon the heath ... with Macbeth' – *Hamlet* begins with fear and uncertainty: 'Who's there?' A 'thing' troubles the night, 'harrows' the rational Horatio, and seems to prophesy 'some strange eruption' to the state. Ghosts are, of course, compelling theatre: Banquo's 'blood-boltered' appearance at Macbeth's triumphal festivities and the apparitions before the battle of Bosworth of Richard III's victims are two notably powerful examples. The Ghost as a key instigator of events is theatrically familiar to Shakespeare's audience, particularly in the context of revenge tragedy.

Supernatural apparitions can be a silent atmospheric presence rather than an agent for retribution: ghostly presences in Webster's plays, for example, contribute to the emotion of a scene rather than make demands on the protagonists. In the most successful and influential play of the period, Kyd's *The Spanish Tragedy* (1587), the ghost of Andrea, slain in battle, emerges from a classical underworld to act as witness, with his guide Revenge, to the 'blood and sorrow' that unfolds. In most performances, Andrea and Revenge remain onstage throughout, adding a metatheatrical dimension to the tragic events of the plot. At the end of the play Andrea catalogues the various deaths he has witnessed, expresses his satisfaction and anticipates the further tortures of his enemies in the underworld. At no point, however, does Andrea's Ghost address or interact with the onstage characters. The ghost of Hamlet's father is unusually eloquent: a presumed earlier version (the *Ur Hamlet*) was memorable to Thomas Lodge for 'a ghost which cried so miserably at the Theatre, like an oyster-wife, *Hamlet*, revenge' (cited in Thompson and Taylor, 44). Shakespeare suggests an extraordinary proximity between the mortal world and the afterlife, as if the murdered king can come and go at will, within or outside his castle. The restless spirit suggests medieval Roman Catholic ideas about Purgatory and the tradition and practice of offering prayers, alms or Masses to ease the sufferings of the departed. Thomas More adumbrates the Catholic attitude of his time in his tract, 'The Supplication of Souls' (1529) where he addresses the living on behalf of the suffering souls themselves, imploring remembrance and pity for 'your late [recent] acquaintance, kindred, spouses, companions, play felowes, and frends' (cited in Duffy, 349). More's intention was to attack the anticlerical author of 'A Supplication for the Beggars' – an argument against the buying and selling of indulgences. His fervent tone, however, testifies to a fear that the living might forget the departed, cease to pray and intercede for them, a fate worse than the pain of the purgatorial fire itself. By the time Shakespeare's play was first performed, though, the Church of England had decisively rejected Purgatory: 'The Romish Doctrine concerning Purgatory, Pardons, Worshipping and Adoration, as well of Images, as of Reliques and also invocation of Saints is a fond thing vainly invented and grounded upon no warranty of Scripture, but rather repugnant to the Word of God' (*Book of Common Prayer*, 'Articles of Religion', 22).

Belief in Purgatory as a Catholic doctrine is fully defined in the various official Catholic encyclopaediae and websites. Derived from the Latin, *purgare*, to cleanse, it is a temporary condition where venial or unabsolved sins can be atoned for or expiated; where the soul is not sufficiently purged of the frailties and transgressions of life. The efficacy of the prayers of the living to remit the sufferings of Purgatory was universally believed (and, indeed, still is official Catholic doctrine). The bond between the living and the dead is thereby real: mourning the dead is lamenting the loss of the departed; praying for the dead is actively ameliorating their passage through Purgatory. Catholic historian Eamon Duffy emphasizes the importance of family bonds and 'the natural ties of affection, blood kinship and obligation' (Duffy, 349) in sixteenth-century thinking about Purgatory. While the dead in Purgatory 'continued to care for their families on earth', they were 'at the mercy of their kindred' to ensure their 'speedy release [from] torment' (Duffy, 349). In terms of Reformation theology, belief in Purgatory was the antithesis of Calvinist belief which seals off any possibility of reform, renewal, or transformation for the *un*elect.

The Ghost of Hamlet's father, then, would seem to personify orthodox views of Purgatory:

Unhouseled, disappointed, unaneled,
No reckoning made but sent to my account
With all my imperfections on my head.

1.5.77–9

'Unhouseled' and 'unaneled' are peculiarly Catholic terms, referring to the last rites of the dying, the receiving of the

Sacrament, and Extreme Unction, anointing with holy oil. Beatrice Groves, in common with other writers, observes that *Hamlet* 'can be read as an extended meditation on maimed funeral rites' (Groves, 3). Laertes objects to the lack of ceremony accorded to Ophelia and roars into the court demanding revenge for his father's 'obscure' funeral: 'No trophy, sword nor hatchment o'er his bones,/No noble rite, nor formal ostentation' (4.5.205–7). Yet Hamlet's father, as king, has clearly received the most ceremonious of rituals, befitting his status, and his appearance disturbs Hamlet, in part, because of the violation of this formality. His first direct question to the Ghost requires him to 'tell

> Why thy canonized bones hearsed in death
> Have burst their cerements, why the sepulchre
> Wherein we saw thee quietly interred
> Hath oped his ponderous and marble jaws
> To cast thee up again.
>
> 1.4.47–51

Clearly, all has been performed with due propriety and, above all, finality: Hamlet, like Horatio, does not expect the appearance of the revenant.

'So have I heard and do in part believe it.' Horatio's Renaissance scepticism

To Barbara Everett, the first appearance of the Ghost is 'perhaps the most quietly startling moment in all Elizabethan drama' (Everett, 134), in part because the Ghost silently appears in Barnardo's narrative of itself and thus 'alters the temporal dimension of the moment':

> As Barnardo remembers, and the bell beats, and the Ghost comes and stands in the darkness, the present moment dissolves into a receding sequence of shadows, of haunted

imagined nights all reaching back for their meaning to a time
when 'the king that's dead' really lived ... For the whole of the
rest of the play it will be foolish to think that the past is past.

EVERETT, 134-5

Horatio's responses to the appearance of the Ghost are
crucial in establishing an intellectual and theological context
in which Hamlet's later reaction can be assessed. At the outset
Horatio is openly dismissive – ''twill not appear' – until the
appearance of the Ghost forces him instantly to reconsider.
Horatio's Protestant perspective can be inferred from his status
as a student of the University of Wittenberg, famous for
Lutheran and Anabaptist theology. He is characterized as the
model Renaissance thinker: he will not believe without 'the
sensible and true avouch/Of mine own eyes' (1.1.56–7). To
Horatio's mind the apparition is an aberration within Nature,
'usurp[ing]' the tranquillity of night and presaging national
disaster. Yet his initial assumption is that the martial figure
attired in the royal armour is 'like' the king, not necessarily the
king himself. His commands typify contemporary attitudes
towards troubled revenants: 'If there be any good thing to be
done ... If thou art privy to thy country's fate ... if thou hast
uphoarded in thy life/Extorted treasure' (1.1.129, 132, 5–6).
Even here Horatio expresses himself cautiously; these are
reasons '*they say* your spirits oft walk in death' (1.1.137, my
emphasis). And when he reports the event to Hamlet, he
adheres to his judgement that the apparition is 'a figure like
your father' (1.2.198). The nature of Horatio's Wittenbergian
philosophy is evident in these opening scenes: he expresses
with real urgency to Hamlet the possibility that the Ghost may
be no more than an evil spirit intent on luring Hamlet to
destruction. Horatio is certainly not an unbeliever – he swears
'Before my God' and he believes that 'Heaven will direct'
Denmark – yet he refuses to accept the supernatural without
empirical evidence. When the Ghost disappears, as convention
requires, with the morning cockcrow, he again interrogates
received wisdom, concluding 'of the truth herein/This present

object made probation' (1.1.154–5), seeking for and establishing proof as if he were debating a precept in logic. After the traumatic events of the night, it is Marcellus who produces the reassuringly sentimental legend that the cock 'singeth all night long' on Christmas night to mark the 'hallowed and ... gracious' time (1.1.159, 163). Horatio's response is characteristic: 'So have I heard and do in part believe it' (1.1.164). He cannot willingly subscribe to mythology – yet he is prepared to believe 'in part'.

So the Ghost has appeared to a Protestant audience – both onstage and in the theatre itself – and unfolds a Catholic tale of judgement and Purgatory. By the time Hamlet encounters the Ghost, the audience have been presented with a familiar theatrical convention and Horatio's Renaissance distrust.

Now read 1.5 and the Ghost's speeches to Hamlet.

- *Look closely at the language he uses to describe the afterlife.*
- *To what extent does he speak as a father to Hamlet?*

Two contemporary dramatic comparisons shed interesting reflections upon Shakespeare's text: the first, John Marston's *Antonio's Revenge* shares similarities with *Hamlet* (entered in the Stationer's Register, October 1601). Here, the Ghost of Andrugio appears to his grieving son to reveal the truth of his murder and demand justice:

> And lo, the ghost of old Andrugio
> Forsakes his coffin. Antonio, revenge!
> I was empoison'd by Piero's hand;
> Revenge my blood! Take spirit, gentle boy.
> Revenge my blood!
>
> 3.1.33–7

Marston roots his play firmly in the Senecan mould by quoting directly from Seneca's *Thyestes* at the climax of the speech where the Ghost urges his son to 'Remember this:/*Scelera non ulcisceris, nisi vincis*' (3.1.50–1) which translates, troublingly, as 'Injuries are only revenged when they are exceeded'. The Senecan reference, like Kyd's classical underworld, distances the play from Christian morality – unquestioning revenge becomes the *raison d'être* of the drama. Tourneur's later *The Atheist's Tragedy* supplies an intriguing contrast: here, the Ghost of Montferrers appears, as in a dream, to his son Charlemont:

> Return to France, for thy old father's dead
> And thou by murder disinherited.
> Attend with patience the success of things,
> But leave revenge unto the King of kings.
>
> 2.6.20–3

In citing biblical authority ('Vengeance is mine; I will repay, saith the Lord' (Rom. 12.19 KJV), Tourneur shapes a radically different revenge play and an infinitely more paternal figure in the Ghost. Back in the world of Elsinore, Hamlet confronts an uncompromising figure in a scene which raises unanswerable questions. In the opening **stichomythic** exchanges, the Ghost establishes his purgatorial sufferings, demanding not pity and prayer, as might be expected, but a filial obligation to revenge. He begins with a narrative he is forbidden to disclose, the 'secrets of my prison-house' (1.5.14) which has the effect of intensifying the horror. This precedes his conditional; 'If thou didst ever thy dear father love ... Revenge his foul and most unnatural murder' (1.5.23, 25). The two striking uncertainties here must be the key question of the drama: should Hamlet trust the word of an apparition? He later comments, the 'spirit that I have seen/May be a de'il' (2.2.533–4), clearly echoing the convictions of Horatio and his fellow guards earlier. Secondly, why would the King desire his son – his sole heir – to be damned in pursuit of revenge? Shakespeare has emphasized the Christian world of the play from the opening; the play does not operate in a Senecan, classical setting. The scene is urgently emotional: the Ghost's passionate jealousies and resentment elicit Hamlet's horror and intensify his existing despair. In Michael Almereyda's film (2000), the scene is powerful and disturbing: a very real and physical Ghost fervently embraces Hamlet but also stands menacingly above him demanding loyalty. Interestingly, Almereyda retains the Ghost's purgatorial references in full even though the filmgoer of 2000 might not connect with concepts of 'unhouseled' and 'unaneled'. The desire to retain the liminality of the supernatural is a significant aspect of the film; indeed, the Ghost appears more frequently than in the play. Almereyda was influenced by Russian director Tarkovsky for whom 'the Ghost ought to be the most real, concrete character in the play. All the pain is now concentred in him, all the suffering of the world' (Tarkovsky, 381). The Ghost exemplifies the ultimate horror of the afterlife – that all the anguish of life might not be dispelled, but intensified.

Choosing damnation

Before the first 'real' death is witnessed, Hamlet's impulsive and ill-judged murder of Polonius, the play offers narratives and enactments of revenge and violent death, establishing vicarious images of slaughter that impact on the primary world of the play's action. A complex morality of historic cause and effect emerges in the opening scene when Horatio describes the medieval conflict between the aggressor, Old Fortinbras, and the victorious Old Hamlet. The young Fortinbras, 'Of unimproved mettle, hot and full' (1.1.95) appears to replicate the warlike ambitions of his father and seeks a military revenge against Denmark. The play is haunted by a tale of historic defeat and a son's revenge before the Ghost has even appeared to Hamlet. In Horatio's description, young Fortinbras is a fiery youth choosing to make his mark by rewriting history; later, Hamlet admires Fortinbras for his insouciant disregard of 'death and danger' when 'honour's at the stake' (4.4.51, 55). In the context of war and revenge of a father's death, 'the hellish Pyrrhus' is described as the archetypal revenger, face and armour coated with congealed blood, mercilessly slaughtering the elderly Priam. For Pyrrhus revenge is an absolute, a compulsion that cannot be denied; he operates in a legendary classical context, remote from any claims of Christian morality. For Hamlet, the crucial narrative is, of course, the Ghost's blood-curdling tale, addressed only to him. Yet it will be visually realized for the entire court in the dumbshow. Before 'The Murder of Gonzago' can be acted and interrupted, the dumbshow offers a vision, often highly stylized, of Claudius' crime. This layering of dramatic effects and levels of illusion connects always with Hamlet himself, complicating the plot and offering a spectrum of comparisons. Violent death and the impulse towards revenge are mirrored and duplicated.

In this context, Laertes' unreflecting and immediate assumption of the role of revenger is telling: Laertes defies damnation but does so knowingly and this has a significant bearing on his final exchanges with Hamlet. The parallels and contrasts between Hamlet and Laertes are revealing: Laertes opts to leave the court of Denmark and return to Paris, a request graciously granted by Claudius. He roars back ready to murder – unlike Hamlet, he is not troubled by a need for proof: 'O thou vile king,/Give me my father' (4.5.115–16). Neither loyalty to the monarch nor the fate of his immortal soul will stand in his way:

> To hell allegiance, vows to the blackest devil,
> Conscience and grace to the profoundest pit.
> I dare damnation. To this point I stand –
> That both the worlds I give to negligence.
>
> 4.5.130–3

Hamlet too initially distances himself from the court; his 'inky cloak' separates him from the new *régime* and connects him with the liminal world of the night and the Ghost. But Hamlet has evidently expressed a choice in favour of life: he wishes to leave Denmark and return to the University of Wittenberg. His request is refused by Claudius; it would be far too dangerous for a rival claimant to the throne to be in a neighbouring country where he might, like Fortinbras, 'shark up lawless resolutes'. In terms, then, of the death-obsessed Hamlet idolized by Romantic poets, it is worth remembering that his initial choice is to pursue a life elsewhere. The two father figures that dominate prevent this: Claudius for political reasons and the Ghost for reasons of personal honour and revenge. In terms of accepting his destiny, however, Hamlet is as resolute as Laertes; he threatens Horatio and the guards and will speak to the Ghost 'though hell itself should gape' (1.2.243). In the **Folio** text of the play, Hamlet expresses his own recognition of the parallelism between his situation and Laertes': 'by the image of my cause I see/The portraiture of his (Thompson and Taylor, 472–3, lines 10–11).

The final encounter between the two achieves the extraordinary: in their dying exchanges a resolution is achieved which moves the play beyond the old Catholic vision of Purgatory that commences the action. In Hamlet's dramatic return to Denmark in Act 5, there seems to be a profound paradox: he is certainly the active revenger, the deaths of Rosencrantz and Guildenstern 'are not near my conscience' (5.2.57); neither the Queen nor Horatio can stop him fighting Laertes in the graveyard, and he accepts the challenge delivered by Osric despite its obvious dangers. For Hamlet it is now a moral obligation – 'perfect conscience' – to rid Denmark of Claudius. Yet although he assumes agency, he expresses an acceptance of the Protestant idea of Providence:

> There's a divinity that shapes our ends,
> Rough-hew them how we will.
>
> 5.2.10–11

This is inherently biblical; when Hamlet says later that there is 'special Providence in the fall of a sparrow' (5.2.197–8) he is recalling the words of Christ that 'two sparrows are sold for a farthing' and 'one of them shall not fall on the ground without your Father' (Mt. 10.29, KJV). Hamlet articulates a Protestant concept of destiny in which he must accede to God's wider and unknown purpose.

In the final duel Hamlet seeks Laertes' forgiveness in language which is strangely distanced and evasive: 'His madness is poor Hamlet's enemy' (5.2.217). The response he receives from Laertes is equally obfuscatory while making specific reference to revenge. Yet it is Laertes who reveals to Hamlet the murderous plot that destroys them and thereby re-establishes publicly for the court a degree of justice. Following the confusion over the poisoned rapier, Laertes' judgement is self-accusing: 'I am justly killed with mine own treachery' (5.2.292). He repeats the identical pronouncement when Claudius dies with the same poisoned weapon: 'He is justly served' (5.2.311). His final words, in a play concerned so frequently with damnation, are highly significant:

> Exchange forgiveness with me, noble Hamlet,
> Mine and my father's death come not upon thee,
> Nor thine on me. [*Dies*]
>
> 5.2.313–15

Laertes echoes the words of the Lord's Prayer, part of the Elizabethan catechism and central to every child's education: 'forgive us our trespasses as we forgive them that trespass against us.' His dying words absolve Hamlet while seeking pardon for himself. In Protestant terms there is no need for priestly intervention: inner conscience and sincere repentance will secure grace. Hamlet's response, 'Heaven make thee free of it' (5.2.316) is altruistic; Laertes, too, is deserving of forgiveness. Horatio's pious hope that 'flights of angels sing thee to thy rest' (5.2.344) signifies the soul's journey to Heaven rather than to Purgatory: in medieval angelology the souls of the blessed are accompanied by angels, a tradition deriving from the New Testament account of the beggar who 'was carried by the angels into Abraham's bosom' (Lk. 16.22 and see Keck, 203–7). In the Ghost's terms, Hamlet's death is certainly 'unhouseled . . . unaneled' yet Reformation theology has moved away from the necessity of the church's rites to bestow salvation. The play that begins *in memoriam* Catholic rituals of death and remembrance concludes in a dramatic exchange of Protestant individualism. Hamlet and Laertes are revengers – they have impliedly chosen damnation; they die attaining forgiveness and redemption.

A Soviet *Hamlet*: Grigori Kozintsev (Lenfilm, 1964)

For Grigori Kozintsev (1905–73) as for the later Russian stage and film director, Andrei Tarkovsky (1932–86), Shakespeare is the consummate tragic playwright, dramatizing the struggle of the individual against the implacable forces of an oppressive state. Kozintsev's engagement with *Hamlet* typifies the changing ways in which Russian artists appropriated Shakespeare across the turbulent years of the twentieth century. Kozintsev's roots were in 1920s revolutionary agitprop, avant-garde Constructivism and the Factory of the Eccentric Actor (FEKS) – the Petrograd theatre collective formed by Kozintsev and fellow film director Leonid Trauberg. Shakespeare's writing was highly esteemed by radical artists and political theorists: both Marx and Lenin had written positively about Shakespeare, seeing in the tragedies a proto-revolutionary dynamic of class struggle and resistance to tyranny. Kozintsev became engaged with the idea of FEKS performing an experimental staged version of *Hamlet* as early as the Bolshevik 1920s but, in fact, it was not until 1954, some months after the death of Stalin, that he first directed the play at the Pushkin Academic Theatre in Leningrad. For Joseph Troncale, historian of Russian culture, Kozintsev's Shakespearean films form part of the Soviet memory of 'the Great Patriotic War' where *Hamlet* can be seen as 'a treatise on the tyranny of fascism and the consequent dehumanization of humanity' (Troncale, 196). In this context '[a] modern Elsinore would have no objection to closing the barbed wire of concentration camps around humanity like a crown of thorns' (Kozintsev, cited in Troncale, 197). Stalinism created a deeply repressive cultural climate, however, in which Shakespeare's tragedies were taken to epitomize the bourgeois reactionary art of the West with Hamlet no more than an effete aristocrat. Tragic experience was deemed to be incompatible with the progressive world of Soviet Communism. Artists and writers deemed unacceptable to the Party were exiled, imprisoned, murdered or simply ignored. Shostakovich's sexually anarchic opera *Lady Macbeth of the Mtsensk District* (1932) was highly popular in Russia until Stalin's vociferous dislike led to *Pravda* attacking the opera for petit-bourgeois formalism. The opera disappeared and the composer lived in fear of his life. In this context, Hamlet becomes the dissident artist-hero, 'hunted, exiled, murdered for his views, yet determined ... to speak the truth through art, specifically theater' (Moore, 20).

Appropriating *Hamlet* as an attack on Stalinism was facilitated by the writings of Jan Kott, Polish academic and writer (1914–2001), a seminal influence on dissident Soviet intellectuals amongst whom his works circulated in *samizdat* form. For Kott, Shakespeare offers a way into 'our modern experience, anxiety and sensibility' (Kott, *Contemporary*, 48). A key production of *Hamlet* in Cracow in 1956 is described as 'tense and sharp, modern and consistent ... a political drama *par excellence*' (Kott, *Contemporary*, 46). Writers of the totalitarian mid-century found in *Hamlet* the workings of a repressive state, a world contaminated by political crime, tyranny and fear, where relations between lovers, families and friends could be undermined and corroded by an evil system. In this context there is no mistaking the complex web of surveillance and spying in the play. As Kott argues, '*Hamlet* is like a sponge ... it immediately absorbs all the problems of our time (Kott, *Contemporary*, 52). As Moore suggests, writers and directors operating in a context of brutal repression and censorship become adept at strategies of 'resistance and critique' (Moore, 8). The Cracow *Hamlet* dramatized a hero of political resistance: 'Every Hamlet has a book in his hand ... Hamlet in the Cracow production of late autumn, 1956, read only newspapers. He shouted that "Denmark's a prison" and wanted to improve the world. He was a rebellious ideologist' (Kott, *Contemporary*, 56). Kozintsev did not identify with the melancholy tormented soul created by Goethe and the Romantic poets and he, too, produced an oppositional Hamlet, appropriate to the Soviet-Communist mid-twentieth century, a youth 'deeply involved in politics, rid of illusions, sarcastic, passionate and brutal' (Kott, *Contemporary*, 51).

Kozintsev's film dates from a period generally recognized as the Khrushchev 'thaw', the post-Stalinist period which saw a revival of cultural life and new possibilities of creative expression. Kozintsev chose to shoot the film in widescreen format and in black and white to reflect the 'cold greys of the North'. As with *King Lear* (1971), the music, composed by Kozintsev's contemporary, Shostakovich, plays a highly significant role in the film. Pasternak's prose translation of the text is a significantly curtailed version and, as Neil Taylor observes, the musical score 'accompanies 236 out of the film's 434 shots' (Taylor, 'Hamlet', 185). Indeed, the film is remarkable for the sequences in which there is no speech: Kozintsev creates a visual and musical aesthetic with recurring symbolic *leitmotifs*:

> **Stone:** the walls of Elsinore, the firmly built government prison
> **Iron:** weapons, the inhuman forces of oppression, the ugly steel faces of war
> **Fire:** anxiety, revolt, movement ... raging fiery tongues
> **Sea:** waves, crashing against the bastions, ceaseless movement, the change of the tides, the boiling of chaos ...
> **Earth:** the world beyond Elsinore, amid stones – a bit of field tilled by a ploughman, the sand pouring out of Yorick's skull, and the handful of dust in the palm of a wanderer-heir to the throne of Denmark.
>
> KOZINTSEV, 266

The film opens with an **establishing shot** of the sea beneath the huge and forbidding edifice of the fortress – the late-medieval castle of Ivangorod on the Russian–Estonian border. Throughout, the fortress both creates and symbolizes the dehumanizing world of Elsinore; as Hamlet first gallops towards the castle, huge banners are flung from the battlements to announce the death of the king, as if the mighty stone walls are shrouded in mourning. And as he enters the castle, the drawbridge is painfully drawn up and the terrifying teeth of the portcullis descend. Within, the architecture is oppressive: 'Elsinore does not consist in walls, but in the ears which the walls have' (Kozintsev, 225). Hamlet, played by Innokenti Smoktunovski, is seen in his first court appearances to distance himself from Claudius, 'a barrel-chested cross between Stalin and Henry VIII' (Crowl, *Hamlet*, 109) and his first soliloquy is a voice-over as he passes through crowds of smiling and sycophantic courtiers. Kozintsev's choice of protagonist was itself significant: Smoktunovski had fought with the Red Army from 1943, was briefly a German POW before escaping to fight with Russian partisans against the retreating German troops, but was judged as potentially subversive and exiled in Siberia for some years after the war. Kozintsev's intention was that he should play Hamlet not as a 'tender young man' but a 'heretic who attacks, burning with the intoxicating joy of struggle' (Moore, 72). A wider political world is also suggested in the film – unlike the earlier Olivier (1948) which remains within the enclosed and claustrophobic world of Elsinore throughout. Here, although the fortress frequently dominates the mise-en-scène, Kozintsev is also concerned to depict peasants, villagers, animals – and thereby, a sense of the wider fabric of life. The arrival of the players is vividly carnivalesque and 'The Murder of Gonzago' is performed as a grand public spectacle performed by torchlight. Long **tracking shots** reveal Fortinbras' army as if approaching from a vast distance, just as Hamlet is being dispatched to England. The film concludes with Fortinbras' victorious return. Interestingly, the depiction of the numinous is a key part of the film, despite official Soviet atheism: the scene between Hamlet and the Ghost is one of the most cinematically striking. The appearance of the Ghost is powerfully evoked by a disturbing full score with brass and percussion fanfare; there is nothing spectrally ethereal, rather a powerful and commanding effect. The camera initially looks down on Hamlet as the Ghost strides above, cloak billowing against the night sky, then, as the Ghost speaks, the camera pans down to reveal the terrified Hamlet shrinking against the castle walls, the surging waves breaking beneath him. The Ghost does not reappear but the repetition of the characteristic music, with dislocating light effects signal Hamlet's recall of the Ghost's words. In complete contrast, Ophelia is associated with delicate and melodic harpsichord music. She is first seen, in white, dancing 'like a mechanical doll to the tune of a tinkling child's music box' (Rothwell, 178) and stands, similarly stiffly when her female attendants dress her in mourning clothes and an iron corset. She is consistently the innocent victim of the machinations around her and, as she descends into madness, poignantly repeats the stylized dance movements.

Modern adaptations of *Hamlet* include *Haider* (Vishal Bhardwaj, 2014) where a story of violence and betrayal rooted in Kashmiri separatist politics is refracted through the essence of *Hamlet*. The film received considerable attention in India where it proved highly controversial for its depiction of brutality within the Indian army and the desecration of Kashmiri sacred sites. There would seem to be little in common between the politics of India–Pakistan border disputes and Shakespeare's Renaissance text yet there are also key similarities, and the ways in which Bhardwaj has interpreted the text for his contemporary context is provocative and perceptive. Here, too, in common with Kozintsev and Almereyda, there is a troubled Ghost haunting Haider and his mother, Ghazala. One of the scenes which translates powerfully to a troubled Muslim and Hindu context is Haider's failure to kill his uncle when – as a good Muslim – he is kneeling in prayer. And the film ends with a violent shoot-out in a snow-covered Kashmir graveyard.

Further reading

Martin Coyle (ed.), *Hamlet: Contemporary Critical Essays* (Basingstoke, 1992)

Maurice Hindle, *Shakespeare on Film* (Basingstoke, 2015)

Alison Shell, *Shakespeare and Religion* (London, 2010)

Emma Smith (ed.), *Five Revenge Tragedies: Kyd, Shakespeare, Marston, Chettle, Middleton* (London, 2012)

Robert N. Watson, 'Tragedy', in A.R. Braunmuller and Michael Hattaway (eds), *English Renaissance Drama* (Cambridge, 1994)

GLOSSARY OF CRITICAL TERMS USED IN THIS BOOK

Alliteration	repeated consonants especially at the beginnings of words
Anaphora	patterned repetition of a word or group of words
Antimetabole	words in an initial clause repeated in reverse grammatical order in a succeeding clause
Antithesis	words or ideas set up in contrast to each other, usually in balanced constructions
Apostrophe	an exclamatory address, usually to an object, abstract idea or a person who is absent or dead
Aptronym	a name that is suited to a character's status, identity or personality
Aubade	literally 'dawn song'; usually lovers' farewell
Blank verse	unrhymed iambic pentameter
Blazon	a speech of praise to a woman, itemizing her beauty feature by feature; closely associated with the courtly love convention

296 GLOSSARY OF CRITICAL TERMS USED IN THIS BOOK

Caesura	a break or pause in a poetic line; **medial caesura** is where this occurs exactly in the middle of the line
CGI	computer-generated image
Close-up shot	shot of the head or face and shoulders, often used to capture a character's reaction
Deixis	a linguistic concept related to words and phrases that situate what is spoken in time and space (e.g. 'this', 'that', 'here', 'now')
Diegetic sound	in film terms, the sound, music or voice effects that form part of the screen world
Ekphrastic	poetry about a visual art work and, more generally, a rhetorical device whereby aesthetic objects are brought alive by verbal description
Emblem	pictorial depiction of symbols/personifications, often for the purpose of moral instruction
Enjambement	running on of one line of verse to the next with no punctuation break
Epithalamium	wedding song
Epithet	verbal label (often a noun or adjective) defining a characteristic of a person or thing
Establishing shot	usually a distant shot which establishes character(s) in a particular setting
Euphuism	highly wrought rhetorical language

Folio	printed work (literally 'leaf' where the printer's sheet is folded once to create four pages).
The Gaze	usually used of male voyeuristic scrutiny of women
Heptameter	a line of fourteen syllables (seven metrical feet)
Hyperbole	conscious use of verbal exaggeration
Hypermetrical	a line which has one or more extra syllables
Iambic pentameter	the basic metre of Shakespeare's verse: five iambic feet (five stresses per line)
Illeism	the act of referring to oneself in the third person
In medias res	literally, 'in the middle of things'; often used for openings of plays or scenes where characters seem to be involved in discussion
Long-shot	refers to the relative size of an object filling the screen; 'long-shot' frames a human figure within the screen; 'medium-long shot' frames most, but not all, of an adult figure
Metaphor	comparative figure of speech where one thing is described in terms of another
Motif	recurring image, theme, idea or verbal pattern in an art work (usually film, literature or music)
Non-diegetic	in film, non-diegetic sound is background music or any sound not represented on screen

298 GLOSSARY OF CRITICAL TERMS USED IN THIS BOOK

Oxymoron — figure of speech where two opposing words are side by side, e.g. 'fair devil' (*Othello*)

Paralinguistic — elements of spoken communication that lend emphasis to the words articulated (e.g. gesture, facial expression, tone, volume and pitch)

Paratext — text that surrounds the main text, such as a preface, introduction or footnotes

Pentameter — five strong stresses in a verse line

Performative language — speech acts which 'perform' a specific function; e.g. swearing an oath, exchanging marriage vows

Personification — attributing human qualities to inanimate objects

Petrarchism — language influenced by the fourteenth-century Italian poet, Petrarch; associated with courtly love and characterized by elaborate rhetorical flourishes

Plosive — in phonetics, a consonant which creates a 'stop' in the sound; e.g. 'mob'

Polyptoton — the repetition of a word with the same root in a different form; e.g. 'love is not love/Which alters when it alteration finds' (Sonnet 116)

Polysemy — a sign (such as a word or symbol) that holds multiple meanings

Polysyllabic — having several syllables

Quarto — printed text where printer's sheets are folded twice to make eight pages

GLOSSARY OF CRITICAL TERMS USED IN THIS BOOK

Scopophilia	connected with the 'gaze'; a form of voyeurism
Sententia(e)	pithy statement(s) of received wisdom
Sibilance	repeated 's' sounds in a verse line
Stichomythia	dialogue of alternate single lines, often a kind of verbal parrying
Tracking shot	a camera shot that moves forwards, backwards or sideways
Transferred epithet	figure of speech where the epithet (usually an adjective) modifies a noun to which it cannot be literally attached; e.g. 'incestuous sheets' (*Hamlet*)
Trochee	metrical foot which is the reverse of iambic; i.e. a stressed, followed by an unstressed syllable
Trope	figurative language including metaphor, simile and personification
Two-shot	a shot which frames two persons (usually medium close-up or medium shots)

REFERENCES

Adler — Renata Adler, '*Doctor Faustus* (1967) Screen: Faustus Sells His Soul Again: Burtons and Oxford Do the Devil's Work', *New York Times*, 7 February 1968. Available online: www.nytimes.com/movie/review?res=9B02EED91439E63ABC4F53DFB4668383679EDE (accessed 5 August 2015)

Aebischer — Pascale Aebischer, 'Silence, Rape and Politics in *Measure for Measure*: Close Readings in Theatre History', *Shakespeare Bulletin*, 26 (2008), 1–23

Aers — David Aers, 'A Whisper in the Ear of Early Modernists; or, Reflections on Literary Critics Writing the "History of the Subject"', in David Aers (ed.), *Culture and History 1350–1600: Essays on English Communities, Identities and Writing* (New York and London, 1992)

Arshad — Yasmin Arshad, 'The enigma of a portrait: Lady Anne Clifford and Daniel's "Cleopatra"', in *The British Art Journal*, 11 (2011), 30–6

Auden — W.H. Auden, *The Dyer's Hand and Other Essays* (London, 1975)

Bacon — Francis Bacon, *Francis Bacon: The Major Works*, ed. Brian Vickers (Oxford, 2002)

Barber	John Barber, 'The pre-Shakespeare bloodbath', *Daily Telegraph*, 23 September 1982, n.p.
Barker	Francis Barker, *The Tremulous Private Body: Essays on Subjection* (London, 1984)
Bartels *Moor*	Emily C. Bartels, *Speaking of the Moor: from* Alcazar *to* Othello (Philadelphia, 2008)
Bartels '*Tis Pity*'	Emily C. Bartels, '*'Tis Pity She's a Whore*: the play of intertextuality', in Emma Smith and Garrett A. Sullivan, Jr (eds), *The Cambridge Companion to English Renaissance Tragedy* (Cambridge, 2010)
Barton	Anne Barton, *Ben Jonson: Dramatist* (Cambridge, 1984)
Basse	William Basse, *Sword and Buckler, or, Serving-mans Defence* (London, 1602)
Bate *Ovid*	Jonathan Bate, *Shakespeare and Ovid* (Oxford, 1994)
Bate *Titus*	*Titus Andronicus*, ed. Jonathan Bate, Arden Shakespeare (London, 1995)
Bawcutt	*The Changeling*, ed. N.W. Bawcutt (Manchester, 1991)
Beilin	Elaine V. Beilin, *Redeeming Eve: Women Writers of the English Renaissance* (Princeton, 1987)

Belsey	Catherine Belsey, *The Subject of Tragedy: Identity and Difference in Renaissance Drama* (London, [1985] 1993)
Bergeron	David Bergeron, *Textual Patronage in English Drama, 1570–1640* (Aldershot, 2006)
Bevington	David Bevington, 'The Performance History', in Sara Munson Deats (ed.), *Doctor Faustus: A Critical Guide* (London, 2010)
Billington *Faustus*	Michael Billington, 'Carry On Doctor', *The Guardian*, 13 March 2002, available online: www.theguardian.com/stage/2002/mar/13/theatre.artsfeatures (accessed 10 August 2015)
Billington *Malfi*	Michael Billington, 'The Duchess of Malfi', *The Guardian*, 16 January 2014, available online: www.theguardian.com/stage/2014/jan/16/the-duchess-of-malfi-review (accessed 10 August 2015)
Bloom	Harold Bloom, *The Invention of the Human* (London, 1999)
Blumenthal	Eileen Blumenthal, *Julie Taymor: Playing With Fire: Theater, Opera, Film*, 3rd edn (New York, 2007)
Boehrer	Bruce Boehrer, *Environmental Degradation in Jacobean Drama* (Cambridge, 2013)
Botero	Giovanni Botero, *The Greatness of Cities*, in D.P. Waley (ed.), *The Reason of State* (London, 1956)

Bowdler	Thomas Bowdler, *The Family Shakespeare* (London, 1863)
Braudel	Fernand Braudel, *The Mediterranean and the Mediterranean World in the Age of Philip II*, trans. Siân Reynolds (New York, 2002)
Britland	*The Tragedy of Mariam*, ed. Karen Britland (London, 2010)
Brockbank	Philip Brockbank (ed.), *Players of Shakespeare* (Cambridge, 1985)
Bromley and Stockton	James M. Bromley and Will Stockton (eds), *Sex Before Sex: Figuring the Act in Early Modern England* (Minneapolis, 2013)
Brook	Peter Brook, *The Empty Space* (London, 1968)
Brown *Renaissance*	Alison Brown, *The Renaissance* (London, 1999)
Brown 'Thing'	Bill Brown, 'Thing Theory', *Critical Inquiry*, 28 (2001), 1–22
Brown 'Sexuality'	John Russell Brown, 'Representing Sexuality in Shakespeare's Plays', in Catherine M.S. Alexander and Stanley Wells (eds), Shakespeare and Sexuality (Cambridge, 2001)
Brown *Venetian*	Patricia Fortini Brown, *Venetian Narrative Painting in the Age of Carpaccio* (London, 1988)
Bryson	Anna Bryson, *From Courtesy to Civility: Changing Codes of Conduct in Early Modern England* (Oxford, 1998)

Buckley	George Buckley, *Atheism in the English Renaissance* (Chicago, 1932)
Bulman	James C. Bulman, *Shakespeare in Performance: The Merchant of Venice* (Manchester, 1991)
Burnett *Changeling*	Mark Thornton Burnett, 'The Changeling and Masters and Servants,' in Garrett A. Sullivan, Patrick Cheney, Andrew Hadfield (eds), *Modern English Drama: A Critical Companion* (Oxford, 2006)
Burnett *Servants*	Mark Thornton Burnett, *Masters and Servants in English Renaissance Drama and Culture* (Basingstoke, 1997)
Burton	Robert Burton, *The Anatomy of Melancholy* (Oxford, 1632)
Butler *Gender*	Judith Butler, *Gender Trouble: Feminism and the Subversion of Identity* (London, 1990)
Butler 'Performative'	Judith Butler, 'Performative Acts and Gender Constitution: An Essay in Phenomenology and Feminist Theory', *Theatre Journal*, 40 (1988), 519–31
Caldwell	Ellen Caldwell, 'Invasive Procedures in Webster's *The Duchess of Malfi*', in Linda Woodbridge and Sharon Beehler (eds), *Women, Violence, and English Renaissance Literature: Essays Honoring Paul Jorgensen* (Arizona, 2003)
Callaghan	Dympna Callaghan, 'Re-reading Elizabeth Cary's *The Tragedie of Mariam, Faire Queene of Jewry*', in

	Margo Hendricks and Patricia Parker (eds) *Women, Race and Writing in the Early Modern Period* (London, 1994)
Calvo and Tronch	*The Spanish Tragedy*, eds Clara Calvo and Jesús Tronch, Arden Early Modern Drama (London, 2013)
Carlson	Marvin Carlson, *Performance: A Critical Introduction* (Oxford, 1996)
Carpenter	Julie Carpenter, 'First night review: *Othello*', *Daily Express*, 25 April 2013 (n.p.), available online: www.express.co.uk/entertainment/theatre/394507/First-night-review-Othello-National-Theatre-London (accessed 10 August 2015)
Cartmell	Deborah Cartmell, 'Franco Zeffirelli and Shakespeare' in Russell Jackson (ed.), *The Cambridge Companion to Shakespeare on Film*, 2nd edn (Cambridge, 2007)
Cavendish	Dominic Cavendish, 'Frantic Assembly's *Othello*', *Daily Telegraph*, 27 October 2008, available online: www.telegraph.co.uk/culture/theatre/drama/3562596/Neil-Bartletts-Romeo-and-Juliet-and-Frantic-Assemblys-Othello-reviews.html (accessed 10 August 2015)
Cerasano	S.P. Cerasano and Marion Wynne-Davies, *Renaissance Drama by Women: Texts and Documents* (London, 1996)
Clare	Janet Clare, *Revenge Tragedies of the Renaissance* (Tavistock, 2006)

Cleaver	Robert Cleaver, *A Godly Form of Householde Governement* (London, 1598)
Clerico	Terri Clerico, 'The Politics of Blood: John Ford's *'Tis Pity She's a Whore*, *English Literary Renaissance*, 22 (1992), 405–34
Coleridge	S.T. Coleridge, *Lectures 1808–1819 On Literature*, ed. R. A. Foakes, 2 vols (London, 1987)
Cook	*The Roaring Girl*, ed. Elizabeth Cook (London, 1996)
Cooper	Helen Cooper, *Shakespeare and the Medieval World* (London, 2010)
Corbin	Peter Corbin, 'Performing *Measure for Measure*', in Nigel Wood (ed.), *Measure for Measure* (Buckingham, 1996)
Coryate	Thomas Coryate, *Coryate's Crudities* (London, 1611)
Cox	John D. Cox, *The Devil and the Sacred in English Drama 1350–1642* (Cambridge, 2000)
Creaser	*Volpone, or, the Fox*, ed. John W. Creaser (London, 1978)
Crooke	Helkiah Crooke, *Microcosmographia* (London, 1615)
Crosse	Henry Crosse, *Vertues Common-wealth or the High-way to Honour* (London, 1603)

Crowl *Hamlet*	Samuel Crowl, *Screen Adaptations: Shakespeare's Hamlet* (London, 2014)
Crowl 'Shylock'	Sam Crowl, 'Looking for Shylock' in Mark Thornton Burnett and Romona Wray (eds), *Screening Shakespeare in the Twenty-First Century* (Edinburgh, 2006)
Curran	Kevin Curran, *Marriage, Performance and Politics at the Jacobean Court* (Farnham, 2009)
Cust	Richard Cust, *Charles I and the Aristocracy, 1625–1642* (Cambridge, 2013)
Dawson and Minton	*Timon of Athens*, eds Anthony B. Dawson and Gretchen E. Minton, Arden Shakespeare (London, 2008)
Derrida	Jacques Derrida, 'Aphorism Countertime', trans. Nicholas Royle, in Derek Attridge (ed.), *Acts of Literature* (London, 1992)
DiGangi	Mario DiGangi, 'John Ford', in Arthur F. Kinney (ed.), *A Companion to Renaissance Drama* (Oxford, 2002)
Dillon	Janette Dillon, *The Cambridge Introduction to Shakespeare's Tragedies* (Cambridge, 2007)
Dollimore *Radical*	Jonathan Dollimore, *Radical Tragedy* (Basingstoke, 2010)
Dollimore 'Subversion'	Jonathan Dollimore, 'Subversion through Transgression, *Doctor Faustus*', in David Scott Kastan and Peter

	Stallybrass (eds), *Staging the Renaissance: Reinterpretations of Elizabethan and Jacobean Drama* (London and New York, 1991)
Donne	*The Complete Poems of John Donne*, ed. Robin Robbins (Harlow, 2010)
Dromgoole	Dominic Dromgoole, 'The Next Stage', Guardian Saturday Review, *The Guardian*, 15, 11 January 2014, available online: www.theguardian.com/stage/2014/jan/11/shakespeare-globe-new-stage-dromgoole (accessed 10 August 2015)
Duffy	Eamon Duffy, *The Stripping of the Altars: Traditional Religion in England 1400–1580* (New Haven and London, 1992)
Duncan-Jones	Katherine Duncan-Jones, *Ungentle Shakespeare: Scenes from his Life* (London, 2001)
Dusinberre	Juliet Dusinberre, *Shakespeare and the Nature of Women* (London, 1975)
Edelman	Charles Edelman, *The Merchant of Venice: Shakespeare in Production* (Cambridge, 2002)
Eliot	T.S. Eliot, *Selected Essays* (reprinted London, 1986)
Empson	William Empson, *Faustus and the Censor: The English Faust-book and Marlowe's Doctor Faustus*; recovered and edited by John Henry Jones (Oxford, 1987)

Erne	Lukas Erne, *Beyond* The Spanish Tragedy: *A Study of the Works of Thomas Kyd* (Manchester, 2001)
Everett	Barbara Everett, *Young Hamlet: Essays on Shakespeare's Tragedies* (Oxford, 1992)
Faustbuch	*The English Faust Book: A Critical Edition, Based on the Text of 1592*, ed. John Henry Jones (Cambridge, 1994)
Fernie	Ewan Fernie, *Spiritual Shakespeares* (London, 2005)
Findlay	Alison Findlay, *Illegitimate Power: Bastards in Renaissance Drama* (Manchester, 1994)
Fitter	Chris Fitter, *Radical Shakespeare: Politics and Stagecraft in the Early Career* (New York, 2012)
Fitzmaurice	James Fitzmaurice, 'Shakespeare, Cavendish, and Reading Aloud in Seventeenth-Century England', in Katherine Romack and James Fitzmaurice (eds), *Cavendish and Shakespeare, Interconnections* (Aldershot, 2006)
Foster	Verna Foster, '*'Tis Pity She's a Whore* as City Tragedy', in Michael Neill (ed.), *John Ford: Critical Re-Visions* (Cambridge, 1988)
Foucault 'Nietzsche'	Michel Foucault, 'Nietzsche, Genealogy, History', in Paul Rabinow (ed.), *The Foucault Reader* (London, 1986)

Foucault *Will*	Michel Foucault, *The Will To Knowledge* (Harmondsworth, 1990)
Freedman	Penelope Freedman, *Power and Passion in Shakespeare's Pronouns: Interrogating 'you' and 'thou'* (Aldershot, 2007)
Freud	Sigmund Freud, 'On the Introduction of Naricissism', in *Beyond the Pleasure Principle and Other Writings*, trans. John Reddick (London, 2003)
Fudge	Erica Fudge, *Perceiving Animals: Humans and Beasts in Early Modern English Culture* (Urbana, 2002)
Garber *Age*	Marjorie Garber, *Coming of Age in Shakespeare* (London, 1981)
Garber *Culture*	Marjorie Garber, *Shakespeare and Modern Culture* (New York, 2008)
Gibbons	Brian Gibbons, *Jacobean City Comedy* (London, 1980)
Gibson	Colin Gibson, '"The Stage of My Mortality": Ford's Poetry of Death', in Michael Neill (ed.), *John Ford: Critical Re-Visions* (Cambridge, 1988)
Gill	*Doctor Faustus*, based on the A text, ed. Roma Gill (reprinted London 2013)
Goethe	Johann Wolfgang Goethe, *Faust Part Two*, trans. and ed. Philip Wayne (London, 1959)
Gouge	William Gouge, *Of Domesticall Duties, Eight Treatises* (London, 1622)

Gowing	Laura Gowing, *Common Bodies: Women, Touch and Power in Seventeenth-Century England* (New Haven, 2003)
Gras and Gras	Vernon Gras and Marguerite Gras (eds), *Peter Greenway: Interviews* (Jackson, Mississippi, 2000)
Greenaway	Peter Greenaway, *The Cook, the Thief, his Wife and her Lover* [filmscript] (Paris, 1989)
Greenblatt *et al.*	Stephen Greenblatt, Walter Cohen, Jean E. Howard, Katharine Eisaman Maus (eds), *The Norton Shakespeare* (New York, 1997)
Greenblatt *Hamlet*	Stephen Greenblatt, *Hamlet in Purgatory* (Princeton, 2002)
Greenblatt *Self-fashioning*	Stephen Greenblatt, *Renaissance Self-fashioning: From More to Shakespeare* (Chicago and London, [1980] 2005)
Griffiths	Sian Griffiths, 'Bard can help make migrant children British', *Sunday Times*, 9 February 2014 (n.p.), available online: www.thesundaytimes.co.uk/sto/news/uk_news/National/article1373565.ece (accessed 10 August 2015)
Groves	Beatrice Groves, *Texts and Traditions: Religion in Shakespeare 1592–1604* (Oxford, 2007)
Guillemeau	Jacques Guillemeau, *Childbirth, or, The Happy Delivery of Women*, trans. unknown (London, 1635)

Gurr *Playgoing*	Andrew Gurr, *Playgoing in Shakespeare's London*, 3rd edn (Cambridge, 2004)
Gurr *Spanish*	*The Spanish Tragedy*, ed. J.R. Mulryne, with Introduction and Notes by Andrew Gurr, New Mermaids (London, 2009)
Haber	Judith Haber, *Desire and Dramatic Form in Early Modern England* (Cambridge, 2009)
Harding	Sarah Harding, '*Compulsion*: A View from the Director's Chair', *Shakespeare Bulletin*, 29 (2011) 605–16
Harness	*The Dramatic Works of John Ford*, ed. William Harness, 2 vols (London, 1831)
Harrison	William Harrison, *The Description of England*, ed. George Edelen (Washington, DC and New York, 1994)
Hatchuel and Vienne-Guerrin	Sarah Hatchuel and Nathalie Vienne-Guerrin, 'Nationalizing *Volpone* in French Cinema and Television: Mediating Jonson through Molière, Shakespeare and Popular Screen Comedy', *Shakespeare Bulletin*, 29 (2011), 509–23
Hattaway	Michael Hattaway, *Elizabethan Popular Theatre: Plays in Performance* (London, 1982)

Hazlitt *Characters*	William Hazlitt, *Characters of Shakespear's Plays* (London, 1818)
Hazlitt *Lectures*	William Hazlitt, *Lectures on the Dramatic Literature of the Age of Shakespeare*, 2nd edn (London 1821)
Healy	Thomas Healy, 'Marlowe's biography', in Emily C. Bartels and Emma Smith (eds), *Christopher Marlowe in Context* (Cambridge, 2013)
Hic Mulier	*Hic Mulier: Or, The Man-Woman*, anon. (London, 1620)
Hindle	Maurice Hindle, *Studying Shakespeare on Film* (Basingstoke, 2007)
Hirschfield	Heather Hirschfield, *The End of Satisfaction: Drama and Repentance in the Age of Shakespeare* (Ithaca, 2014)
Hodgdon	*The Taming of the Shrew*, ed. Barbara Hodgdon, Arden Shakespeare (London, 2010)
Hodgson-Wright	Stephanie Hodgson-Wright, 'Beauty, Chastity and Wit: Feminising the Centre-stage', in Alison Findlay and Stephanie Hodgson-Wright with Gweno Williams, *Women and Dramatic Production, 1550–1700* (Harlow, 2000)
Honigmann	*Othello*, ed. E.A.J. Honigmann, Arden Shakespeare (London, 1997)
Hope	Jonathan Hope, *Shakespeare and Language: Reason, Eloquence and Artifice in the Renaissance* (London, 2010)

Hopkins *Hero*	Lisa Hopkins, *The Female Hero in English Renaissance Tragedy* (Basingstoke, 2002)
Hopkins 'Incest'	Lisa Hopkins, 'Incest and Class: *'Tis Pity She's a Whore* and the Borgias', in Elizabeth Barnes (ed.), *Incest and the Literary Imagination* (Gainesville, 2002)
Horowitz	Arthur Horowitz, 'Shylock after Auschwitz: *The Merchant of Venice* on the post-Holocaust stage – subversion, confrontation, and provocation', *Journal for Cultural and Religious Theory*, 8 (2007), 7–20
Hortmann	Wilhelm Hortmann, *Shakespeare on the German Stage: the Twentieth Century* (Cambridge, 1998)
Howard	Jean Howard, '*The Taming of the Shrew*', in Greenblatt *et al.* (eds), *The Norton Shakespeare: Comedies* (New York, 2008)
Hunter and Lichtenfels	Lynette Hunter and Peter Lichtenfels, *Negotiating Shakespeare's Language in* Romeo and Juliet: *Reading Strategies from Criticism, Editing and the Theatre* (Farnham, 2009)
Jameson	Anna Jameson, *Characteristics of Women: Moral, Poetical, and Historical*, 2 vols (London, 1832)
Jankowski	Theodora A. Jankowski, 'Hymeneal Blood, Interchangeable Women, and the Early Modern Marriage Economy in *Measure for Measure* and *All's Well That*

Ends Well', in Richard Dutton and Jean E. Howard (eds), *A Companion to Shakespeare's Works, Volume 4: The Poems, Problem Comedies, Late Plays* (Oxford 2005)

Jardine Lisa Jardine, *Worldly Goods* (London, 1996)

Jones Eldred Jones, *Othello's Countrymen: the African in English Renaissance Drama* (London, 1965)

Jonson *The Devil is an Ass*, ed. Peter Happé (Manchester, 1994)

Jorgens Jack J. Jorgens, *Shakespeare on Film* (London, 1979)

Kahn Coppélia Kahn, *Man's Estate: Masculine Identity in Shakespeare* (Berkeley, 1981)

Karim-Cooper Farah Karim-Cooper, 'The performance of early modern drama at Shakespeare's Globe', in Pascale Aebischer and Kathryn Prince (eds), *Performing Early Modern Drama Today* (Cambridge, 2012)

Karim-Cooper and Stern Farah Karim-Cooper and Tiffany Stern, *Shakespeare's Theatres and the Effects of Performance* (London, 2013)

Kastan *Doctor Faustus: A Norton Critical Edition*, ed. David Scott Kastan (New York and London, 2005)

Keck David Keck, *Angels and Angelology in the Middle Ages* (Oxford, 1998)

Keesey	Douglas Keesey, *The Films of Peter Greenaway: Sex, Death and Provocation* (Jefferson, 2006)
Kernan	Alvin Kernan, *The Cankered Muse* (New Haven, 1959)
King and Davidson	Pamela King and Clifford Davidson (eds), *The Coventry Corpus Christi Plays* (Kalamazoo, Michigan, 2000)
Knapp	James A. Knapp, 'Penitential Ethics in *Measure for Measure*', in Ken Jackson and Arthur F. Marotti (eds), *Shakespeare and Religion: Early Modern and Postmodern Perspectives* (Notre Dame, Indiana, 2011)
Knight	G. Wilson Knight, *The Wheel of Fire: Essays in Interpretation of Shakespeare's Sombre Tragedies* (London, 1930)
Ko and Shurgot	Yu Jin Ko and Michael W. Shurgot (eds), *Shakespeare's Sense of Character: On the Page and From the Stage* (Farnham, 2012)
Kott *Contemporary*	Jan Kott, *Shakespeare our Contemporary*, trans. Boleslaw Taborski (London, 1965, reprinted 1983)
Kott 'Kozintsev'	Jan Kott, 'On Kozintsev's *Hamlet*', *The Literary Review*, 22 (1979), 385–407
Kozintsev	Grigori Kozintsev, *Shakespeare, Time and Conscience* (London, 1967)
Kristeva *'Romeo'*	Julia Kristeva, 'Romeo and Juliet: Love-Hatred in the Couple' ['Le couple amour-haine selon *Roméo et Juliette*'], in

	R.S. White (ed.), *Romeo and Juliet* (Basingstoke, 2001)
Kristeva 'Women's Time'	Julia Kristeva, 'Women's Time', in Robyn R. Warhol and Diane Price Herndl (eds), *Feminisms* (New Brunswick, 1991)
Lake	Arthur Lake, *Sermons with Some Religious and Divine Meditations* (London, 1629)
Leavis	F.R. Leavis, *The Common Pursuit* (London, 1952)
Leggatt	Alexander Leggatt, *Shakespeare's Tragedies: Violation and Identity* (Cambridge, 2005)
Lemnius	Levinus Lemnius, *The Secret Miracles of Nature: in Four Books* (London, 1658)
Letts 'Globe'	Quentin Letts, 'McInnerny is the darling of the Globe', *Daily Mail*, 25 May 2007, available online: www.dailymail.co.uk/tvshowbiz/reviews/article-457622/McInnerny-Darling-Globe.html (accessed 10 August 2015)
Letts 'Isabella'	Quentin Letts, 'Sensual? This Isabella is as sexy as a bar of soap', *Daily Mail*, 25 November 2011 (n.p.), available online: www.dailymail.co.uk/tvshowbiz/reviews/article-2065963/Measure-For-Measure-review-This-Isabella-sexy-bar-soap.html (accessed 10 August 2015)
Lever	*Measure for Measure*, ed. J.W. Lever, Arden Shakespeare (London, 1965)

Levin	Richard Levin, *The Multiple Plot in English Renaissance Drama* (Chicago, 1971)
Levith	Murray J. Levith, *Shakespeare's Italian Settings and Plays* (Basingstoke, 1989)
Lindley	David Lindley, *The Trials of Frances Howard: Fact and Fiction at the Court of King James* (London, 1993)
Little	Arthur L. Little Jr, *Shakespeare Jungle Fever: National-Imperial Re-Visions of Race, Rape, and Sacrifice* (Stanford, California, 2000)
Lyly	John Lyly, *Euphues: The Anatomy of Wit and Euphues and His England*, ed. Leah Scragg (Manchester, 2003)
Macaulay	Alastair Macaulay, 'A grievous attack of nobility', *Financial Times*, 9 May 1997, 13
McCabe	Richard A. McCabe, *Incest, Drama and Nature's Law, 1550–1700* (Cambridge, 1993)
McCandless	David McCandless, *Gender and Performance in Shakespeare's Problem Comedies* (Bloomington, 1997)
MacCulloch	Diarmaid MacCulloch, *Reformation: Europe's House Divided 1490–1700* (London, 2004)
McDonald	Russ McDonald, *Shakespeare and Jonson, Jonson and Shakespeare* (Brighton, 1988)

McEvoy	Sean McEvoy, *Ben Jonson, Renaissance Dramatist* (Edinburgh, 2008)
MacFaul	Tom MacFaul, *Problem Fathers in Shakespeare and Renaissance Drama* (Cambridge, 2012)
McLuskie	Kathleen McLuskie, *Renaissance Dramatists* (London, Hemel Hempstead, 1989)
McPherson	David C. McPherson, *Shakespeare, Jonson, and the Myth of Venice* (London, 1990)
McRae	Andrew McCrae, *Renaissance Drama* (London, 2003)
Magnusson	Lynne Magnusson, *Shakespeare and Social Dialogue: Dramatic Language and Elizabethan Letters* (Cambridge, 1999)
Mahood	*The Merchant of Venice*, ed. M.M. Mahood (Cambridge, 2013)
Malcolmson	Cristina Malcolmson, '"As Tame as the Ladies": Politics and Gender in *The Changeling*', *English Literary Renaissance*, 20 (1990), 320–39
Mountford	Fiona Mountford, 'Groundlings aren't gripped', *Evening Standard*, 25 May 2007, formerly available at: www.standard.co.uk/goingout/theatre/groundlings-arent-gripped-7395516.html
Marcus *Duchess*	*The Duchess of Malfi*, ed. Leah S. Marcus, Arden Early Modern Drama (London, 2013)

Marcus *Puzzling*	Leah S. Marcus, *Puzzling Shakespeare: Local Reading and its Discontents* (Berkeley, 1988)
Marotti	Arthur Marotti, 'Shakespeare and Catholicism', in Richard Dutton, Alison Findlay and Richard Wilson (eds), *Theatre and Religion: Lancastrian Shakespeare* (Manchester University Press, 2003)
Marowitz	Charles Marowitz, *The Marowitz Shakespeare* (London, 1978)
Marston	John Marston, *Antonio's Revenge*, ed. W. Reavley Gair (Manchester, 1978)
Massai	*'Tis Pity She's a Whore*, ed. Sonia Massai, Arden Early Modern Drama (London, 2011)
Maus *Inwardness*	Katharine Eisaman Maus, *Inwardness and Theater in the English Renaissance* (Chicago, 1995)
Maus *Norton*	Katharine Eisaman Maus, Introduction to *Measure for Measure*, in Stephen Greenblatt, Walter Cohen, Jean E. Howard, Katharine Eisaman Maus (eds), *The Norton Shakespeare* (New York, 1997)
Milton	John Milton, *Paradise Lost*, ed. Alastair Fowler, 2nd edn (Harlow, 1998)
Milward	Peter Milward, SJ, 'Shakespeare's Jesuit Schoolmasters', in Findlay *et al.* (eds), *Theatre and Religion: Lancastrian Shakespeare* (Manchester, 2003)

Moody	A.D. Moody, *Shakespeare: The Merchant of Venice* (London, 1964)
Moore	Tiffany Ann Conroy Moore, *Kozintsev's Shakespeare Films: Russian Political Protest in Hamlet and King Lear* (Jefferson, North Carolina, 2012)
Mulryne	J.R. Mulryne, 'History and Myth in *The Merchant of Venice*', in Michele Marrapodi *et al.* (eds), *Shakespeare's Italy: Functions of Italian Locations in Renaissance Drama* (Manchester 1997)
National Theatre	*National Theatre Learning:* Othello *Background Pack* (The Royal National Theatre Board, 2013)
Neely	Carol Thomas Neely, *Distracted Subjects: Madness and Gender in Shakespeare and Early Modern Culture* (Ithaca and London, 2004)
Neill *Changeling*	*The Changeling*, ed. Michael Neill (London, 2006)
Neill *Death*	Michael Neill, *Issues of Death: Mortality and Identity in English Renaissance Tragedy* (Oxford, new edn 1999)
Neill *History*	Michael Neill, *Putting History to the Question: Power, Politics, and Society in English Renaissance Drama* (New York, Chichester, 2000)
Neill 'Riddle'	Michael Neill, 'What Strange Riddle's This?: Deciphering *'Tis Pity She's a Whore*', in Michael Neill (ed.), *John Ford: Critical Re-Visions* (Cambridge, 1988)

Nightingale	Benedict Nightingale, 'First to cry for revenge', *The Times*, 9 May 1997, 33
'Old Titus'	'Old Titus makes them swoon at Stratford', *Daily Mail*, 24 October 1955, 3
Orlin	Lena Cowen Orlin, 'The Performance of Things in "The Taming of the Shrew"', *The Yearbook of English Studies*, 23 (1993), 167–88
Pacino	'Q & A With Al Pacino', by Ivor Davis, *Jewish Journal*, posted 6 January 2005, available online: www.jewishjournal. com/arts/article/q_a_with_al_ pacino_20050107 (accessed 4 August 2015)
Painter	William Painter, *The Palace of Pleasure*, ed. Joseph Jacobs, 3 vols (London, 1890)
Parker	Brian Parker, 'Jonson's Venice' in J.R. Mulryne and Margaret Shewring (eds), *Theatre of the English and Italian Renaissance* (Basingstoke, 1991)
Pater	Walter Pater, *Appreciations* (London, 1889)
Peter	John Peter, '*Othello*', *Sunday Times*, 5 October 2008 (n.p.) www. thesundaytimes.co.uk/sto/culture/arts/ theatre/article239790.ece (accessed 10 August 2015)
Potter 'Marlowe'	Lois Potter, 'Marlowe in theatre and film', in Patrick Cheney (ed.), *The Cambridge Companion to Christopher Marlowe* (Cambridge, 2004)

Potter *Othello*	Lois Potter, *Shakespeare in Performance: Othello* (Manchester, 2002)
Powell	Raymond Powell, 'The Adaptation of a Shakespearean genre: *Othello* and Ford's *'Tis Pity She's a Whore*', *Renaissance Quarterly*, 48 (1995), 582–92
Purkiss	Diane Purkiss, *Three Tragedies by Renaissance Women* (London, 1998)
Quarshie	Hugh Quarshie, *Second Thoughts About Othello* [International Shakespeare Association Occasional Paper, no.7] (Chipping Campden, 1999)
Quinn and Ryan	David Quinn and A.N. Ryan, *England's Sea Empire* (London, 1983)
Raber	Karen Raber, *Dramatic Difference: Gender, Class, and Genre in the Early Modern Closet Drama* (London, 2001)
Rackin 'Androgyny'	Phyllis Rackin, 'Androgyny, Mimesis, and the Marriage of the Boy Heroine on the English Stage', *PMLA*, 102 (1987), 29–41
Rackin *Women*	Phyllis Rackin, *Shakespeare and Women* (Oxford, 2005)
Radford	'Michael Radford – The Merchant of Venice – 12/11/04', interview in *Groucho Reviews*, available online: www.grouchoreviews.com/interviews/38 (accessed 4 August 2015)
Reynolds	John Reynolds, *The Triumphs of Gods Revenge Against the Crying and Execrable Sinne of Wilfull and Premeditated Murther* (London, 1621)

Rieger	Gabriel A. Rieger, *Sex and Satiric Tragedy in Early Modern England: Penetrating Wit* (Farnham, 2009)
Righter	Anne Righter, *Shakespeare and the Idea of the Play* (London, 1967)
Roberts	Sasha Roberts, *Romeo and Juliet* (Plymouth, 1998)
Rothwell	Kenneth S. Rothwell, *A History of Shakespeare on Screen: A Century of Film and Television*, 2nd edn (Cambridge, 2004)
Rutter *Child's Play*	Carol Chillington Rutter, *Shakespeare and Child's Play: Performing Lost Boys on Stage and Screen* (London, 2007)
Rutter *Voices*	Carol Rutter, *Clamorous Voices: Shakespeare's Women Today* (London, 1988)
Ryan *Comedies*	Kiernan Ryan, *Shakespeare's Comedies* (Basingstoke, 2009)
Ryan *Shakespeare*	Kiernan Ryan, *Shakespeare*, 3rd edn (Basingstoke, 2002)
Sanders	Julie Sanders, *Caroline Drama: The Plays of Massinger, Ford, Shirley and Brome* (Plymouth, 1999)
Santayana	George Santayana, *Interpretations of Poetry and Religion* in *The Works of George Santayana* III (Cambridge, MA, 1989)

Sawday	Jonathan Sawday, *The Body Emblazoned: Dissection and the Human Body in Renaissance Culture* (London, 1995)
Schafer *THE*	Liz Schafer, 'Intimate horror for the front-row elite', *Times Higher Education*, 46–7, 16 January 2014, available online: https://www.timeshighereducation.co.uk/features/culture/review-the-duchess-of-malfi/2010517.article (accessed 10 August 2015)
Schafer *Witch*	*The Witch*, ed. Elizabeth Schafer (London, 1994)
Schoenfeldt	Michael C. Schoenfeldt, *Bodies and Selves in Early Modern England: Physiology and Inwardness in Spenser, Shakespeare, Herbert, and Milton* (Cambridge, 1999)
Scott Holland	Henry Scott Holland, 'Death is nothing at all', line 2, available online: www.poemhunter.com/poem/death-is-nothing-at-all/ (accessed 7 August 2015)
Shapiro	James Shapiro, *Shakespeare and the Jews* (New York, 1996)
Shuger	Deborah Kuller Shuger, *Habits of Thought in the English Renaissance: Religion, Politics, and the Dominant Culture* (Berkeley, 1990)
Sidney	Philip Sidney (Sir), *An Apology for Poetry (or The Defence of Poesy)*, revised edn, ed. R.W. Maslen (Manchester, 2002)

Sinfield *Authority*	Alan Sinfield, *Shakespeare, Authority, Sexuality* (London and New York, 2006)
Sinfield *Faultlines*	Alan Sinfield, *Faultlines: Cultural Materialism and the Politics of Dissident Reading* (Oxford, 2001)
Smith 'Shakespeare'	Emma Smith, 'Shakespeare and early modern tragedy', in Emma Smith and Garrett A. Sullivan, Jr (eds), *The Cambridge Companion to English Renaissance Tragedy* (Cambridge, 2010)
Smith *Spanish Tragedie*	*The Spanish Tragedie*, ed. Emma Smith (Harmondsworth, 1998)
Sofer	Andrew Sofer, 'Absorbing Interests: Kyd's Bloody Handkerchief as Palimpsest', *Comparative Drama*, 34 (2000), 127–53
Solga	Kim Solga, *Violence Against Women in Early Modern Performance* (Basingstoke, 2009)
Spencer	Charles Spencer, 'Unhappy mix of sex toys and silliness', 28 November 2011 (n.p.), available online: www.telegraph.co.uk/culture/theatre/theatre-reviews/8913932/Measure-for-Measure-RSC-Swan-Theatre-Stratford-upon-Avon-review.html (accessed 10 August 2015)
Steggle	Matthew Steggle, *Volpone: A Critical Guide* (London, 2011)
Stone *Crisis*	Lawrence Stone, *Crisis of the Aristocracy* (Oxford, 1965)

Stone *Family*	Lawrence Stone, *The Family, Sex and Marriage In England 1500–1800*, abridged edn (Harmondsworth, 1979)
Straznicky	Marta Straznicky, 'Private drama', in Laura Lunger Knoppers *The Cambridge Companion to Early Modern Women's Writing* (Cambridge, 2010), 247–59
Stubbes	Philip Stubbes, *The Anatomie of Abuses* (London, 1585)
Tanner	Tony Tanner, *Prefaces to Shakespeare* (London, 2010)
Tarkovsky	Andrei Tarkovsky, *Time Within Time: the Diaries, 1970–1986* (London, 1994)
Taylor *Self*	Charles Taylor, *Sources of the Self: The Making of the Modern Identity* (Cambridge, 1989)
Taylor 'Hamlet'	Neil Taylor, 'The films of *Hamlet*', in Anthony Davies and Stanley Wells (eds), *Shakespeare and the Moving Image: the plays on film and television* (Cambridge, 1994)
Taylor 'MM'	Paul Taylor, *The Independent*, 'Measure for Measure', 29 November 2011 (n.p.), available online: www.independent.co.uk/arts-entertainment/theatre-dance/reviews/measure-for-measure-swan-theatre-stratforduponavon-6267240.html (accessed 10 August 2015)
Thompson and Taylor	*Hamlet*, eds Ann Thompson and Neil Taylor, Arden Shakespeare (London, 2006)

Tourneur	Cyril Tourneur, *The Atheist's Tragedy*, in *Four Revenge Tragedies*, ed. Katharine Eisaman Maus (Oxford, 1995)
Tricomi	Albert Tricomi, *Anti-court Drama in England, 1603–42* (Charlottesville, 1989)
Tromly	Fred B. Tromly, *Fathers and Sons in Shakespeare: The Debt Never Promised* (Toronto, 2010)
Troncale	Joseph Troncale, 'The War and Kozintsev's Films *Hamlet* and *King Lear*', in Anna Lawton (ed.), *The Red Screen: Politics, Society, Art in Soviet Cinema* (London, 1992)
Veltruský	Jiří Veltruský, 'Dramatic Text as a Component of Theater', in Ladislav Matejka and Irwin R. Titunik (eds), *Semiotics of Art* (Cambridge, MA, 1976)
Vickers	Brian Vickers (ed.), *William Shakespeare: The Critical Heritage 1693–1733* (London, 1974)
Watson *Silence*	Robert N. Watson, *The Rest is Silence: Death as Annihilation in the English Renaissance* (Berkeley, 1994)
Watson *Volpone*	*Volpone*, ed. Robert N. Watson (reprinted London 2013)
Webster	John Webster, *The White Devil*, ed. Christina Luckyj (London, 2014)
Weis	*Romeo and Juliet*, ed. René Weis, Arden Shakespeare (London, 2012)

Weller and Ferguson	Barry Weller and Margaret Ferguson (eds), *'The Tragedy of Mariam, The Fair Queen of Jewry' with 'The Lady Falkland: Her Life,' by One of Her Daughters* (London, 1994)
Wells	Stanley Wells, 'The Challenges of *Romeo and Juliet*', *Shakespeare Survey*, 49 (1996), 1–14
White	*Arden of Faversham*, ed. Martin White (London, 2007)
Wilson *Ground*	August Wilson, *The Ground on Which I Stand* (London, 2001)
Wilson *Discourse*	Thomas Wilson, *A Discourse Upon Usury* (London, 1572)
Woodbridge 'Malfi'	Linda Woodbridge, 'Queen of Apricots: The Duchess of Malfi, Hero of Desire', in Naomi Conn Liebler (ed.), *The Female Tragic Hero in English Renaissance Drama* (Basingstoke, 2002)
Woodbridge *Revenge*	Linda Woodbridge, *English Revenge Drama: Money, Resistance, Equality* (Cambridge, 2010)
Woods	Gillian Woods, 'The Confessional Identity of *'Tis Pity She's a Whore*', in Lisa Hopkins (ed.), *'Tis Pity She's a Whore: A Critical Guide* (London 2010)
Woolf	Virginia Woolf, *The Common Reader 1* (London, 1925)
Worthen	W.B. Worthen, 'Drama, Performativity, and Performance', *PMLA*, 113 (1998), 1093–107

Wray	*The Tragedy of Mariam*, ed. Ramona Wray, Arden Early Modern Drama (London, 2012)
Wrightson	Keith Wrightson, *Earthly Necessities: Economic Lives in Early Modern Britain, 1470–1750* (London, 2002)
Zweig	Stefan Zweig, *Ben Jonson's Volpone* (freely adapted), trans. Ruth Langner (London, 1928)

INDEX

Aaron (*Titus Andronicus*) 203–4
acting companies xii
   King's Men 35–6
Almeida Theatre Company
   Measure for Measure (2010)
   233–4
Almereyda, Michael
   Hamlet (film) 285
Angelo (*Measure for Measure*)
   225–30
Annabella (*'Tis Pity She's a
   Whore*) 243–7
anti-Semitism 56, 58, 61–4, 118
Antonio (*Duchess of Malfi*) 28–9
   (*Merchant of Venice*) 42,
   47–51, 57–8, 61, 63–4
Arden of Faversham (anon) 116
authorship viii–xi,
   and *Spanish Tragedy, The*
   189–91

Bacon, Francis 45, 176–7, 184,
   194, 258
Bassanio (*Merchant of Venice)*
   52–4
Basse, William
   *Sword and Buckler, or,
   Serving-man's Defence*
   (poem) 136–7, 139–40
BBC Shakespeare (1978–85)
   Othello 145
   Titus Andronicus 209
BBC *Shakespeare Retold*
   The Taming of the Shrew 108

beast fable 79–83
Beatrice-Joanna (*Changeling)*
   152–62, 165–8
Beaumont, Francis *Knight of the
   Burning Pestle, The* 154
Bhardwaj, Vishal
   Haider (film) 86, 293
Bianca (*Taming of the Shrew*)
   94–7, 103–4, 106
Bible, the 115, 213
   1 Corinthians 214
   Deuteronomy 236, 238
   Ephesians 131
   Genesis 26, 57–8, 71, 214, 238
   1 John 263
   Leviticus 214, 238
   Mark 256
   Matthew 255, 287
   Psalms 268
   Revelation 256, 272–3
   Romans 263
   1 Timothy 44
Blackfriars playhouse 35–9, 120,
   126
Bosola (*Duchess of Malfi*) 32–3,
   152
Bradley, A.C. 7
Brook, Peter xiv, 195–6, 208,
   219, 222
Brooke, Arthur
   *Tragical History of Romeus
   and Juliet, The* (poem) 7,
   8, 9, 10, 12
Burton, Richard (actor)

INDEX

in *Taming of the Shrew, The* 105
in *Doctor Faustus* 275–7
Burton, Robert (*Anatomy of Melancholy*) 49, 215

Calvin, John (and Calvinism) 256, 268, 271, 280
Cary, Elizabeth 109–11,
   Tragedy of Mariam, The ix, 109–23
Cassio (*Othello*) 141–2
celibacy 215
   in *Measure for Measure* 220, 224–6
censorship 65, 132, 171–2, 290
   bowdlerization 14, 218–19
   and *Doctor Faustus* 271
   Master of the Revels viii, 135
   Shakespeare film 205
character 5–6, 90, 123, 133, 231, 233
   in Ben Jonson 70, 74
Cheek By Jowl (theatre company)
   'Tis Pity She's a Whore (Barbican, 2014) 243
Chicago Shakespeare Theater 148
closet drama 116, 123–7
Coghill, Nevill (director)
   Doctor Faustus 275–6
Coleridge 79, 133
colour-blind casting 147
comedy 47, 65–7, 79
   city comedy xi, 8, 69, 75–6, 88
   Shakespearean 93, 218, 230
commedia dell'arte 82–3, 96
Corpus Christi plays 113, 256
Coryate 41–2, 77
courtship 154

in *Duchess of Malfi, The* 27–8
in *Merchant of Venice, The* 52
in *Taming of the Shrew, The* 94–9

Davenant, William
   Law Against Lovers, The 222
Deflores (*Changeling*) 151–63, 165–6
Dekker, Thomas 236
   Honest Whore, The 221, 237
   Shoemaker's Holiday, The 8
   (with John Ford and William Rowley)
   Witch of Edmonton, The 8, 265, 276
   (with Thomas Middleton)
   Roaring Girl, The 88–9, 126
Donne, John
   'Divine Meditations' 254–5, 270
   Sermons 255
Duchess of Malfi (*Duchess of Malfi*) 25–35, 247

Eliot, T.S. x, 79, 83, 240

Faustbuch (anon) 261, 271, 273
Faustus (*Doctor Faustus*) 261–77
First Folio (1623) ix, 20, 90, 140, 173, 287
Fletcher, John
   The Woman's Prize; or, The Tamer Tamed 104–5
Ford, John
   Broken Heart, The 240, 242
   Christ's Bloody Sweat (poem) 245–6

'Tis Pity She's a Whore 33, 173, 207, 217, 234–51
Foucault, Michel 3–4, 212–13
Frantic Assembly (theatre company) 148
  Othello (2009) 148–9
Freestone, Elizabeth (director)
  Doctor Faustus 274–7

Garrick, David 13, 14
Gildon, Charles
  Measure for Measure; or Beauty the Best Advocate 222
Giovanni ('Tis Pity She's a Whore) 239–44
Globe playhouse (see also Shakespeare's Globe) xi, 36, 38, 88, 136–7
Goethe, Johann Wolfgang von
  Faust 271
Gouge, William 31–2, 117, 131–2, 144
Greenaway, Peter
  The Cook, the Thief, his Wife and her Lover (film) 247–51
Greenblatt 3–4, 63, 257, 266
Griffi, Giuseppe Patroni
  Addio, fratello crudele (film) 241
Gurr, Andrew x, 37, 85, 179

Hamlet (Hamlet) 281–9, 292–3
Harding, Sarah
  Compulsion (film) 164–8
Hazlitt, William x, 8, 13–14, 271
Herod (Tragedy of Mariam) 111–15, 117–23

Hieronimo (Spanish Tragedy) 176, 179, 183–94, 200, 201, 204

Iago (Othello) 116, 133–45, 168
incest 217, 237–8, 244–6
  in 'Tis Pity She's a Whore 235, 238–9, 244–6
Isabella (Changeling) 161–4
Isabella (Measure for Measure) 224–9, 231–4

Jameson, Anna 14
Jews 42, 60, 114–15, (see also anti-Semitism)
Jonson, Ben
  Alchemist, The 66
  Devil is an Ass, The 277
  Epicoene or The Silent Woman 89
  Every Man in his Humour 65–6
  'On my First Sonne' (poem) 186
  Volpone 65–84
Juliet (Romeo and Juliet) 11–19, 25, 28, 211, 241, 244
Junger, Gil
  Ten Things I Hate About You (film) 107–8

Katherina (Taming of the Shrew) 93–4, 97–104, 106–7
Kott, Jan 262, 290–1
Kozintsev, Grigori
  Hamlet (film) 289–93
Kyd, Thomas
  Spanish Tragedy, The 174–6, 178–95, 200, 201, 279

Lavinia (*Titus Andronicus*)
    206–10
Lemnius, Levinus 30, 34, 213–14
Luhrmann, Baz
    *William Shakespeare's Romeo
    + Juliet* (film) 19–24
Lumley, Lady Jane
    Iphigenia at Aulis 110, 123–4
Lyly, John *Euphues* 98

madness
    in *Changeling, The* 160
    in *Hamlet* 288, 293
    in *Spanish Tragedy, The*
        189–90
Marcus (*Titus Andronicus*)
    207–10
Mariam (*Tragedy of Mariam*)
    111–15, 118–23
Marowitz, Charles 102
Marlowe, Christopher 260–2
    Doctor Faustus 260–78
    Jew of Malta, The 56–7, 71
    Tamburlaine Part 1 xi
    Tamburlaine Part 2 263–4
marriage 163–4, 212, 214
    in *Duchess of Malfi, The*
        29–32
    in *Measure for Measure*
        229–30
    in *Taming of the Shrew, The*
        96–104
    in *Tragedy of Mariam, The*
        117, 120–1
Marston, John
    Antonio's Revenge 283–4
    Dutch Courtesan, The 221,
        223–4
masques 113, 123–6
Mephastophilis (*Doctor Faustus*)
    264–9, 271, 275–6

Middleton, Thomas 25, 132
    Revenger's Tragedy, The x,
        31, 157, 173, 180, 183,
        207, 237, 248–9
    Women Beware Women 237
    (and Dekker) *Roaring Girl,
        The* 88–9, 126
    (and Rowley) *Changeling,
        The* 150–69
Milton, John
    Comus 124–5
    Paradise Lost 75, 255, 264,
        267
money 43–5, 47, 49, 53–4, 70–6
Mosca (in *Volpone*) 72–9
music 53, 55
    in *Hamlet* (film) 291, 293
    in *William Shakespeare's
        Romeo + Juliet* (film) 22–3

National Theatre Company,
        London
    The Changeling (1988) 168
    National Theatre Live xiii–xiv
    Othello (2013) 146, 148
    The Spanish Tragedy (1982)
        188
new historicism 4

Othello (*Othello*) 136, 142,
    146–50
Ovid 93, 96

Painter, William
    Palace of Pleasure, The 25,
        26–7, 31
Parker, Oliver
    Othello (film) 138
Pater, Walter 218, 222–3
Peele, George
    David and Bethsabe 237

Performativity 85–90,
    and gender 12, 87–90
Perkins, William 268
Petruccio (*Taming of the Shrew*)
    98–104, 106–7
Portia (*Merchant of Venice*)
    51–6, 58–61, 64
Prynne, William 82, 126, 276
psychoanalytic theory 2, 8, 212, 225
Purgatory 279–80, 283, 287–8

racism
    in *Merchant of Venice, The*
        52, 56, 58, 64
    in casting *Othello* 145–50
    in *Othello* 135–6
    in *Titus Andronicus* 203–4
Radford, Michael
    (*Merchant of Venice* film)
        61–5
rape 154, 157, 206, 216
    in *Compulsion* (film) 167
    in *Measure for Measure* 217, 226, 230
    in *Titus Andronicus* 201–2, 207–10
Ravenscroft, Edward
    Rape of Lavinia, The 203
revenge tragedy 171–210,
    248, 249–51, 279, 281,
    283–9
Roderigo (*Othello*) 136–8, 144
Romeo (*Romeo and Juliet*) 7,
    10–11, 17
Royal Shakespeare Company 147
    RSC Swan xiii
    Doctor Faustus (1974) 275
    Measure for Measure
        (Stratford Memorial
        Theatre, 1950) 219
    Measure for Measure (RSC
        Swan, 2011–12) 231–3
    Othello (2015) 146
    Richard II (2013–14) 6
    The Spanish Tragedy (RSC
        Swan, 1997) 188
    Titus Andronicus (Stratford
        Memorial Theatre, 1955)
        195–6, 205, 208

Salome (*Tragedy of Mariam*)
    111–12, 115–18, 121
Seneca, Lucius Annaeus 123, 172
    Senecan rhetoric 119, 180, 187
    Senecan tragedy 111
    Thyestes 283–4
Shakespeare, William
    All's Well That Ends Well 99, 230
    Antony and Cleopatra ix, 24, 25, 120, 134, 204
    As You Like It 47
    Cymbeline 174, 189–90
    Hamlet viii, ix, 4, 5,6, 31,
        134, 173, 178, 180, 189,
        237, 278–89
    Henry VIII 36
    King Lear 31, 134, 201, 202,
        205, 258
    Macbeth ix, 31, 186, 257, 278
    Measure for Measure
        218–34, 255
    Merchant of Venice, The
        42–3, 47–61
    *Midsummer Night's Dream,
        A* xiv, 91, 188, 218
    Much Ado About Nothing
        98, 99, 180
    Othello 43, 114, 133–50,
        157, 168, 236

INDEX

Pericles 221–2, 237
Richard II 134
Richard III 113, 278
Romeo and Juliet 7–24, 25, 28, 134, 211–12, 236, 239, 241, 246
Sonnets 28, 220, 257
Taming of the Shrew, The 90–108
Tempest, The ix, 94, 266
Timon of Athens 76
Titus Andronicus 175, 178, 195–210, 250
Twelfth Night 26, 47, 93, 154, 218
Shakespeare's Globe x, 37, 86, 148, 191
 Othello (2007) 149–50
Shylock 49, 51, 56–61, 63–4
Sidney, Lady Mary 110, 124
Sidney, Sir Philip 66, 124
Sly, Christopher (*Taming of the Shrew*) 90–4
soliloquy
 in *Doctor Faustus* 262, 265, 271–3, 277
 in *Duchess of Malfi, The* 26
 in *Hamlet* 292
 in *Measure for Measure* 225, 227–9
 in *Othello* 135
 in *Romeo and Juliet* 12–16, 25
 in *Spanish Tragedy, The* 186–8
 in *'Tis Pity She's a Whore* 247
 in *Tragedy of Mariam, The* 116–17, 119–20, 122
 in *Volpone* 72, 75
Stubbes, Philip 89, 214–15

Tabori, George
 The Merchant of Venice as Performed in Theresienstadt (adaptation) 62
Taming of a Shrew, The (anon) 90–1, 94
Taylor, Elizabeth (actor) 105–6
 in *The Taming of the Shrew* (film) 105–7
Taymor, Julie
 Titus (film) 205–10
thing theory 192–3
Titus (*Titus Andronicus*) 197–203
Tourneur, Cyril
 Atheist's Tragedy, The 258–9, 284

Ur-Hamlet (anon) 279
usury 44–5, 58

Venice 41–7, 49, 51–2, 65, 67–9, 75, 81
Volpone (*Volpone*) 69–79

Wanamaker Playhouse xiii, 37
 The Duchess of Malfi (2014) 38–9
 'Tis Pity She's a Whore (2014) 234–5, 239
Webster, John
 Duchess of Malfi, The 24–39, 152, 174, 233, 259
 White Devil, The 36

Zeffirelli, Franco
 The Taming of The Shrew (film) 103–7

Zweig, Stefan 79